THE SELF AND COMMUNICATIVE THEORY

The Self and Communicative Theory

GREGORY HEATH
RMIT University

Routledge
Taylor & Francis Group
LONDON AND NEW YORK

First published 2000 by Ashgate Publishing

Reissued 2018 by Routledge
2 Park Square, Milton Park, Abingdon, Oxon OX14 4RN
711 Third Avenue, New York, NY 10017, USA

Routledge is an imprint of the Taylor & Francis Group, an informa business

A Library of Congress record exists under LC control number: 99076356

ISBN 13: 978-1-138-71330-7 (hbk)
ISBN 13: 978-1-138-71324-6 (pbk)
ISBN 13: 978-1-315-19925-2 (ebk)

Contents

Acknowledgments

I would like to thank John Rundell and Horst Imberger for their comments and constructive criticisms of parts of the manuscript and for their support with the project. I also wish to thank Fiona Wahr and Nicole McLaughlin for their help in the preparation of the typescript.

I would also like to acknowledge the dedication and support of my wife Jilly Heath during the entire project.

1 Introduction: Transcendental Selves

Charles Taylor in *Inwardness and the Culture of Modernity* identifies a particularly modern philosophical problem. The problem that he identifies is that the modern disengaged self is based on a paradox. The paradox is that the disengaged, objective self of modernity is only comprehensible through a radical subjectivity; that self which is claimed to serve as a point for objective judgement is itself only accessible by the path of subjectivity. He says that: '...this [modern, disengaged] self which emerges from the objectification of and separation from our given nature cannot be identified with anything in this given [our given nature]'.[1] He further claims that 'this is the source of a continuing philosophical discomfort in modern times' and suggests that various solutions have been tried including reductionism, 'transcendental theories' and returns to dualism, but that the problem remains unresolved. This book seeks to address this key problem which is at the heart of many unresolved current issues. The proposed solution will show that this modern "antinomy", identified by Taylor, reveals that such a basis for the self is incoherent, and also that an intersubjective theory of the self is required to resolve the "antinomy". The strategy of resolution will be to develop a form of "transcendental" perspective that sets out the conditions for a reflexive self-identifying consciousness. The expressivist view proposed by Taylor himself will be discussed as a background to the major theme of transcendental theory, but it will be shown that such a theory is, in itself, inadequate.

The problem is similarly identified by Jurgen Habermas, but with the difference that Habermas, in a more Kantian mould, places the emphasis on individuation as contrasted with universal species membership, rather than Taylor's subjectivity contrasted with objectivity. Habermas says, 'Sociological interpreters lack the concepts that would enable them to capture descriptively a specific experience of modernity, one that is present to them intuitively. The individual is supposed to be distinguished as that which is essential, yet can only be defined as the accidental; namely, as that which deviates from the exemplary embodiment of a generic universal'.[2] Yet the underlying problem is the same, it is the tension between a universal humanity and the individual instantiation of that humanity in autonomous beings.

This work develops a proposal for a transcendental theory of the self which is essentially intersubjective and reflexively self-critical. In this proposal, the introspective "I" which has constituted the linchpin of so many theories ranging initially from Plato through to the "inwardness" of Augustine and Descartes, to the subjective pointillism of Locke, and further to the expressive self of Schiller and Charles Taylor, is superseded.

The proposal for a transcendental theory of the self presents a framework for the self which includes the elements of freedom and imagination as essential conditions. The theoretical framework alone does not of itself provide a substantive self. However, it does provide the fabric for a substantive self allowing for what Benhabib calls the "concrete other" in an intersubjective framework.[3] The elements of freedom and imagination, in conjunction with intersubjectivity, as determinants of the self, indicate that the substance of each self is determined by the reality of each person's life and their set of intersubjective connections.

The strategy of the exposition is a development of Kantian theory via recent discussions by Apel, Taylor and to a lesser extent, Habermas. Further discussion involves consideration of Charles Sanders Peirce and George Herbert Mead for the introduction of the pragmatic perspective and the dimension of the socially constructed self. Then the insights of the later philosophy of Wittgenstein are employed to lay the ground for an intersubjective theory. Finally, an intersubjective theory of self is offered, that draws upon the later philosophy of both Kant and Wittgenstein and is based on intuitions, in the Kantian sense, of freedom and imagination in an engaged social context.

It will be argued that, whilst an intersubjective theory is necessary to overcome the paradox of inwardness and to support communicative theory, those offered to date have been inadequate to the task. It will be further argued, following Kant, that the additional elements of freedom and imagination, particularly imagination, must be added as a ground for intersubjective theory to be successful and to overcome the misleading Cartesian perspective on the self.

The transcendental theory of the self requires certain essential elements. These are; freedom (especially practical freedom); reason as a principle for communication (communicative rationality); pragmatism as a theory of truth; reflexivity and re-identification in consciousness, and imagination as the principle of a language using subject. Each of these elements will be discussed in the exposition of the transcendental position proposed.

The reasons for choosing the transcendental path here are: firstly that such a path is seen to be the most likely to produce a coherent account of the self that supports communicative theory and provides an intersubjective self-understanding on which the human sciences can find a ground which is non-subjective, but at the same time one that does not incur all the problems of "objective" theories. Secondly, it is also seen as the path most likely to overcome the Kantian dilemma of individuation against a background of universal humanity. And finally, it is a path can clearly overcome the problems Cartesian radical subjectivity that inevitably lead to problems of "methodological solipsism".

Communicative theory, as a modern transcendental theory, and as a general theoretical approach to philosophical and social theoretic problems is also supported. The reasons for this are that communicative theory offers an approach that overcomes, or promises to overcome, many of the problems encountered by traditional approaches from naturalism to phenomenology. It also offers a genuine emancipatory force through discursive theories of ethics and action. However, it is recognised that communicative theory still has many serious unresolved problems.

Two of the major problems are, firstly, the failure to establish a normative basis, in that it is not clear that communicative theory provides an orientation to the good. Secondly, that to date, no adequate account of the subject of communicative transactions has been provided. The latter problem is the more serious and fundamental in that the furnishing of an account of the subject would lay the ground for an ethical theory leading to an orientation to the good. Such an ethical theory will not be developed in this book as it lies beyond the scope of the enquiry. However, in later chapters clear indications will be given as to the starting points of such a theory. Clearly a Cartesian theory of the self is unsatisfactory for communicative theory in that it presupposes a self-referential precommunicator behind the communicator. Such a theory is ultimately incoherent in that it leads either to an assertoric solipsism or an infinite regress of selves behind the self. The alternative is to provide a non-Cartesian account of the type that intersubjective theory attempts. In this connection, Habermas for instance, appropriates Mead's theory of a community generated self, but with limited success, as Mead still assumes a second order ego behind the self. Apel presupposes an "ideal communication community" and Benhabib opts for "egalitarian reciprocity" of a socially situated self. However, all these theories and intersubjective theory in general, require a further grounding as a basis for intersubjective consciousness and it is this grounding which is addressed in this book. The communicative transcendental approach is the only approach that allows for the development of a non-Cartesian critical reflective view of the self, which at the same time allows for that self to be a socially engaged self.

Communicative theory takes its origin from Kant, via pragmatism to the contemporary discussions of communicative rationality, communicative action and communicative ethics. The Kantian origin, establishes the critical reflective base for a subjective consciousness which participates in the structuring of experience. The path, via philosophical pragmatism, provides a theory of truth, or at least provides for the validation of truth claims, based on agreement rather than some absolute or subjective criterion, yet one which can accept that reflective consciousness plays a role in the structuring of the objects of experience. It is important to note, that for the theory of pragmatism it is the conditions of agreement rather than agreement as such, that establish criteria for judgements as to the validity of truth claims.

Communicative theory was originated in separate ways, first by Karl-Otto Apel, and then in a more comprehensive social context by Jürgen Habermas.[4] It has recently been taken up and used more broadly in philosophy and social theory by writers such as Seyla Benhabib and Albrecht Wellmer. It offers the opportunity for progress in democratic social theory, but has struggled to find an adequate philosophical grounding. A major problem faced by communicative theory has been its failure to give an account of the subject adequate to support an intersubjectivity sufficient to ground communicative concepts related to reason, orientation to the good, and a new social democracy free of the dominations of late capitalism which include gender, ethnicity and dominant power structures.

Habermas reinforces the need for a transcendental perspective in a discussion of individuation in which he claims that certain conditions must pertain in order for self-consciousness to be established.

> The universal pragmatic presuppositions of communicative action constitute semantic resources from which historical societies create and articulate, each in its own way, representations of mind and soul, concepts of the person and of action, consciousness of morality, and so on.[5]

He continues in a similar vein, referring this time to Mead with approval:

> Kant's Kingdom of Ends must be *supposed* here and now as a context of the interaction and as a communication community in which everyone is capable of taking up the perspective of everyone else and is willing to do so.[6]

The transcendental perspective is taken up much more vigorously by Karl-Otto Apel who repeatedly and most emphatically asserts that the self has a transcendental basis that can be found in a transformation of Kantian philosophy. Apel as one of the founders of modern communicative theory presents a strongly foundationalist view.[7] It will be shown that whilst Apel makes a strong contribution to communicative theory and to the framework for a theory of intersubjectivity, he does not free himself from a grounding in Kantian idealism.

The work of Immanuel Kant figures prominently in the discussion. There are a number of reasons for this. Firstly, Kant is the originator of both the method of critique and the transcendental method of argument as it is understood today. But more importantly, Kant's development of an understanding of the subject of consciousness proves to be a most enlightening development. This development has not been fully discussed in the literature. There is an interesting discussion in published lectures by Hannah Arendt which relates to the *Critique of Judgement* and the later political essays, but it was unfortunately not further developed.[8] It is necessary to trace out the development of Kant's discussion of the subject of consciousness from the *Critique of Pure Reason* to the very last works because it changes and develops so profoundly. This change is not recognised by Kant himself who sees his work as unified whole. It is not just a matter of development, or the unfolding of an idea, because Kant introduces many radical new elements in successive works, such as the idea of freedom in the *Critique of Practical Reason* and the idea of communicability in the *Critique of Judgement.* Each of these stages needs consideration in the development of the very remarkable full Kantian picture of the self.

The picture of the self, as subject of consciousness that is usually attributed to Kant is that of the first *Critique* only, based on the unity of apperception. However a series of intriguing and more sophisticated developments emerges in the later works. These include the idea of being a member of the Kingdom of Ends in the *Fundamental Principles of the Metaphysic of Ethics*, being a personality that exercises freedom in the *Critique of Practical Reason*, being a member of a communicating sociality in the *Critique of Judgement*, and being possessed of the transcendental reflective capacity in the *Opus Postumum.* In many of these iterations of the self, elements of later thought are presaged. These include the idea of a self-creating being to be found in Hegel and his followers, an argument for the non-privacy of subjective states similar to that of Wittgenstein and an account of communicability as a transcendental ground of judgement in general, similar to that of communicative theory. Each of these elements in the development of Kantian thought form an integral part of the development of the central argument of the work.

The Kantian perspective is doubly important as it involves, firstly, the establishment of the modern sense of the self via the "Transcendental Deduction" of the *Critique of Pure Reason.* The importance of this move for the whole discussion of the modern self from Hegel to Freud and Nietzsche to the contemporary debates, cannot be underestimated. Secondly, following the development of Kant's thinking constitutes a fascinating study of the importance of transcendental thinking through the establishment of the cognitive powers and the development of an imaginative, self-creating, socially situated, communicative self. The originality and creative power of Kant is quite awe inspiring as he moves through the consequences of the method of critique from a defence of metaphysics to a new radical way of conceiving conscious beings in the world; or as Kant would have said in "the universe". Of particular significance for this discussion is Kant's instatement of communicability as a transcendental ground in the *Critique of Judgement.* His claim, as will be discussed in detail, is not just that communicability is necessary for aesthetic judgements, because of the subjective element, but that communicability is necessary for cognition, and therefore knowledge, in general.[9]

The contribution of Wittgenstein is important to complete the picture. Many writers have drawn attention to parallels between Kant and Wittgenstein, Pears, Taylor, Rorty and Putnam being amongst the most recent, although the discussion by Apel is probably the most significant. None of these discussions, however, bring out the full significance of the later philosophy of Wittgenstein in extending the lines of development established in Kant's thought. Discussions of Wittgenstein have been largely unsatisfactory due both to the failure to come to terms with his idiosyncratic philosophical style and the failure of commentators to place his work in context. His work is a multi-dimensional philosophical mosaic.[10]

At issue here is Wittgenstein's contribution to the discussion of "inner" states and their communicability. It will be claimed that these states presuppose public criteria and thus place intersubjectivity in a position of precedence over subjectivity in a theory of the self. The role of language will also be discussed with development of the notion of the conditions required for language use which, it will be argued, is implicit in Wittgenstein's work. Wittgenstein's discussions of the relationship between language and the inner/outer will also be linked to earlier discussion of the relationship between signs and consciousness by Charles

Sanders Peirce. Peirce's claim that the self is a sign will be related to Wittgenstein's broad claim that we are language.

The term "transcendental" has a number of meanings and its use in the context of this work requires some explanation. "Transcendental" here, in the first instance, is meant in the sense that follows Kant's "transcendental deduction" and used by Karl-Otto Apel, Habermas and others writing today in a broadly post-Kantian tradition. The usage of the term refers to the conditions required for possible experience and for the possibility of understanding. Kant defines a transcendental principle as 'one which we think the universal *a priori* condition under which alone things can become objects of our cognition in general'.[11] These conditions are transcendental in the sense that they transcend the subjective or individual conditions of human experience, and are objective and universal with respect to that experience. As shown in *The Critique of Pure Reason* where time and space, as intuitions, are the transcendental conditions necessary for experience of the world. Here the inquiry will take up the issue of the transcendental conditions necessary for the existence of selves and show that an interpersonal perspective is required.

"Transcendental", however, does have a further connotation of "extraworldliness" which, along with Taylor, I would not want to deny altogether; although it is peripheral to the main argument where the focus will be on the Kantian interpretation. Kant himself in fact defines transcendental variously. In *The Critique of Pure Reason* he tends to define the transcendental as the a priori system. However, in his later philosophy there are many, and somewhat confusing, variations in specification of the transcendental. Caygill comments that the term is used 'ubiquitously to qualify nouns such as logic, aesthetic' etc., to signify that the noun is 'being considered in terms of its conditions of possibility'.[12] Later Kant is much more likely to align the transcendental with God and the divine intuition. For example:

> Transcendental philosophy is the system of knowledge, which presents *a priori* all objects of pure reason necessarily combined in one system.
>
> These objects are God, the world, man in the world, subject to the concept of duty. Totality of beings.[13]

But it is also notable that he suggests that we share that divine intuition as the "noumenon within", which is the basis of understanding and realisation of the universe.

Charles Taylor provides an instructive recent discussion of transcendental arguments. These arguments, he says, come down to us from Kant and have been tried in various forms by contemporary writers. He says:

> The arguments I want to call "transcendental" start from some feature of our experience which they claim to be indubitable and beyond cavil. They then move to a stronger conclusion, one concerning the nature of the subject or the subject's position in the world. They make this move by a regressive argument, to the effect that the stronger conclusion must be so if the indubitable fact about experience is to be possible (and being so, it must be possible).[14]

This statement provides a good exposition of how transcendental arguments work, but it is misleading in some respects. Transcendental arguments do not necessarily require that some feature of experience needs to be indubitable. What they do require is that there be some general feature of experience that is acknowledged as such a feature. Indubitability is too strong a claim and not required as part of the argument. The features of experience can be as general as an acknowledgment that sensory experience occurs, or that words can have meaning. They do not have to be tied down to a specific experience or meaning and subjected to a test of indubitability.

The other feature that may be misleading is to claim that transcendental arguments work by a process of regressive argument. Whilst the general form of argument could be said to be regressive, there is a further essential element to the arguments and that is the critical-reflective element. It is true that the mechanism of the argument works in the following way; if one concedes *y* then one must accept that *x*, where *x* is a condition for *y*. But there is more to it than this, the critical-reflective element is essential to make the bridge from the experience to the haver of the experience. It is this feature that makes the argument transcend the level experience only. A transcendental argument can step from one order to another via the critical-reflective move. Thus one can step from the experience to a conclusion about the consciousness required for the experience and not just another dimension of experience. It is this element that tends to make transcendental arguments so powerful.

Taylor shows awareness of the critical reflective element in his discussion of the "embodied agent" in the world, but does not fully represent the critical-reflective element in his discussion.

The distinctions between the terms "self", "subject", "consciousness" and "self-consciousness" and a range of other terms, such as "person" and "ego", have formed the basis for great confusion in discussions in this most complex area. Distinctions are not easily drawn and not consistently applied in the literature. Here, "the self" will be discussed as the primary case and the term distinguished from the other subjective terms where appropriate. The sense attached to "self" and the other terms will only emerge in the fuller discussion of freedom, reason, imagination and reflexivity. It is neither possible, nor appropriate, to attempt to prescriptively define these terms. As with any attempt to tightly define terms which are also part of common usage, a certain artificially must develop and thus inhibit the scope and force of the discussion. Many significant philosophical distinctions are to be found in the nuances of these discussions.

Nevertheless, every effort will be made maintain a consistency in the application of these terms, and the contexts of their employments by various authors adequately explained.

The second chapter gives an account of the origins of communicative theory outlining the importance of Kant and Peirce in its foundation and discussing Apel and Habermas in their contributions to its recent development. This chapter also establishes the central problematic by outlining the inadequacy of the accounts of the self and subjectivity in communicative theories.

The third chapter offers a consideration of Kant's early critical views and gives an account of the origin of the modern theory of the self. It is also pointed out that what is called the modern theory of the self differs from what is termed the "conventional theory" of possessive individualism, which is still rooted in a Cartesian framework and lacks the critical reflective element introduced by Kant.

In the following chapter the modern view of the self is expanded through an examination of the way Kant replaces the sovereignty of reason with a radical view of freedom. The essential element explored here relates to the development of autonomy as a key to the constitution of the self.

The fifth chapter moves to examine Apel's proposed linguistic transformation of Kantian philosophy and his claims to have transformed philosophy yet retained a transcendental framework. It also introduces the discussion of communicative theory.

In chapter six consideration is given to the intersubjective theory of the self with discussions of George Herbert Mead and Jürgen Habermas. Mead's basis for an intersubjective theory of the self is critically evaluated but it is argued that it ultimately fails to allow for a post-Cartesian subjectivity. It is also argued that for this reason it will not serve Habermas' purposes in securing the intersubjective dimension of communicative theory.

Chapter seven provides a critical evaluation of the importance of the expressive component in a transformed transcendental view. The recent perspective on the self, presented by Charles Taylor is evaluated against a Kantian background. It is argued that whilst Taylor contribute to an overall theory of the self, and provides an alternative transcendental view, the expressivist view is in itself inadequate to account for intersubjectivity. It is acknowledged however that the expressive and imaginative dimensions must be accommodated in any comprehensive theory.

Kant's late writings have not been widely discussed in the context of a discussion of his views on self and subjectivity. In these writings and in particular the *Critique of Judgement* he introduces a radical new element of communicability as a transcendental ground for the self. This element is discussed and related to his overall project in chapter eight.

Chapter nine traces and comments upon the remarkable parallels between the later philosophy of Kant and Wittgenstein that allow for a new evaluation of the importance of Wittgenstein's late writings and particularly of his understanding of the subject. A parallel is also drawn between Wittgenstein and Peirce in their respective treatments of signs and language as they relate to sign and language users.

In the concluding chapter a theory of the self is outlined which encompasses intersubjectivity. This theory is a transcendental theory that provides a framework for a substantive self. It is argued that whilst intersubjectivity is a requirement for a theory of the self such a theory needs certain conditions of subjectivity to be met in order to be successful. It is proposed that these conditions are imagination, freedom and communicability. With these conditions in place communicative theory can be secured and fulfill its claims.

Notes

1 Taylor, Charles (1992), "Inwardness and the Culture of Modernity", in *Philosophical Interventions and the Unfinished Project of the Enlightenment*, ed. Axel Honneth et. al., The MIT Press, Cambridge, Mass, p. 102.

2 Habermas, Jurgen (1992), "Individuation Through Socialization", in *Postmetaphysical Thinking*, trans. William Mark Hohengarten, MIT Press, Cambridge, Mass., p. 150.

3 Benhabib, Seyla (1992), *Situating the Self*, Polity Press, Cambridge, p.164.

4 Habermas was influenced by the Frankfurt School and Theodore Adorno in particular, and also by the German Social Democratic movement and later by

the lectures of Apel. Apel took a more conventional approach through the study of Kant and the American pragmatists. See Wiggershaus, Rolf (1994), *The Frankfurt School*, trans. Michael Robertson, MIT Press, Cambridge, Mass., p. 537ff and p. 636ff.

5 Habermas, Jurgen (1992), *Postmetaphysical Thinking*, chapter 7, "Individuation Through Socialization: On George Herbert Mead's Theory of Subjectivity", trans William Mark Hohengarten, Polity Press, Cambridge, p. 190.

6 Ibid., p. 185.

7 See Apel, Karl-Otto (1980), "From Kant to Peirce", in *Towards a transformation of philosophy*, trans. Glyn Adey and David Frisby, Routledge and Kegan Paul, London, p. 77ff, for a statement of Apel's Kantian foundationalism.

8 Arendt, Hannah (1982), *Lectures on Kant's Political Philosophy*, ed. Ronald Beiner, University of Chicago Press, Chicago. Beiner notes that Arendt's premature death prevented a further development of the themes outlined in the lectures.

9 See Kant, Immanuel (1987), *The Critique of Judgement*, trans. Werner S. Pluhar, Hackett, Indianapolis, p. 153. Kant claims the problem of critique of judgement is part of the general problem of transcendental philosophy.

10 Recent discussions by David Pears, *The False Prison*, and Paul Johnston, *Wittgenstein: Rethinking the Inner*, provide excellent discussions of the subjective dimensions but they do not take full account of the hermeneutic dimension of Wittgenstein's thought.

11 Kant, Immanuel (1987), *Critique of Judgement*, trans. Werner S. Pluhar, Hackett, Indianapolis, p. 20.

12 Caygill, Howard (1995), *A Kant Dictionary*, Basil Blackwell, Oxford, p. 399.

13 Kant, Immanuel (1993), *Opus Postumum*, ed. Eckart Föster, trans. Eckart Föster and Michael Rosen, Cambridge University Press, Cambridge, p.247.

14 Taylor, Charles (1995), *Philosophical Arguments*, Harvard University Press, Cambridge, Mass., p. 20.

2 Communicative Theory

Communicative theory has its origins jointly in American pragmatism and critical theory. The term "communicative theory" is intended to include the group of more specific theories developed primarily by Jürgen Habermas and Karl-Otto Apel, including the theory of communicative action, the theory of communicative rationality and communicative ethics. There is, underlying these theories, a more basic communicative theory of truth which has its origins in pragmatism. This aspect is more evident in Apel, due mainly to his detailed study of Peirce, than in Habermas.[1]

But communicative theory is not simply a theory, but a whole approach to both philosophising and social theory. It is, like many movements in theory, such as critical theory itself, not amenable to a precise encapsulation. There are a number of themes, debates, commonalities and differences in the totality of the ongoing movement. Also communicative theory is, in philosophical terms, relatively young and undergoing continuing creative development and refinement. As an instance of this development one should note Seyla Benhabib's recent work *Situating the Self* as an impressive example of the extension of communicative theory into gender issues and contemporary ethics.[2]

The two bases of communicative theory are the dimension of intersubjectivity, derived indirectly from pragmatism, and the reflexive use of language, derived primarily from critical theory and speech act theory in Habermas case and from the hermeneutic interpretation of Wittgenstein in Apel's case.

The origin of communicative theory clearly resides with Kant in the *Critique of Judgement.* In fact, his establishment of communicability as a transcendental ground for judgement clearly presages much that has been developed in recent decades. Kant argues that communicability is not only necessary for aesthetic judgements, because of the subjective element, but also that it is necessary for cognition, and therefore knowledge, in general.[3] The origins of communicative theory and its "consensus theory" of truth lie with the Kantian "Copernican revolution" in philosophy.

In order to appreciate the importance of communicative theory as a major development in philosophical and sociological understanding it is useful to place it in the context of the development a genuinely new perspective on truth, and thus a new perspective on rationality, meaning and action.

Prior to Kant, philosophy had maintained a basic Platonic or neo-Platonic view of truth. This view was, very broadly speaking, that cognitive contents, expressed as propositions, must correspond with an external reality. In the case of Plato it was the Forms that had independent, external existence. Truth was achieved when experience of the world corresponded with the pure perception of the Forms which were knowable through recollection, the purest form of cognition.

Aristotle maintained a broadly Platonic model which influenced medieval scholars such as St Thomas Aquinas and later indirectly Descartes. Aristotle still believed in the existence of independent Universals which, however, did not have the divine status of Plato's Forms. Aristotle relied on the notion *nous* or a form of epistemic intuition to establish whether or not experience of particulars fell under a universal. Aristotle thus allowed room for some empirical content in knowledge but truth was to be found in the "reasoned facts" falling under rationally determined Universals. Truth was discoverable by a process of logical deduction, determining whether or not certain cognitions fell under one or another Universal. Whilst sense perception could lead us towards the discovery of Universals it was reason, along with Aristotles categories that determined Universals.

Descartes' move to radical subjectivity created problems for a theory of truth. His problem was how to maintain the objective certainty required for truth within framework of knowledge based on radical introspection. Descartes introduced the notion of "clear and distinct ideas" to solve his dilemma. A statement was true when what was observed corresponded with what could be deduced from self evident first premises. Thus, reason alone could come up with "clear and distinct" ideas of the basic properties of substance, such as extension and mass. Descartes, however, was faced with a problem similar to that which Aristotle solved by appealing to *nous*. It was that of determining whether or not certain experiences fell under this or that "clear and distinct ideas". Descartes could not rely solely on introspection or a form of intuition. In the end he had to rely on his proof for the existence of God to rule out the possibility of being deceived by either our own subjective processes or an "evil demon" to rescue his theory of truth.[4]

The empiricists, whilst trying to retain an objective notion of truth, finally broke with the notion that truth was to be found in some underlying correspondence between cognition and an independent reality. They argued that all knowledge came from experience and not innate ideas. Yet they did not abandon or reject the broad Platonic metaphysical model, nor did they replace it with an alternative scheme. Locke was forced to admit that the underlying "real essence" of objects could never be known, yet he did not deny its existence. All we could be aware of were the "ideas" which formed the basis of his epistemology or the "nominal essences" which were things represented by words, which he saw as symbols for abstract ideas. Whilst Locke had made such a significant breakthrough he could not accept that the certainty of truth did not hold and argued, rather unconvincingly, that a type of "reasoned fact" based on the clarity of the "ideas" still gave certain knowledge and thus could serve as a criterion of truth.

Hume took the implications of the empiricist program to a more consistent conclusion, arguing that no matter of fact could be demonstrated to be true and restricted truth to logical relations. It was not that Hume thought that truth about matters of fact was not possible, but rather that truth in these circumstances could not be the absolute truth claimed by Plato, Aristotle and Descartes.[5]

Kant in meeting Hume's scepticism proposed that the objects of knowledge were created by our innate capacities as humans in accordance with the "intuitions", or forms, of space and time and the categories. Thus, for Kant, we could have a priori knowledge about some features of the world because our cognition constructed certain features of experience. On the basis of the forms of intuition to structure experience, he could, by the synthetic a priori, guarantee the truth of synthetic a priori statements, as well of course, analytic statements. However, at the same time, Kant in the *Critique of Pure Reason*, asserted that things-in-themselves, the noumena, were beyond the scope of both sense and reason. Whilst reason could deduce the necessity of there being things-in-themselves, it was utterly powerless to make any determinations about them. The things-in-themselves were not the objects of knowledge and not the objects of truth judgements which were restricted to the realm of human cognitive powers. It was this insight that started the movement towards communicative theory, because another way of approaching the issues of truth and knowledge, and the place of reason and judgement, had to be developed. Also, as a consequence, a new understanding of the self and subjectivity had to be incorporated into an overall perspective, which is the focus of this book.

Kant through his "Copernican revolution" had created a situation which was to require a completely non-Platonic response to the issue of the determination of both truth and knowledge. Kant himself went quite some distance towards working out the implications of his insights in later works, where he first recognises the importance of freedom to guide the actual employment of reason in the *Critique of Practical Reason* and then later in the *Critique of Judgement* recognises the importance of reflexivity and communicability for the exercise of imagination in the creation of freedom. Kant did not achieve the non-Platonic response that his critical philosophy necessitated. The situation which he left to be addressed was one where truth was determined by our cognitive powers, yet had to be universal, and avoid both scepticism and subjectivism.

There will be much more detailed discussion of Kant later in later chapters, which will support the requirements for an interpersonal theory of the self which is in turn, required to support communicative theory. At this point it is sufficient to identify the point where the underpinning of communicative theory is established.

Kant's critical philosophy required, as a further step, a theory of truth that was genuinely new and non-Platonic in its ontology and methods. What became necessary was a theory of truth that did not make assumptions about the existence or nature of an external reality with which cognitions had to correspond. It was Charles Sanders Peirce, who proposed a theory that could respond to the dilemma left by the Kantian insight that paved the way for the development of communicative theory.

Peirce's philosophy is notoriously difficult to deal with, due to its complexity, eccentricity and lack of clear unifying themes; Hausman describes it as 'like entering a labyrinth with as many entrances as passages'.[6] A detailed analysis of it is well beyond the scope of this work. However, it is important to sketch some of Peirce's principle ideas as a foundation to communicative theory and, interestingly, also as one basis of Wittgenstein's later philosophy.

Much of the difficulty in dealing with Peirce results from the fact that he developed his ideas in isolation from the academic community of his day. He was for only a few years employed at John Hopkins University, gave some lectures at Harvard, but despite his friendship with Royce and William James, worked in isolation.[7] Another reason for Peirce's isolation was his philosophical commitment to a scientific objectivist view which ran counter to the academic orthodoxy of the conservative American academy of his day.

Wiener comments:

> One reason that Peirce insulated himself from the psychological approach of James and the idealists (from Berkeley to Hegel) was that he condemned the subjectivism that tinged all such philosophies.[8]

This isolation, in part, made it possible for Peirce to develop a genuinely new approach to solving philosophical problems that would result in what he called "pragmaticism" to distinguish it from "pragmatism" as espoused by William James.[9] The difference in approach is emphasised in the 1905 essay published in *The Monist* where Peirce emphasises his logical approach in contrast to James' psychological point of view. Pragmaticism was not just a method for determining the truth of beliefs, it also involved a much more elaborate theory of meaning based on the reality of signs.

Peirce's philosophy is rich and diverse, spanning a wide range of topics in logic, the philosophy of science, phenomenology and semiotics and ranging further over virtually all the philosophical topics of his day. If there is a unifying thread to be found in his philosophy it stems his concern with methodology. Particularly the methodology of science and its relation to epistemology. It is out of this concern that the theory of pragmaticism developed. Peirce saw himself as building an "architectonic" to supersede, in particular, Kant, but also Hegel and the idealism which followed Kant. Peirce recommended a transformation of Kantianism on many fronts and claimed there was a need for the "Kantist" to abjure from the bottom of his heart the proposition that a thing-in-itself can, however indirectly, be conceived. It is clear that one of the motivations in Peirce's scheme was to preserve the Kantian insights into the constitution of knowledge and experience and thus secure the "Copernican revolution" yet do away with the vestiges of metaphysics, and the idea that knowledge, especially scientific knowledge, rested on the existence of imperceivable, yet deducible things-in-themselves.

Peirce sought to develop an overall "architectonic" for understanding the world. Such an architectonic would have structural and dynamic elements which would include a new set of categories, his Firstness, Secondness and Thirdness,[10] a metaphysics of realism, a method and a semiotic. This architectonic in Peirce's philosophy turns out to be an unwieldy beast indeed, but it represents the scale of his project. The origin of communicative theory is essentially bound up with the theory of truth and the method of pragmaticism within this architectonic.

In his early essays he made a clear break with the Cartesian method of establishing truth and with Cartesianism in general. His main line of attack focussed on doubt of the power of introspection, as a power of consciousness, to determine that anything is self-evident and that 'modern science and modern logic require us to stand upon a very different platform to [Cartesianism]'.[11] He was of the view that 'philosophy ought to imitate the successful sciences in its methods, 'and that knowledge began with a process of cognition about an external world, and not from any 'self consciousness'.[12]

In an essay entitled "Some Consequences of Four Incapacities" he sets out an anti-Cartesian program which was to lead to the philosophy of pragmatism and to the underpinnings of communicative theory. The four "Incapacities" he summarises as follows:

> 1. We have no power of Introspection, but all knowledge of the internal world is derived by hypothetical reasoning from our knowledge of external facts.

2. We have no power of Intuition, but every cognition is determined logically by previous cognitions.

3. We have no power of thinking without signs.

4. We have no conception of the absolutely incognizable.[13]

The final "Incapacity" is clearly aimed at Kant, but would, in Peirce's view, include all those philosophies the claimed to rely on an underlying absolute ground for knowledge, whether discernible by intuition or implied by deduction. Peirce then embarks upon a long and meandering justification of the four "premises" tracing by consequences the establishment of the first two and then by deduction the following two. The justification is not relevant to the purpose of this discussion, but the conclusion points to the notion of the "final community" that was to become an essential factor in the pragmatic theory as it was the putative "final community" that served as the truth-critical criterion. Peirce says:

> Finally as to what anything really is, is what it may finally come to be known to be in the ideal state of complete information, so that reality depends on the ultimate decision of the community.[14]

In the essay "Critical Review of Berkeley's Idealism", Peirce extends the notions of the "community of minds". It is in this essay that he also began to elaborate his theory of semiotics that was later adapted by Apel as a further precursor to communicative theory.

Peirce held that Berkeley was to be recognised for his understanding that the notion of the thing-in-itself was insupportable, but that he erred in his support for a radical subjectivist alternative. In attacking Berkeley's subjectivism Peirce enlists Kant and his "Copernican step" in the service of a pragmatic theory of reality. Peirce says of Kant: 'It was the essence of his philosophy to regard the real object as determined by the mind.[15] But Peirce had already denied the validity of introspection as a method of establishing both truth and reality, so he had to look to non-subjective criteria for a reality that was "determined by the mind". What such a realist wants, Peirce argues, is a 'consensus or common confession which constitutes reality'.[16]

These notions are further developed in two of Peirce's best known essays "The Fixation of Belief" and "How to Make our Ideas Clear" which are generally regarded as setting out the basis of the pragmatic view of truth. In these essays he rejects two methods for gaining clearness. Firstly, he rejects the Cartesian method of clarity by acquaintance because it is not possible to rule out contingencies.[17] Secondly, he rejects distinctness because it depends on definition and is subject to the criticisms he levels at nominalism. The rule proposed for attaining the third grade of clearness that Peirce required is stated thus:

> ...consider what effects, which might conceivably have practical bearings, we conceive the object of our conception to have. Then, our conception of these effects is the whole of our conception of the object.[18]

He thus espoused not only criteria for truth, but also a method of science based on investigating the consequences or "sensible effects" of bodies. He illustrated his "rule" by demonstrating that if two concepts have the same effects then they are the same concept. This was to become known as the "pragmatic maxim". He realised however, that just what the effects are perceived to be was not a simple matter, as they were subject to the beliefs of the interpreter. Thus, it was necessary to establish how it could be that a belief was sufficiently clear and distinct to provide for scientific knowledge according to his method. It is here that he introduces the other side of the "pragmatic maxim" with the notion that the beliefs of informed investigators will tend to converge toward the truth over time, even if each individual is in error. The beliefs, that turn out to be beliefs that are about real things, and therefore true, are those whose results 'will move steadily together towards a destined centre'.[19]

Peirce says, in as clear a statement as he makes about the object of the final opinion,

> The opinion which is fated to be ultimately agreed to by all who investigate, is what we mean by the truth and the object represented in this opinion is the real.[20]

Whilst debate continues as to the extent to which Peirce was a realist or idealist, the feature that interests us here is that he had committed himself to intersubjective criteria for truth.[21] It is also clear that Peirce was committed to some criteria of agreement that would lead to truth and "the real". In this latter dimension there is a precursor of the normative aspect of communicative theory.

A major problem with Peirce's theory here is that he seems not only not provide any reason the long run agreement should lead to truth, but also parts of his overall theory would preclude such grounds. For instance the view that there can be no underlying or imperceivable grounds. Another possibility, for which Peirce gives no support, is that a subjective pragmatism is implied here and truth is just what is agreed. However Peirce elsewhere rejected such subjective views. He seemed to hold a belief in a metaphysics that guaranteed that the long run of investigation would tend towards a final opinion. Hausman attributes this to the view that Secondness, the second of Peirce's three categories that applied to meaning, 'sustains a bit of unintelligibility'.[22] The unintelligibility referred to relates to the unknowable element of things-in-themselves. Hausman says; 'Thus, the end of enquiry is an ideal, a regulative ideal justifying continued attempts to bring the results of inquiries together for a community of investigators'.[23] And continues, that what we might call the '"finalizing opinion", is an ideal limit that is regulative, inspiring heuristically the continued pursuit of inquiry'.[24] Yet even at this "proto" stage of communicative theory it is clear that Peirce had no sufficiently developed theory of self to account for membership of the "community of investigators".

We find here many of the elements in place necessary for the development of communicative theory, including the regulative element so important for Habermas's claims for a normative basis for communicative ethics and Apel's idealising communities.

The link between Peirce and communicative theory can be directly established through the work of Apel. Apel in the post-war years studied both in the German and Anglo-American philosophical traditions. Apel's interest in Peirce was generated through his interest in the philosophy of science, and particularly fallibilism, which he saw as an inadequate methodology. He was also interested in Peirce's attempt to reconstruct Kant and in particular the *Critique of Pure Reason*. But he says 'Peirce finally became important for me primarily as an ally in the systematic undertaking of a "transformation of (transcendental) philosophy".[25]

Apel's own transformation of philosophy will be examined in later chapters. Here it will be sufficient to indicate what he took from Peirce to establish his own version of communicative theory.

Apel identifies two aspects of Peirce's elaborate theory, of which the further theoretical development will form basis for communicative theory. The first is the idea that the notion of a "final community of investigators" constitutes a transcendental ground, not just for communication but for philosophy in general. It is this aspect that leads to the "ideal communication community" which Apel hopes will provide the grounds for a transformation of transcendental philosophy.[26] The second aspect is more complicated and relates to Apel's interpretation of Peirce's semiotics. The fundamental idea involved here is that the meaning of a sign must involve (a priori) the understanding of an interpreter.

In the case of the first aspect Apel combines the concept of the "unlimited community of investigators" with the notion of the "uncurtailed" nature of sign interpretation to establish an ideal communication community that, he claims, has a regulative base, which in the case of science is aimed at knowledge and in the case of ethics has a normative base. This regulative principle can be applied to all the areas of human concern, where, for instance, in the case of the social sciences it is liberation and agreed policy based on the ideals of unconstrained argumentation.[27] His claim is that there is an a priori implicit in the process of entering into a process of inquiry or debate that presumes an ideal outcome in an unlimited situation. Those who engage in ethical debate presuppose that the good is the ultimate outcome, and this, he says, is seen to be a priori by a critical-reflexive judgement.[28]

In the second aspect of Peirce's theory that Apel was to adapt to the basis of communicative theory is to be found in the complex theory of semiotics. Peirce revised his semiotic theory on many occasions and it is the latter revisions where Peirce stressed the autonomy of the sign process that Apel focuses on. Apel sees it as a "crucial" point that Peirce recognised that '*cognition, as a sign mediated function, is a triadic relationship that cannot be reduced to a dyadic relationship*'(Apel's italics).[29] Put as simply as possible, this means that a sign cannot relate to an object without interpretation. At the next level Peirce took the view that the representational function of sign presupposed the existence of the real world for consciousness; the sign was not generated by the mind but rather related the mind to the object. Thus, the sign was general and not privileged to any one subjectivity but was open to all subjectivities relating signs to objects. So here was a semiotic that opened up a community of interpretation and, to that extent, was genuinely intersubjective in its determination of reality.[30] Apel in his discussion explores at length the reinterpretation of Kant that Peirce's semiotics provides.[31] Here he sees an opportunity to achieve Kant's aims in the *Transcendental Deduction* via a semiotic transformation, where it is the force and dynamic of the sign rather than the form of the cognitive faculties that give structure and meaning to experience.

Peirce had a theory of the self and subjectivity that basically reversed the previously received relationship between subjectivity and the sign. It was the sign, imported into consciousness, that determined or generated subjectivity. Subjectivity was a composite of signs, inwardly reflected, and the self a sign to consciousness. It is significant however that Apel does not import from Peirce anything more than a weak theory of the self and intersubjectivity to support his transformation; perhaps Peirce was too radical for Apel's transcendentalism. There is even some confusion as to whether or not he supports Royce's version of an historically embedded self or Peirce's "semiotic" self.[32] Apel is attracted to Royce because his view supports a hermeneutic interpretation, and such an interpretation would undermine the generality of Peirce's theory of the sign. For Peirce, in contrast to Royce, it is the sign rather than the context of its interpretation that carries the shape and embodiment of meaning and in this context, as Colapietro says, 'The self itself is a sign'.[33]

The other and much better known joint originator of communicative theory is Jürgen Habermas. Habermas was also influenced by Peirce and the pragmatists. This influence came in large part through Apel. Wiggershaus says, 'During his years at Heidelberg, Habermas had studied the American pragmatists at the suggestion of his friend Karl-Otto Apel and had learned the value of their work as a democratic American variant of the philosophy of praxis'.[34] Habermas attended Apel's lectures on Peirce and, as Wiggershaus further claims, was persuaded by Apel to look to a critical rationality as a basis for a critical social theory, rather than Adorno's more culture based approach.[35]

There was, however, a fundamental difference between the approach taken by Habermas and that of Apel. Whereas Apel has always insisted on a form of transcendentalism with respect to the communication community, Habermas has denied the actuality of such a foundation. In this respect Habermas says:

> Apel uses the vivid image of the interlocking of the ideal communication community and its real counterpart, which sounds almost too Kantian. ...The structure of the use of language oriented toward reaching understanding demands idealizing suppositions on the part of the communicative actors; yet these notions function as social facts and are, as is language *per se,* constitutive for the form in which socio-cultural life reproduces itself.[36]

Here Habermas is reinforcing his view that sufficient grounds for communicative theory, and therefore communicative action, can be found in the life-world and language itself.

Habermas was, of course, strongly influenced by both Adorno and the more orthodox approach to rationality found in the German tradition following Weber.[37] This influence can be seen in Habermas's early work such as *Structural Transformation of the Public Sphere.* However with the publication of *Legitimation Crisis* and *Knowledge and Human Interests* during the 1970s Habermas's approach to reason, both as the central theme of German philosophy and as basis for a critical social theory had begun to shift. In the Kantian reflections of *Knowledge and Human Interests* Habermas acknowledges Kant's insight that 'The practical interest of reason could assume the role of a knowledge-constitutive interest'.[38] However he does not accept that Kant was able to establish the practical interest of reason because he could not unite practical and theoretical reason. This move, he claims was left to Fichte who established 'speculative reason's dependence in principle on practical reason'.[39] through the element of self-reflection. To this insight Habermas added further insights into the nature and use of language gained from hermeneutics and speech act theory emphasising the historical and socially embedded nature of language, particularly its practical interest in intersubjective understanding. It was from this point of development that Habermas produced his fully developed communicative theory expressed comprehensively in *The Theory of Communicative Action.*

Habermas' presentation of his elaborated communicative theory in *The Theory of Communicative Action* is, as Charles Taylor describes it, 'exceptionally rich and dense'.[40] It is a work of great breadth and complexity with many strong core themes, some of which centre around reason and rationalisation and the critique of instrumental reason, the foundations of communication and its place in a critical social theory and the normative basis of social action. Brand succinctly encapsulates the key theme when he says that 'his analysis here amounts to an argument for the replacement of [the paradigm of the philosophy of consciousness] with an altogether different one, that of communicative theory'.[41] To this end Habermas proposes a transformation of reason from all its external manifestations from Kant through Weber to the instrumental reason of scientific rationality, to a reason that is based in subject to subject relations. The crucial point in the theory centres around the point of the subject of consciousness in the process of rational action.

Habermas says:

> The phenomena in need of explication are no longer, in and of themselves, the knowledge and mastery of an objective nature, but the intersubjectivity of possible understanding and agreement - at both the interpersonal and intrapsychic levels. The focus of investigation thereby shifts from cognitive-instrumental rationality to communicative rationality. And what is paradigmatic for the latter is not the relation of a solitary subject to something in the objective world that can be manipulated, but the intersubjective relation that speaking and acting subjects take up when they come to an understanding with one another about something.[42]

Habermas correctly identifies the link between the philosophy of consciousness and the construction of reason that has led to the form of rationalisation and the breakdown of meaning and freedom in modern Western society. His view that an intersubjective paradigm of consciousness leading to communicative theory will continue the "project of the enlightenment" and bring about appropriate forms of democracy and social organisation would appear to be the most promising development in recent social theory. However the failure in the theory Habermas presents is the failure to fully articulate an intersubjective paradigm. This is a failure shared by Apel, and could be said to apply to Peirce as well. Habermas turns on two occasions, in *The Theory of*

Communicative Action[43] and *Postmetaphysical Thinking*[44] to Mead to provide an intersubjective paradigm for replacement of the philosophy of consciousness. But he does not succeed in establishing an intersubjective paradigm via Mead because Mead himself remained locked within a quasi-Cartesian model of the theory of consciousness. Habermas acknowledges the limitations of the theory in his second essay on Mead, where he says: 'Mead examined social individualization solely from the point of view of progressive individuation'.[45] And the conflict remains between intersubjectivity and autonomy which Mead cannot resolve. Mead's interest in social psychology provides a model of intersubjective self-formation without an adequate philosophical theory to support it. It is significant that in this essay on Mead, Habermas uses the language of Apel in referring to 'the agreement of an unlimited communication community' rather than his earlier characterisation of the "ideal speech situation", to support the notion of an intersubjective identity.

Habermas' primary interest in the sociology of communicative action rather than its philosophical basis shows through here. His reliance in the later writing on the concept of the lifeworld emphasises the embedding of language and communicative rationality. Whilst this serves his purpose to explain the symbolic structure of social reproduction it obscures to an extent his further claim that language use commits one to rationality, which must in turn be communicative rationality. The bind here is that the lifeworld presupposes language as part of its symbolic structure, but, in turn, language also structures the lifeworld; language cannot be in the life world and its basis at the same time. It is these consideration that confound Habermas attempt to produce a theory of intersubjective consciousness sufficient to support his notion of language and communicative theory.

Following this point Charles Taylor makes a strong related criticism of Habermas conception of language. This criticism, related to Taylor's own expressivist account of the self, which will be discussed in a later chapter, is that Habermas ignores, or largely fails to account for, the expressive use of language in communicative situations; most particularly in the presentation of the self. As a background to this criticism, Taylor accuses Habermas as having a totally proceduralist normative theory in contrast to Taylor's own substantialist ethics. Habermas takes issue with Taylor claiming communicative ethics has an orientation to the good. But what is really at issue in this discussion is the scope of language. Taylor says, that it is a 'severe mistake' to limit language to the domain of rationality.[46]

Taylor continues:

> Language plays an indispensable role as an expressive medium in the overall domain of practical reason. We express our moral ends and our understanding of ourselves as humans by at the same time understanding and justifying our ends.
>
> Furthermore, language plays a constitutive role with regard to these ends, norms and customs: it is only through their articulation in language that our norms and purposes can also be changed. Yet language effects this only by disclosure, ie. by lending expression to a part of our pre-understanding of these ends and norms either affirmatively or critically.[47]

In reply, Habermas acknowledges that there is a significant difference between Taylor's view of language and his own. He claims, that Taylor, in basing his view on von Humboldt's theory of language, emphasises "the figures of thought" which are taken from the theory of the subject, that are inherent in the "presuppositions of language" rather the their grounding in a theory of intersubjectivity. Whilst the differences between Taylor and Habermas must remain largely unreconciled as they are based on different paradigms of language it must be acknowledged that Habermas does not adequately deal with the expressive and disclosive uses of language in his theory. Not all valid uses of language entail validity claims that are redeemable in the context of an ideal communication situation.

Habermas struggle here with the scope of language and its relation to the lifeworld in a context communicative theory reveal again that the subject in intersubjectivity behind communicative theory is not given an adequate account. It will be demonstrated in the following chapters that a return to Kant and a reconstruction of Kantian theory in the light of Wittgenstein and communicative theory is necessary to produce a theory of the self that supports both intersubjectivity and a communicative theory that will, in turn, support discursively redeemable validity claims.

Notes

1 See for instance Karl-Otto Apel (1993), "The Challenge of the Totalizing Critique of Reason", in *Reason and Its Other*, eds. Dieter Freundlieb and Wayne Hudson Berg, Providence, p.31. Also see Apel, Karl-Otto (1981), *Charles Sanders Peirce; From Pragmatism to Pragmaticism*, trans. John Michael Krois, University of Massachusetts Press, Amherst.

2 Benhabib, Seyla (1992), *Situating the Self*, Polity Press, Cambridge.

3 See Kant, Immanuel, The *Critique of Judgement*, trans. Werner S. Pluhar, Hackett Indianapolis, p. 153. Kant claims the problem of critique of judgement is part of the general problem of transcendental philosophy.

4 See Trusted, Jenifer (1981), *An Introduction to the Theory of Knowledge*, Macmillan, London, Chapter 4.
5 See Trusted, Jenifer, op. cit., Chapter 7.
6 Hausman, Carl R. (1993), *Charles S. Peirce's Evolutionary Philosophy*, Cambridge University Press, Cambridge, p. 1.
7 See Brent, Joseph (1993), *Charles Sanders Peirce: A Life*, Indiana University Press, Bloomington. This fascinating and excellent work charts the life and work of this "most original and versatile thinker" against the background of a complex and flawed personality.
8 Peirce, Charles Sanders (1958), *Selected Writings*, ed. Philip P. Wiener, Dover, New York, p. xi.
9 William James promoted Peirce as the founder of pragmatism, but Peirce disagreed with James' interpretation and coined the term "pragmaticism" to distinguish his theory from the James version which he thought dealt inadequately with semiotics. Peirce is claimed to have said that the term "pragmaticism" ought to be ugly enough not to be appropriated by anyone else.
10 See Hausman, Carl R. (1993), *Charles S. Peirce's Evolutionary Philosophy*, Chapter 3 especially pp.93 - 97, for an explanation of the categories.
11 Peirce, Charles Sanders, *Selected Writings*, p.40.
12 Ibid., p.41.
13 Ibid.
14 Ibid., p. 72. Also note that Peirce's syntax frequently leaves much to be desired; so much so that Hartshorne, one of his early editors, claims that some key ideas are rendered incomprehensible.
15 Peirce, Charles Sanders, *Selected Writings*, p.84.
16 Ibid.
17 He may here have misunderstood Descartes' notion of "clear and distinct ideas" as he seems to relate them to that which is clearly perceived alone rather than the notion ideas which are clear and distinct before the mind.
18 Ibid., p.124.
19 Ibid., p.133.
20 Ibid.
21 The debate about realism versus idealism has been far reaching in Peirce scholarship and centres around the degree to which Peirce can be read as a naturalist or positivist or as a Kantian idealist. This issue is discussed, for instance, by Christopher Hookway and Carl Hausman in various writings.
22 Hausman, Carl R., *Charles S. Peirce's Evolutionary Philosophy*, p. 167.
23 Ibid.
24 Ibid., p. 168.
25 Apel, Karl-Otto (1981), *Charles S. Peirce: From Pragmatism to Pragmaticism*, University of Massachusetts Press, Amherst, p. ix.
26 A clear statement of this development can be found in the essay "The Communication Community as the Transcendental Presupposition for the Social

Sciences" in Apel, Karl-Otto (1980), *Towards a Transformation of Philosophy*, trans. G. Adey and D. Frisby, Routledge and Kegan Paul, London.

27 For a more detailed account of Apel's position see Apel, Karl-Otto (1984), "The situation of Humanity as an Ethical Problem" in *Praxis*, vol. 4, no. 3.

28 Ibid., pp. 136 – 147.

29 Apel, Karl-Otto (1980), *Towards a Transformation of Philosophy*, p. 101.

30 See Colapietro, Vincent M. (1989) *Peirce's Approach to the Self*, State University of New York Press, Albany. Chapter one provides an excellent exposition of Peirce's theory of signs.

31 Apel, Karl-Otto, Charles S. Peirce: *From Pragmatism*, pp. 35-47.

32 See Karl-Otto Apel, *Towards a Transformation of Philosophy*, pp. 114 - 118.

33 Colapietro, Vincent M. (1989), *Peirce's Approach to the Self*, p. 68.

34 Wiggershaus, Rolf (1994), *The Frankfurt School; Its History, Theories, and Political Significance*, trans. Michael Robertson, MIT Press, Cambridge, Massachusetts, p. 571.

35 Ibid., p. 639.

36 Habermas, Jürgen (1991), "A Reply", in *Communicative Action*, eds. Axel Honneth and Hans Joas, trans. Jeremy Gaines and Doris L. Jones, MIT Press, Cambridge, Mass., p. 243.

37 Habermas was Adorno's research assistant at the "Institute for Social Research" during the 1950s. Adorno was proud of him but Horkheimer could not accept him, regarding him as too left wing and regarding his activism in the "Students for a Democratic Society" with suspicion. Horkheimer prevented him from taking his Habilitation at Frankfurt, but in spite of all this Habermas respected Horkheimer's work.

38 Habermas, Jürgen (1971), *Knowledge and Human Interests*, trans. J. Shapiro, Beacon Press, Boston, p. 205.

39 Ibid.

40 Taylor, Charles (1991), "Language and Society", in *Communicative Action*.

41 Brand, Arie (1990), *The Force of Reason*, Allen and Unwin, Sydney, p. 3.

42 Habermas, Jürgen (1984), *The Theory of Communicative Action, Vol 1*, trans. Thomas McCarthy, Beacon Press, Boston, Mass., p. 392.

43 Habermas, Jurgen (1987), *The Theory of Communicative Action, Vol II*, Polity Press, Cambridge, Part V.

44 Habermas, Jürgen (1992) "Individuation through Socialization: On Mead's Theory of Subjectivity", in *Postmetaphysical Thinking*, trans. William Mark Hohengarten, MIT Press, Cambridge, Mass.

45 Ibid., p. 192.

46 Taylor, Charles (1991), "Language and Society", in *Communicative Action*, p.34.

47 Ibid.

3 Kant: The Unity of Apperception and the Modern Self

The discussion of the modern sense of the self relevant to the concerns to be discussed here begins with Kant. However, as Taylor[1] in *Sources of the Self* notes the recognition of "inwardness" as a category of experience owes its origins, in the first instance, to Augustine and somewhat later to Descartes. Thence, Locke and Hume can be credited with a telling critique of introspective theory, yet one that sought to give an empirical grounding to inwardness; not to deny it. The modern sense of the self, still incorporating an inwardness, arises clearly with Kant in the "Transcendental Deduction"[2] and thence is further articulated in the *Critique of Practical Reason*[3] and later works.

Pre-Kantian views of the self were based on the themes established by Plato and developed by Augustine, Descartes and the empiricists. Taylor points out that there is a significant difference between the ground breaking theory of Plato and the "revolution" of inwardness brought by Augustine and Descartes.[4] For Plato reason was an external set of rules which the mind could grasp and accept by a process of "reminiscence". When we live by these rules we attained self-mastery and self-understanding. When we lived by appetite and desire we failed of self-mastery and self-understanding. The self, as far there was such a thing, for Plato was the inner reflection of a set of external Forms. Taylor further makes the point that this model is quite familiar to us and is still today easily comprehended. It has formed a basis for a model of the Christian moral code passed down to today. The "revolution", or turn to inwardness, that comes with Augustine and then much later with Descartes, does not deny the importance of reason but rather finds it within. Augustine replaced the Platonic Ideas with God; and it is God who we find within, 'In the inward man dwells truth', he says. God becomes the inner light of reason that allows us to see the world aright. [5]

The familiar picture of inwardness proposed by Descartes extends the reflexivity of Augustine to a radical reflexivity in the *cogito.* Descartes claims that the process of doubt leads to the situation where, by reflexive reasoning I cannot doubt that at the time of doubting that I am conscious. And that, if conscious, I must be a conscious being that is capable of a range of cognitions, including doubt, memory, belief, etc.

Here Descartes maintains that we find the "self within" by a process of radical reflexive introspection. This model of the self, only recently under serious challenge, has been enormously influential in establishing the picture of the discrete inner, ontologically self-sufficient, disengaged self.

It is against this background that Kant sought to make his "Copernican revolution" in philosophy with a radically new understanding of reason and the place of the subject. In his revolutionary view the subject, via his or her cognitive powers, is realised in the manifestation of such an understanding.

Kant thought of himself as an empiricist, but as one who would not give up the importance of metaphysics and reason as a basis for philosophy. He accepted much of the force of Hume's empiricist critique but could not accept the scepticism that it implied. Kant accepted Hume's view that introspection did not reveal a "self" or "ego identity" in Descartes' (and Augustine's) sense. It was Hume's view, that when he excluded all impressions, both external and internal, there was no residual impression of an "I"; there was literally, nothing. The "I" was inferred from a continuity and unity of perception rather than being an object of perception. Hume's argument for this position centres on there being no impression of the substance of the mind. The registration of internal impressions leads us assume, falsely, that there must be some substance in which they adhere, but analysis of those impressions does not justify any such conclusion.[6]

Hume's view undermines the introspective ego of Descartes but leaves the self as seeming to be an accidental feature of experience rather than something more substantive. It is from this position that Kant set out to develop the modern sense of the self.

The expression, "the modern sense of the self" has been used by Taylor and others, yet it is clearly the case that there is little consensus about what the modern sense of the self is. In fact, it is clear that there is some theoretical disarray in this respect at present. This theoretical disarray, of course, reflects the pressing need for philosophical solutions. The range of discussion spans from the decentred self such as the recent discussion by Giddens[7] to the newer versions of Lockean individualism.

There is, most importantly, yet mistakenly, a current dominant sense of the self which forms part of a set of norms and beliefs that is based on a post-Cartesian view and implicitly supported by interpretations of Locke and Hume that underpins capitalist social formations and scientific rationalism. Such a view is supported, for instance, by Robert Nozick in *Anarchy State and Utopia.*[8] In this view the Cartesian self becomes an ideal, albeit after Hume an unsustainable ideal, but this is precisely what makes the "myth" work. The very idea of taking "a property in" in Locke's sense depends upon there being a self as owner of the property thus taken. Locke's view of the self derives from his views about the mind and the relationship of consciousness to the world.

He says:

> Let us suppose the mind to be, as we say, white paper void of all characters, without any *ideas*. How comes it to be furnished? Whence comes it by that vast store which the busy and boundless fancy of man has painted on it with an almost endless variety? Whence has it all the materials of reason and knowledge? To this I answer, in one word from *experience*; in that all our knowledge is founded, and from it ultimately derives itself. Our observation, employed either about *external sensible objects, or about the internal operations of our minds perceived and reflected on by ourselves, is that which supplies our understanding with all the materials of thinking.* These two are the fountains of knowledge, from whence all the ideas we have, or can naturally have, do spring.[9]

But for Locke, it was not possible to know the primary qualities directly from experience. They could be deduced by reason from experience. The self however was nothing more than a point of consciousness that registered experience or what Locke called "ideas". The quality-less punctuality of the self makes the reference of properties to such a self, all the less problematic; as long as the illusion of the existence of the punctual self is maintained. This is because the "ideas" before consciousness are undifferentiated with respect to their type of content and all stand in a subject-object relationship to such a self. For the Locke then the individual is individuated by introspection on the "ideas" before the mind. This conventional view is pre-Kantian in essence and not the modern view, which can be found, for instance, in Durkheim and much recent sociological work.

The view of the modern sense of the self to be supported here differs radically from this "conventional view". It is a form of "transcendental view" grounded in communicative theory. The origins of such a theory stem directly and principally from Kant. In using the expression "the modern sense of the self" I am following Habermas' understanding which can be expressed as a socially individuated autonomous being,[10] Habermas acknowledges that: 'Since Kant, the transcendentally revaluated ego has been conceived simultaneously as a *world-generating* and *autonomously acting subject*,'[11] but maintains that for Kant, 'the individuated ego falls through the cracks'.[12] Habermas then claims that Mead offers a full account of the self that permits a construction of an intersubjective yet socially differentiated autonomous being. This discussion will be examined in detail later but is significant here that Habermas acknowledges the turn away from the pure philosophy of consciousness as commencing with Kant's 'transcendental revaluation of the ego'.

Kantian metaphysics claims that there are certain things about the world that can be known a priori, by the process of the mind reflecting upon the conditions necessary for experience; these Kant referred to as 'synthetic a priori statements'. In developing this position he conceded that Hume, in his sceptical attack on Cartesian egoism, was correct. However, he could not accept Hume's sceptical conclusion that the mind really was a form of *tabula rasa* with only the power of association of ideas or impressions.[13] Hume in *A Treatise of Human Nature* had claimed that the act of introspection revealed no "self" or Cartesian ego. Hume's attack on the Cartesian position is quite forthright.

> There are some philosophers, who imagine we are every moment intimately conscious of what we call our SELF; that we feel its existence and its continuance in existence.[14]

Hume is quite sure that such philosophers are deluded, he continues:

> Unluckily all these positive assertions are contrary to that very experience, which is pleaded for them, nor have we any idea of *self,* after the manner it is here explain'd.[15]

And further,

> It cannot, therefore, be from any of these impressions (pleasure, passions, sensation etc.), or from any other, that the idea of the self is deriv'd; and consequently there is no such idea.[16]

All the mind could be aware of were its impressions; remove the impressions and there was literally, nothing. Later in the same chapter Hume asserts, in a remarkable passage with a Wittgensteinian ring to it, that:

> The whole of this doctrine (regarding personal identity) leads us to a conclusion, which is of great importance in the present affair, *viz,* that all the nice and subtle questions concerning personal identity can never possibly be decided, and are to be regarded rather as grammatical than philosophical difficulties.[17]

Hume takes the view that personal identity is not something that has an enduring continuity, but is rather formed by the imagination, memory and the habit of the mind being aware of successive impressions, to the point where there is the belief in continuous identity. However, careful reflection shows that this belief is founded on successive and discontinuous impressions.

Hume's philosophical position has to be carefully assessed. His scepticism is designed to define and explicate our concepts as much as to dump metaphysics. Hume is a keen critic, but he was no nihilist. Hume was not saying that it was wrong to hold a belief in a continuous self, nor that no continuous self existed; he was rather offering an explanation of this belief, which was in fact founded on memory of an episodic and discontinuous string of impressions. For Hume it was the contiguity of the impressions combined with imagination and memory that formed a basis for the belief in personal identity. Later, in amplification of this view, he says in a discussion of the seat of the passions of pride and humility that; 'This object is self, or that succession of related ideas and impressions, of which we have an intimate memory and consciousness'.[18] The self was a matter of reasonably founded belief for Hume, not an indubitable certainty of the Cartesian type; such certainty was not possible and there was no indubitable knowledge of the self.

Hume's position was certainly the most radical of the eighteenth century empiricists and indeed of any empiricist position. He insisted that we should not attribute more to the concept of self, or any other concept, than could actually be established by experience. The self was as it were contingent upon the impressions before the mind and not established by the necessity of any process of reflection. His views are more subtle and profound than is generally received and require more careful consideration than that usually accorded them. Hume is frequently typecast or dismissed as the ultimate proto-positivist; an attribution of which he would no doubt have been proud. However, there is another reading of Hume, which accords with his personal philosophical struggle, in which his views might even be seen to prefigure Hegel in some respects relating to self constitution; although of course the metaphysical basis would not have been shared. Put simply, this view is that we construct our self from the material of our experience. No fixed or enduring self presents to us as humans who have the opportunity for a radical kind of freedom to live in a distinctly human world, which is of our construction. It is a construction from the impressions which are the elements of our experience. It is a special role of the imagination, particularly with respect to the passions, that creates a sense of enduring being that we can call a self.[19] It was a similar notion of imagination that Kant was to develop in the *Critique of Judgement* some years later. The role of imagination, it will later be shown, turns out to be crucial in the individuation of the intersubjective self.

Kant had the greatest respect for Hume and many of the questions Hume raised not only stirred Kant from his "dogmatic slumbers" but set the agenda for Kant's philosophical thought, in metaphysics, epistemology and ethics. In fact the dominant theme in all of Kant's work is the attempt to reply to, and overcome, the powerful sceptical positions established by Hume. Kant's respect for Hume and also for his contemporary, Hutcheson, is perhaps a reflection of Kant's Scottish ancestry.[20] His family were Pietists and although Kant did not share their most austere religious views he nevertheless remained devoutly religious throughout his life.[21] This religious outlook was again opposed to the atheistic scepticism of Hume. Kant, for instance, on many occasions attempted to oppose Hume's view that it was not possible to prove (or to disprove) the existence of God. Whilst Kant claims that the processes of the transcendental deduction and the transcendental logic can be conducted on rational grounds, it is nevertheless clear that the figure of God is at the pinnacle of Kant's transcendentalism.[22] This becomes especially clear in the *Opus Postumum* where Kant links the unity of his system directly to God. Kant was sensitive to the subtlety of Hume's views about the construction of reality from experience and realised that if such a proposal was to succeed and avoid scepticism then a further a priori element was required.

Kant accepted the existence of the Cartesian ego, or something very much like it. Certainly he believed in the existence of an individual soul which also formed the essence of each human person; indeed of each rational being. But he did not accept that it could be established or accessed by the radical reflection of introspection as proposed by Descartes. The element of broad reflective subjectivity runs through all of Kant's critical works and becomes more significant in the later works. It is however, a reflection on the conditions for experience from a transcendental perspective, rather than Descartes' analytic necessity. He variously discusses the elements of subjectivity in its differing modes in a progressive fashion throughout each of the three critiques and the later works. The reason for this clearly stems from his "Copernican revolution" in philosophy where he shifts the structure of experience from external reality to the powers of cognition and to the synthetic a priori in particular.

Kant commences the development of his critical discussion of the powers of cognition in the *Critique of Pure Reason.* He had been trained as a traditional metaphysician in the tradition of Leibniz and Wolff, and thus in doctrines that held that the world was knowable in its entirety a priori via 'truths of reason'.[23] However he became increasingly convinced that this dogmatic rationalism led to antinomies, seeming contradictions, and could not secure metaphysics. He was further, finally dislodged from the complacency of dogmatic rationalism upon reading Hume's *Enquiry.* The *Critique of Pure Reason* is the metaphysician's critical response to these uncertainties.

Our focus here in the discussion of the *Critique of Pure Reason* is on the self and the subjectivity of a priori judgements, on which knowledge is founded. The examination of this issue is complicated by the fact that there is a marked difference between Kant's discussion of the "I" and the "self" in the first and second editions of first *Critique.* This was in part due to the fact that, as Guyer comments: 'the initial response to Kant's argument ...was largely incomprehension'[24] and also the fact that, as Kant acknowledged, 'that part of the *Critique* which should have been the clearest was the most obscure, or even revolved in a circle.'[25] And thus when the second edition was published six years after the first, Kant had completely rewritten the Transcendental Deduction, claiming that the arguments were the same and that only the presentation differed.[26]

However despite Kant's claim there are significant differences in Kant's treatment of consciousness between the editions. It would seem in the first edition he had not fully thought through his position and thus had not recognised either the full importance or complexity of the discussion. Guyer notes that Kant scholars are agreed that the explication of the *Transcendental Deduction* makes for fearful difficulties and would seem to reveal some confusions in his thought. In the first edition he simply sees the deduction as based on, 'This pure original unchangeable consciousness I shall name *transcendental apperception*'.[27] He is then satisfied that a priori and empirical knowledge of the self simply follows from it.

In the second edition the whole context of the discussion has changed. Kant does not repudiate his former position but concentrates his discussion much more upon the transcendental unity of self-consciousness and self-knowledge. Kant takes a position regarding the self and the subject in *The Critique of Practical Reason* that is close to the discussion in the second edition of the first *Critique.* But is also somewhat different in that his stress is on humans as rational agents, rather than the transcendental unity of apperception. This position will be discussed in more detail later. It is perhaps worth noting that despite major shifts in a number of his central theses, Kant never actually repudiates the earlier position but insists on seeing later positions as developments of the earlier position incorporating major tenets. This aspect of his thought can be both frustrating and confusing to the reader. Perhaps the most notorious example of this practice can be illustrated in the *Critique of Practical Reason* where he asserts the precedence of freedom over reason in the order of cognitive powers without any clear acknowledgment that in the earlier *Critique* he had asserted the sovereignty of reason.

Kant's aim in the *Critique of Pure Reason* is to rescue reason from "darkness and contradiction" and, via the transcendental method, to reinstate metaphysics from 'a matron outcast and forsaken' to 'Queen of all the sciences';[28] His strategy was to use the transcendental method to show that experience required an a priori component. This he explored in the

Transcendental Aesthetic, demonstrating that both analytic and synthetic a priori judgements were involved. The analytic a priori gives us access to the truths of reason and the synthetic a priori access to truths about the world. The a priori is based on the intuitions of space and time. The importance of a priori knowledge for Kant, is that it will lead to 'knowledge absolutely independent of all experience'.[29] Thus showing, in the case of a priori synthetic knowledge, that it is possible to have knowledge of the world that is true and universal which does not depend upon experience. By this radical move Kant aims to answer Hume's scepticism and show that reason has a place in knowledge that depends on experience. The radical move was to locate the intuitions of space and time "in us". What is received by the mind is given form by bringing it under the intuitions of space and time. Space is the outer sense that relates the mind to objects[30] and time the inner sense or 'form of our inner intuition' by which we represent our inner dimensions to consciousness.[31]

Having taken the "Copernican step" of locating the generation of experience within, Kant needs to explore the structure of consciousness, self-consciousness and the cognitive faculty of reason to secure his position regarding knowledge and the reinstatement of metaphysics. This he does in the "Transcendental Analytic". The most important section for this discussion, and indeed the key to whole exposition, is to be found in the "The Deduction of the Pure Concepts of the Understanding" of which, in turn, the "Transcendental Deduction" of the second edition is the most important chapter. Having settled the deduction of the categories the further development of the work elaborates the application of transcendental critique to reason in the "The Transcendental Dialectic" and the application of Pure Reason in the "Transcendental Doctrine of Method". But it is the "Deduction" that is the focus of this discussion and, indeed, of most of the recent commentary.

In the "Deduction" Kant sets out to prove the necessity of intellectual principles necessary to establish the basis of certain logical relationships. In particular the relationship of causality; once again having Hume in his sights. Kant has in mind the traditional metaphysical categories such as cause, substance, necessity, etc., which he was seeking to re-establish. Having shown that experience comes from our structuring of the manifold via the intuitions of space and time Kant required a means to put a structure on experience that allowed for the knowledge of the objects of experience. In order for there to be knowledge of objects the objects had to fall under an experience that was generated by us, yet conformed to certain further, eventually metaphysical, principles. Thus the need to deduce the categories. His argument for the categories, between the two editions becomes very confused. The confusion relates to whether or not the categories can be deduced from the unity of thought about objects, the synthetic unity of apperception; or whether the concepts of objects imply, necessarily the unity of thought, apperception, and consequently the self. Kant sets out to prove the former, especially in the first edition and ends up, largely in the second edition, proving the latter.

The matter is further complicated by the fact that, in the exposition, his focus shifts from this intended task of proving the categories, which is still pursued, to the conditions of consciousness required to establish the categories. It is here that the modern sense of the self begins to emerge as Kant turns to the unity of the self and self-consciousness to establish the unity of apperception as a transcendental ground for the establishment of the categories. Discussion of the critique has never been particularly concerned with the categories themselves, but rather focussed on the ground of the categories in self-consciousness.[32] Commentators have not been much concerned with whether or not there are twelve or five or fewer categories, nor with the actual categories themselves, but with the transcendental unity of apperception required by the categories.[33] A later critique by Henrich, Habermas and others reveals that the categories themselves become largely redundant, once the transcendental unity of apperception and thus consciousness, is established. The reason for this is in fact given by Kant himself in the second edition where the transcendental unity of apperception precedes and determines the categories.

Kant says:

> This unity, which precedes *a priori* all concepts of combination, is not the category of unity; for all categories are grounded in logical functions of judgement, and in these functions combination, and therefore unity of given concepts, is already thought.[34]

He adds in a following passage to complete the picture:

> The unity of this apperception I likewise entitle the *transcendental* unity of self-consciousness.[35]

Kant moves from arguing to establish the objective validity of the categories to an argument for the "unity of consciousness" which in turn establishes the "objective validity" of an object. It is the transcendental unity of apperception that gives the concept of an object. As Guyer says: 'The project of discovering conditions that will also be necessary conditions for cognition of objects is thus entirely inverted'.[36] Guyer concludes that: 'Formally speaking, the transcendental deduction is a failure', but that, 'Nevertheless, the transcendental deduction also transformed the agenda of modern philosophy'. Kant had demonstrated that there was a definite connection between self-knowledge and knowledge of the world. It would take the "linguistic turn" and the transformation of Kantian philosophy pioneered by Apel to make this connection explicit.

Many commentators regard Kant's view of the self taken in the first edition of the *Critique of Pure Reason* as the definitive view on consciousness and consequently of the role of the self. Certainly this position does reveal the fundamental step taken by Kant in recognising the transcendental element of consciousness, but it is rather misleading to call this Kant's view. The seconding edition and the later critiques reveal a more complex view of the self as both a free agent and an intersubjective being that go well beyond the powers of the synthesis of the manifold. A closer examination of Kant's position may be developed from a reflection on his treatment of Descartes.

Kant appears to be almost dismissive of Descartes *Cogito*. However, he does not so much dismiss the *Cogito* as false or in some way incorrect, but rather as a relatively trivial insight, which does not, of itself, solve any philosophical problem. He says, in the second edition of *Critique of Pure Reason*: 'It must be possible for the "I think"', to accompany all my representations; 'and not simply the introspective representation accompanied by the expression 'I think'.[37] For Kant it is the unity of the apperception that constitutes a *self*-consciousness and not any intuitive awareness of the "I" or "I think".

Kant says:

> On the other hand, in the transcendental synthesis of the manifold of representations in general, and therefore in the synthetic original unity of apperception, I am conscious of myself, not as I appear to myself, nor as I am in myself but only that I am.[38]

And again it is the unity of apperception that makes possible this thought that "I am".

This is the essence of Kant's direct reply to Hume. Where Hume had said that the unity of the self and consciousness was an illusion, albeit a contingently fortuitous one, Kant says that it must be based in the transcendental synthesis of the manifold as the synthetic unity of apperception. Where Hume claims there was no unifying principle to be discovered; Kant claims there must be an underlying and unifying principle for self-consciousness to exist. Kant's view is that the subject or the ground of the self and self-consciousness is given in the "transcendental apperception" and that the actual self, self-consciousness and self knowledge, is constituted by thought, concept formation and by objective reality, including the possession of empirical knowledge. This is the first statement of what I am calling a characteristically modern view of the self. It is, I stress, a view that has not been universally held in the modern period. Rather, one is likely to find the older conceptions such as the Cartesian/empiricist view, which has supported possessive individualism, materialism and scientific rationalism. However the Kantian view, when fully developed is more completely modern, in that it supports a process of critique and views of discursive and communicative reason in a way that the Cartesian view cannot.

In order to reach an understanding of the basis of the modern view of the self here a more detailed exposition of Kant is required. This exposition will be in two stages representing the episodes in the development of Kant's thought. The first will present the views of the first critique *The Critique of Pure Reason*. The second later view is to be found principally in the second critique *The Critique of Practical Reason* and also in other later writings including the *Critique of Judgement,* the political essays and intriguingly, the fragments of the *Opus postumum*.

In the first critique Kant undertakes a lengthy discussion of the "I think" in the "Transcendental Deduction" he explicitly acknowledges his agreement with Hume, he says:

> Consciousness of self according to the determinations of our state in inner perception is merely empirical, and always changing. No fixed and abiding self can present itself in this flux of inner appearances.[39]

Kant here is explicitly denying Descartes' route of introspection to the discovery of a 'fixed and abiding self'. However, Kant does signal that he has a path to the discovery such a self. He says later in the same paragraph:

> To render such a transcendental presupposition valid, there must be a condition that precedes all experience, and which makes experience itself possible.[40]

It would appear that Kant is trying to maintain a conception very similar to the Cartesian ego, whilst using the transcendental apperception rather than introspection as a route to its discovery. But what exactly Kant's position is here, is not clear; or at least not sufficiently developed. For instance, Dieter Henrich has recently observed;

> For anyone who has tried to follow Kant's justification for his basic theory (of the transcendental unity of apperception) and is familiar with the history of its reception, it is a commonplace that elucidating the form and function of that starting point makes for the most formidable difficulties...[41]

Henrich certainly believes that Kant's position is 'somewhat unclear'. It would seem that Kant himself recognised, to a degree, the problems posed by his account of transcendental deduction as the second edition of the *Critique of Pure Reason* contains a much revised, and somewhat more perplexing account than the first. The account in the first edition is relatively clear but somewhat undeveloped, whilst the account of the second edition is less superficial but raises added difficulties. Much of the difficulty in dealing with Kant's exposition at this point comes, as Henrich observes, from the complexity of his eccentric psychology. Whilst there are these exegetical difficulties with Kant, his overall insight that certain a priori conditions must pertain, is of the utmost importance for the development of a modern theory of consciousness. For it is just what constitutes the nature of the conditions that occupies much contemporary discussion.

Kant's theory, can be better grasped, and falls into clearer relief, if viewed against the background of Hume's sceptical position. Hume, following Locke, claimed that the only power the mind possessed was the power of association of impressions. Kant was disturbed by the radical empiricist position taken by Hume, in much the same way as he had been outraged by Hume's sceptical position on knowledge, which denied the existence of any innate or intuitive knowledge. Even the understanding of cause and effect was derived by habit from experience. It was this denial of any necessary unity of consciousness that so disturbed Kant and it was this point that sought to answer. The two positions are of course linked; there can be no certainty about knowledge if there can be no certainty about the identity and unity of the self, because there would be no locus for the subject of knowledge. In the way in which Kant asserted that there was a transcendental ground for certainty of knowledge based on the synthetic a priori (space and time) there also must be a transcendental ground for the unity of consciousness. These two elements are again, of course, closely bound together but the ground of the self was to prove more elusive.

Kant uses the term "representation" as a near equivalent to Hume's term "impression". Kant says that it must be possible for the "I think" to accompany all representations because otherwise there would be representations which could not be thought, which Kant says, would be impossible. Representation that is given prior to all thought is entitled "intuition". Kant then says: 'All the manifold of intuition has, therefore, a necessary relation to the "I think" in the same *subject* in which the manifold is found'.[42] He then says that he regards this representation as an act of spontaneity which he calls 'pure and original apperception'. Kant continues: 'The unity of this apperception I likewise entitle the *transcendental* unity of self-consciousness, in order to indicate the possibility of *a priori* knowledge arising from it'.[43] This particular passage of the *Critique* makes for great difficulties of interpretation. Kant seems to be saying that in order for there to be representations at all, there must be a transcendental unity of consciousness. But what is most perplexing is his statement that this will be in the "same subject" as the "I think" is found. It is clear that through the relation to the categories and the unity of space and time, he is attempting to answer Hume's scepticism by appealing to a underlying unifying element of perception. In Humean terms Kant's proposition is simply that in order for impressions to be had at all there must be a 'transcendental unity of self-consciousness', and that space and time are indeed part of this unified consciousness. It is important to remember that, for Kant, the impressions were not given, but had to be formed in accordance with our innate intuitions in order to be experienced at all. Kant is here claiming that my representations must, 'conform to the condition under which alone they can stand together in one universal self-consciousness, because [otherwise] they would not all without exception belong to me'.[44] Because intuition is innate to the mind, impressions must presuppose the dimensions of space and time, and consciousness in order to exist as synthetic a priori judgements. If experiences were not being had by one unified self-consciousness they would not be had at all, because, in a real way to Kant, experiences are constructed by consciousness. Experiences must be had by a consciousness and the fact that they are had by me, reflexively establishes the unity of my consciousness. The understanding that experiences are had by such a consciousness implies that the "I think" referred to earlier, could accompany any of the experiences; not just the experience of thinking "I think", as Descartes and Leibniz had assumed. Any experiences (representations) that are had at all must be had by the one and unified consciousness otherwise, as far as "I" am concerned, they would not be experienced at all. If such experiences did exist they would be experiences of another subject(s). Kant says:

> In other words, only insofar as I can grasp the manifold of the representations in one consciousness, do I call them all *mine*. For otherwise I should have as many-coloured and diverse a self as I have representations of which I am conscious to myself.[45]

This insight is at the one time both profound and fraught with exceptional difficulty. Kant says that many consequences follow from it; as indeed they do, but great care needs to be exercised in the drawing of any such consequences. One consequence is that it is the one consciousness that "conjoins" representations rather than Hume's view that conjunction of impressions creates the illusion of one consciousness. Another is that the unity of objects shares the same transcendental ground as the unity of apperception. It is this feature that lays the ground for the establishment of the "noumenon within" which Kant discusses more explicitly in later works, and which will be taken up in later discussion regarding the ground of intersubjectivity.

It is important to consider whether or not Kant's argument at this point actually establishes his conclusion. Guyer for one, as previously indicated, is of the opinion that it does not.[46] The problem relates to a potential circularity in Kant's complex argument; which is at the same time an argument for the twelve categories and the unity of consciousness/self-consciousness, and also late in the "Deduction", the unity of space and time. The complexity and numerous revisions of the argument from the first to the second editions of the *Critique*, to the *Prolegomena,* to the 1787 revision make it very difficult to conduct a formal critical analysis. The circularity may not be a strict circularity, but it involves the issue of whether or not transcendental unity of apperception establishes the unity of the objects of experience via the unity of space and time, or whether the unity of the objects of experience presuppose the synthetic unity of apperception. Ultimately, the question turns on whether the categories can be deduced via the transcendental apperception or whether all synthesis, including judgement, stands under the categories; in which case what is "apperceived" so to speak, can only be judged to be so apperceived because the categories apply. Guyer points to this disparity and suggests a possible source of confusion in Kant's exposition:

> What has not been noticed, however, is that there is a major disparity between the way in which Kant describes the conclusion of the deduction in sections 20 and 21 and the premise from which he set out in section 16. In sections 20 and 21, Kant speaks of the conditions of the unity of the manifold in *a* or *one* given manifold, suggesting that some additional consideration is needed to remove this restriction and prove that *all* of our intuitions can in fact be unified in a *single* manifold. But in section 16 he set out from the claim that *all* of our intuitions are in fact unified in the transcendental unity of apperception.[47]

Guyer here sees that the restricted conclusion of sections 20 and 21 is a tacit recognition on Kant's part that 'all is not well' with the concept of apperception. And that the 'claim that we have we have *a priori* certainty of the numerical identity of the self in all its possible representations is not unimpeachable'.[48]

An analysis of the reasons for the formal failure of the *Transcendental Deduction* involves attempting to deal with some of the most fundamental metaphysical problems that relate consciousness to its objects, to the subject, and to self-consciousness. Kant's partial failure results from the way in which he set up the question(s) that the transcendental deduction was intended to address. The key to the confusion lies where Kant says 'All the manifold of intuition has, therefore, a necessary relation to the "I think" in the same subject in which this manifold is found'. [49] The manifold occurs (spontaneously) in the one subject, yet Kant does not adequately distinguish between this subject of the manifold and the apperception that leads to the transcendental unity of self-consciousness. He confounds the subject which any awareness must presuppose, with self-consciousness which presupposes a unity of apperception. His failure to make such a distinction leads him to beg the question as to whether the unity of apperception presupposes the unity of self-consciousness, and consequently to the failure to deduce the categories from the transcendental unity of apperception.

Kant shows awareness of this difficulty where, in sections 24 and 25, he discusses how the "I" that thinks can be distinct from the "I" that intuits itself. In order to make the distinction Kant returns to the dimensions of space and time and, in this case, specifically to time which is the dimension of inner sense; space being the dimension of outer sense. Significantly, Kant does not, at this point in the argument use the transcendental apperception to distinguish between the "I" that thinks and the "I" that intuits itself. The reason for this seems obscure in that each "I" should, according to Kant's schema, be differentiated within the unity of apperception. It would seem that at this point in the argument Kant did not have confidence that such a distinction could be made within the formulation of the apperception. Kant's avoidance of the conclusion would seem to be well founded. If the unity of apperception gives rise to the unity of consciousness and thus the locus for the ascription of "I" of self consciousness then the "I" could not easily be found within the field of apperception.

However, it would be a mistake to conclude that because the transcendental deduction does not fully succeed that Kant's achievement can be dismissed; quite the contrary. Kant's unsuccessful argument not only 'completely transformed the agenda of modern philosophy'.[50] It in fact set the agenda for the modern understanding of the self, and also of modern epistemology. He had firstly, exposed the inadequacies of Hume's position and shown that the radical scepticism of Hume was incoherent as it stood and that it could be answered by a universalistic, non-solipsistic position. Thus, Kant had shown that it was not possible to maintain a Humean position with regard to the self. There had to be a unifying principle for "impression" or "representation" in order for there to be any impressions as such. Secondly, Kant had completely exposed the inadequacy of the Cartesian position and shown that introspective knowledge of the "I" could not be the sort of priviledged knowledge that Descartes had claimed.

Guyer on this point says:

> Whilst he had difficulty initially spelling it out, Kant clearly perceived that there was some inescapable connection between self knowledge and knowledge of objects, and this completely undermined the Cartesian assumptions that we could have a determinate knowledge of our inner states without any knowledge of the external world at all...[51]

Kant's positive thesis concerning the self in the *Critique of Pure Reason*, remains incomplete. It cannot account for both the subject of experience and the subject of self-awareness. The unity of apperception could, if successful, provide only a passive self, capable of perception and analytical thought but not of action, nor moral reason, nor of aesthetic judgement. Whilst Kant may have achieved his main aim of preserving a place for metaphysics, by defeating both scepticism and solipsism he had raised more questions about the relation of the self to the cognitive powers that would form much of the subject matter of the later *Critiques*. The answers to these questions would, paradoxically, prove more devastating to metaphysics than the scepticism he sought to oppose.

Notes

1 Taylor, Charles (1989), *Sources of the Self*, Cambridge University Press, Cambridge.

2 Kant, Immanuel (1929), *The Critique of Pure Reason*, trans. Norman Kemp-Smith, Macmillan and Company, London, Chapter 2.

3 Kant, Immanuel (1909), *The Critique of Practical Reason*, trans. Thomas Kingsmill Abbot, Longmans, Green and Company, London.

4 Taylor, Charles (1989), *Sources of the Self*, Cambridge University Press, Cambridge.

5 Quoted in, Taylor, *Sources of the Self*, p. 129.

6 Hume, David (1978), *A Treatise of Human Nature*, second edition, ed. L. A. Selby-Bigge, Oxford University Press, Oxford, pp. 132 –136.

7 See, for example, Giddens, Anthony (1991), *Modernity and Self-Identity*, Polity Press, Cambridge. In this work Giddens explores the idea of a highly reflexive self as a means of overcoming the personal meaningless generated by late modernity.

8 See Robert Nozick (1974), *Anarchy State and Utopia*, Basil Blackwell, Oxford. Nozick supports a Lockean version of the self and bases his 'Minimal State' on the notion of Lockean individualism. For instance he states at the very beginning of the work that 'Individuals have rights, and there are things no person may do to them (without violating those rights)'. This book has been most influential in the development of the 'new right' in recent years.

9 Locke, John (1968), *An Essay Concerning Human Understanding*, ed. J. W. Yolton, Everyman, London, II, I 2.

10 See Habermas, Jurgen (1992), 'Individuation Through Socialization', in *Postmetaphysical Thinking*, trans. William Mark Hohengarten, MIT Press, Cambridge, Mass., p. 158ff.
11 Ibid., p. 158.
12 Ibid.
13 Hume, David, *A Treatise of Human Nature*, p. 253.
14 Ibid., p. 251.
15 Ibid.
16 Ibid., p. 252.
17 Ibid., p. 262.
18 Ibid., p. 277.
19 See Ibid., p. 422 ff.
20 There is no evidence that Kant read the *Enquiry Concerning the Principles of Morals* or much of Hume's later work but he was certainly familiar with the ideas of the Scottish enlightenment through the moral and aesthetic works of Francis Hutcheson who also influenced Hume.
21 Abbott observes, "His family was of Scottish origin, his grandfather having been one of many who emigrated from Scotland at the end of the seventeenth century, the spelling in the name was altered from 'Cant' to preserve the pronunciation".
22 Kant also had a more broadly based understanding of many subjects. We are told that from 1755 until 1770 he lectured at the University of Königsberg in natural sciences and mathematics as well as philosophy. This breadth of interest is revealed in his writings which, for instance, show a knowledge of and respect for the work of Sir Isaac Newton.
23 Kant, Immanuel, *The Critique of Practical Reason*, p. xxxi.
24 Guyer, Paul, "The transcendental deduction of the categories" in *The Cambridge Companion to Kant*, ed. Guyer, Paul, Cambridge, Cambridge University Press.
25 Quoted in Guyer, p. 123.
26 Ibid.
27 Kant, Immanuel (1929), *The Critique of Pure Reason*, trans. Norman Kemp-Smith, Macmillan, London, p. 136.
28 Ibid., Preface to First Edition, p. 7.
29 Ibid., p. 43.
30 Ibid., p. 68.
31 Ibid., p. 79.
32 See Guyer's discussion in, Guyer, Paul (1992), "The transcendental deduction of the categories" in *The Cambridge Companion to Kant*, ed. Guyer, Paul, Cambridge University Press, Cambridge, p. 134.
33 Kant at various points suggests that there may be other than the twelve categories proposed in the formal deduction.
34 Kant, Immanuel, *The Critique of Pure Reason*, p. 152.
35 Ibid., p. 153.
36 Guyer, Paul, "The transcendental deduction of the categories", in *The Cambridge Companion to Kant*, p. 151.

37 Kant, Immanuel, *The Critique of Pure Reason*, p. 152.
38 Ibid., p.168.
39 Ibid., p. 136.
40 Ibid., p. 136.
41 Henrich, Dieter (1992), "Origins of a Theory of the Subject", in *Philosophical Interventions in the Unfinished Project of the Enlightenment,* Honneth, Axel et al.(ed.), trans. William Rehig, The MIT Press, Cambridge, Mass.
42 Kant, *Critique of Pure Reason* (B132). p. 153.
43 Ibid. (B132). p. 153.
44 Ibid.
45 Ibid. (B134). p. 154.
46 Guyer, Paul, "The transcendental deduction of the categories" in *The Cambridge Companion to Kant.*
47 Guyer, Paul. op. cit., p. 153.
48 Ibid., p. 154.
49 Kant, Immanuel, *Critique of Pure Reason* (B132), p. 153.
50 Guyer, Paul, *The Cambridge Companion to Kant*, p. 155.
51 Ibid.

4 Freedom: Kant's Critique of Practical Reason and the Primacy of Freedom

It is generally conceded that Kant was mistaken in many respects in *The Critique of Pure Reason.* To take three fundamental objections; first, the elements of the "Transcendental Aesthetic" ie. space and time were both misunderstood and far too rigid for the purpose of framing a priori knowledge; this was in part Hegel's objection. Kant was using them in a strict Euclidean sense, not even taking full account of the development of these concepts made by Newton nearly a century before. Second, the seminal distinction between analytic and synthetic statements has been seriously weakened as the result of critiques by Frege, Quine, and others. The distinction remains useful as a descriptive tool but is no longer viable a categorical logical distinction, which is what Kant's epistemology requires. Thirdly, the concept of "apperception" upon which he based the deduction of the twelve categories is at least unsatisfactory, if not incoherent, especially with respect to self-consciousness in that it would seem to presuppose a single, identical self with the power of representation.

Kant's tripartite division of cognitive powers into pure or conceptual reason, practical reason, and judgement, has been much more durable. For instance, Habermas sees it as a distinction that powered the enlightenment and still sees it as a relevant basis for the domains of rationality elaborated in *Knowledge and Human Interests*[1]

In the *Critique of Practical Reason* Kant makes a much more radical move than any in his first Critique, one that is to form a keystone of the enlightenment, he says that:

> With this faculty [the pure faculty of reason and practical reason], transcendental freedom is also established;

the freedom referred to is an absolute freedom,

> Inasmuch as the reality of the concept of freedom is proved by an apodictic law of practical reason, it is the *keystone* of the whole system of pure reason, even the speculative, and all other concepts (those of God and immortality).[2]

Kant did not actually deny the existence of pure reason, as a distinct cognitive power, in the second *Critique* but subsumed it under practical reason as "pure practical reason". Many commentators have not paid sufficient attention to this radical shift in Kant's later thought. Specifically, they have not paid sufficient attention to Kant's assertion that reflection upon the concept of freedom determines the primacy of practical reason and the fact that pure reason can also be practical. Further, it determines that freedom as a quality of the will is a necessary attribute of all rational beings, and vice versa.

This represents a major step from the discussion of the third antimony in the *Critique of Pure Reason.* In the third antimony Kant supposes that there is a conflict between the causality of freedom on the one hand and the causality of necessity on the other. Kant's solution to the antinomies in general is to appeal to a supersensible world beyond the appearances that shows an intelligible unity where there is apparent contradiction. In the case of freedom just such a solution is proposed. He says that, 'In its empirical character, therefore, this [acting] subject, as appearance, would have to conform to all the laws of causal determination. ... In its intelligible character (though we can only have a general concept of that character) this same subject must be considered to be free from all influence of sensibility and from all determination through appearances'.[3] Further, he explains that thus, '...freedom and nature, in the full sense of these terms can exist together',[4] Then, in a lengthy exposition, Kant explains that it is reason that determines appearances and that it itself is rooted in some transcendental, or supersensible condition. But whilst not claiming at this stage that the 'reality of freedom as one of our faculties has been established',[5] he further states that, 'Freedom is here being treated only as a transcendental idea whereby reason is led to think that it can begin the series of conditions in the field of appearance by means of the sensibly unconditioned'.[6]

Kant does not carry the discussion of freedom any further in the first *Critique,* but it is clear from the foregoing that he has raised a major issue for the relationship between reason and freedom. That is that reason as a cognitive power requires freedom as a transcendental condition for its employment. It is this realisation that both necessitates and provides the grounds for the development of the second *Critique.*

Kant's notion of freedom has been subjected to extensive critique, most recently for instance by Charles Taylor in *Sources of the Self.*[7]

However, despite such criticism it seems to have fared somewhat better than the "Transcendental Aesthetic". The major line of criticism taken by Taylor and others[8] is that the notion of "freedom" as determined by the 'categorical imperative' is far too narrow and prescriptive and would leave all similarly situated rational beings with only one "correct" choice; that dictated by reason. Certainly rational beings could do otherwise but they would only do so out of ignorance, similar to Plato, or as a result of heteronomy of the will; such as being guided by appetite or coercion. Whilst there is substance to this major criticism of the concept of freedom it does not take full account the dimensions of the concept of freedom, particularly as used in the later writings. Kant clearly indicates that both, the notions of reason, including pure reason, and the categorical imperative as a guiding principle of the will, are based on his radical notion of freedom. So, to say that the categorical imperative restricts freedom is to deal only with part of the full understanding of freedom. As we will see in more detail below, it could only restrict the freedom of beings who were not capable of casting their own maxims, that is beings who for whatever reason lacked autonomy.

Despite well founded critiques, much of the framework and method of Kantian analysis remains viable and active in modern philosophy; both in analytic philosophy and critical philosophy. The genealogy of Kantianism in modern philosophy would make a fascinating study. There is a clear strand that runs through the Hegelians, Feyerarbend, Marx, Fichte to the Frankfurt School. There is another strand that was taken up by British, American and Australian analytic philosophers such as Hare, Strawson, Carnap, Anderson, and others. There are less well defined strands such as the influence on both Weber and Durkheim and the whole possibility of a "sociology". And there remains the intriguing question of whether psychoanalysis could have developed without Kant's invention of the 'subjective domain of necessity' in the synthetic a priori.

The major concern here is with the background provided by Kant for arguments about the constitution of the self. The self that emerges in the practical philosophy is the self as agent and as an autonomous being. This is distinct from the rational self, as the unifier of apperception, of the *Critique of Pure Reason*. In order to explore this concern it is necessary to return to Kant's analysis of freedom and reason in *Groundwork of the Metaphysic of Moral* and *Critique of Practical Reason* in order to show how he lays the ground for the constitution of the autonomous self. In Kant's later philosophy he conceives of reason and persons rather differently to the first critique, although there are some indications of a change in the "Transcendental Doctrine of Method".[9] In his discussion of the critique of reason he concludes that, the authority of reason can only be established by persons exercising autonomous self-discipline.

In both the *Groundwork of the Metaphysic of Morals* and *The Critique of Practical Reason* Kant emphasises that humans are rational beings and thus free to act autonomously, but only in accordance with reason. The Categorical Imperative is perhaps the ultimate expression of this principle where we should be able to will that the maxim of our action should become a universal law.[10] Kant in proposing the Categorical Imperative states: 'that everything in nature works according to laws', rational beings only 'have the faculty of acting according *to the conception* of laws'.[11] The will necessitates action from principles deduced by reason. An "Imperative" then is defined as follows:

> The conception of an objective principle, in so far as it is obligatory for a will, is called a command (of reason), and the formula of the command is called an Imperative.[12]

There are two types of imperatives. Hypothetical Imperatives, where 'the action is not commanded absolutely, but only as a means to another purpose'.[13] And Categorical Imperatives, where an action is commanded, 'of itself without reference to another end'.[14] Kant further elaborates each notion but in the case of categorical imperatives he says:

> If the action...; is conceived as good *in itself* and consequently as being necessarily the principle of a will which of itself conforms to reason, then it is *categorical.*[15]

Whilst the notion of the categorical imperative is general and could, in theory. apply to a number of imperatives, it turns out that for the sort of rational beings that we are there is just one such imperative. As Kant says:

> There is therefore but one categorical imperative, namely this: *Act only on that maxim whereby thou canst at the same time will that it should become a universal law.*[16]

This conception of the good has led many commentators to regard Kant as a proceduralist in ethics, without giving any weight to the content of the good or the good life. This criticism has been made, on differing grounds, by both Taylor and MacIntyre. Kant's reply would be that the content derives from the maxims themselves which are specific to the form of each rational being, whilst the imperatives themselves have a transcendental basis in the conditions of the application of reason to the will.

It is the unique capacity of rational beings to act according to maxims. Action according to maxims is distinguished from acting according to instinct or necessity. A maxim is a rule and whilst it should be followed it is not necessitated in the way a law of nature is necessitated. We are free not to act according to maxims whether categorical or hypothetical. It may be irrational and even contrary to our interests to do so but the option remains.

One of the major difficulties, however, with Kant's moral theory, which has long been recognised in the literature, is that it seems to imply that we are free only when we act in accordance with the moral law. That is, that we are only free when we act in accordance with reason, and by implication not free when we do not act in accordance with reason, eg when we act on the basis of appetite or some other "external" factor. What is more, when we act on the basis of reason and are thus free, we (or any rational being) have only one choice; that dictated by reason. It would seem that either Kant is operating with a very formal notion of reason, which is at odds with that developed in the first critique, or with an equally formal and restrictive notion of freedom. Either way the theory first developed in the *Groundwork* and further elaborated in the *Critique of Practical Reason* has significant problems.

For instance, the problem of moral responsibility looms as a major problem here. It would seem that Kant implies, that if we act in any way other than that dictated by reason, say on maxims that could not become a universal law, we are acting *a*rationally or at least outside reason, and thus, as a consequence, could not be held responsible for our actions. Although this interpretation is frequently taken, this is clearly not what Kant intended, as he makes it clear that those who do not act in accordance with the categorical imperative may justifiably be blamed for their actions and, as appropriate, say in the case of causing harm to others, duly punished; as Kant's own example of the lying promise illustrates. Kant does not seem to be aware that there is a problem here regarding moral responsibility. His failure to see a problem may reveal a fundamental weakness in the theory not seen by Kant, or alternatively might indicate that there is an another reading of the relationship between freedom and reason. J. B. Schneewind takes the view that Kant largely overlooked the problem of moral responsibility and gave it only cursory attention in later writing.[17] Schneewind points to the fact that in later writings Kant introduced a distinction, 'between the will and the power of choice (*Wille* and *Willkür)*'; indicating that the power of choice was outside the will. This solution seems to be most unsatisfactory as an account of what constitutes the power of choice, the power to choose the moral law or not, is completely lacking. Even if Kant were to provide an account of the power of choice (*Willkür)* it would not solve his problem as it would still be irrational to choose other than to will in accord with the moral law. The problem, according to Schneewind, is simply pushed back a step; not solved.

Onora O'Neill adopts a different approach in addressing the same problem. She takes the view that there is a reading of Kant, in both the *Groundwork* and *The Critique of Practical Reason* that places the emphasis on autonomy as rational being, not on either freedom or reason. She claims that although there are still difficulties, as Kant was neither consistent in his arguments nor completely lucid in his exposition, there is a defensible interpretation that overcomes the critical objection.[18] The cornerstone of the argument rests on Kant's view that there is only one *reason* 'for it can ultimately be only one and the same reason which has to be distinguished merely in its application'.[19] She poses the question, 'Why does Kant take conformity to desires for heteronomy and conformity to reason for autonomy?'[20] Why is not reason just another form of heteronomy? It is after all external to the will. The answer she suggests is that reason itself is autonomous in Kant's schema and as such constitutes our freedom as rational beings. 'It (Reason) must regard itself as the author of its principles independent of foreign influences'.[21] She claims that Kant is commonly misread and concedes that Kant can be misleading on this point. He in fact argues not from reason to autonomy but from autonomy to reason. In other words, humans are not autonomous beings because they are rational, but rather as autonomous beings they must be rational. This in part accounts for why he puts practical reason ahead of pure (theoretical) reason, although at another level they in fact become one. Humans as ends-in-themselves and thus self-ruling beings must be autonomous. O'Neill says, 'There is no gap between reason and autonomy because the authority of reason is grounded in autonomy'[22] and that, 'It (reason) is merely autonomy in thinking and acting considered in the abstract'.[23] This insight also serves to clarify Kant's view of reason. Reason is the law or rule that autonomous beings give to themselves. There is here a truly radical notion of freedom that goes well beyond the self-ruling claims of other enlightenment thinkers such as Rousseau or Hume.

The realisation that for Kant. 'There is no gap between reason and autonomy' also serves as a crucial step on the path to an autonomous, yet socially individuated, and intersubjective self. The notion of the self can no longer be the Cartesian introspective ego nor the Lockean point but begins to take shape as an autonomous but rule governed being which will later be seen to be essentially connected, via the imagination into an intersubjective domain.

The question to be addressed now is: "How does Kant establish the notion of autonomy?"

Unfortunately the answer is, "not very successfully", although it is possible to construct an outline of Kant's position from the later writings. The key element to the establishment of the notion of autonomy lies in the exposition of "transcendental freedom", but this exposition, although present, is not clearly developed in this connection.

Kant relies less on the transcendental in these writings to establish the autonomy of the self, yet, nevertheless, the transcendental element is inescapably present because he continues to rely on a priori principles. He even claims that pure practical reason can access the *noumenal* relationship between objects in the case of cause and effect. Which places it close to, but beyond, pure theoretical reason.[24]

It is clear in the *Critique of Practical Reason* that Kant has discovered a principle that supersedes the principle of pure speculative reason, or perhaps more accurately, a principle which incorporates it. Kant was very reluctant to concede that the principles of pure speculative reason were in any way redundant and claimed that the *Critique of Pure Reason* was a necessary step to an understanding of pure practical reason. For instance, he says: '... the reader of the Critique of Pure Speculative Reason will be thoroughly convinced how highly necessary that laborious *deduction* of the categories was'.[25] Yet Kant's insistence seems somewhat hollow when the he repeatedly makes it quite clear that the practical employment of pure reason, via the will, takes precedence over speculative reason alone. The key to the fundamental insight of the second critique lies in the concept of "transcendental freedom" which takes priority over reason; an element not recognised in the first critique.

Between first and second critiques, Kant shifted ground from believing that reason or "rational being" was the essential characteristic of human kind to the position that the essential characteristic was freedom. In the *Groundwork* he established the moral law as the governing principle of reason and then in the second *Critique* establishes that comprehension of the moral law by itself determines that such beings must be free. If they were not free, Kant claims, they would not be aware of the moral law as providing imperatives to be enacted by a rational will. They would rather treat the moral law as natural law, or a nature like necessity. Thus, for Kant, humans are not now first of all "rational animals" but "free beings".

The *Critique of Practical Reason* has rightly been seen as a difficult work and thus not given as much attention as other works, particularly the

Groundwork. In certain respects it sits oddly between the *Groundwork* and the *Metaphysic of Morals* and some commentators have seen it as rather the lesser work.[26] Such a view is mistaken and fails to recognise the emphasis that Kant placed on the method of critique. He believed that unless reason, and the consequences thereof, were subjected to a process of critique they would remain merely formal and sterile with respect to both knowledge and the *summum bonum*. It was, for Kant, what was revealed by the process of critique that was philosophically fundamental. The whole of Kant's philosophy displays an immense creativity. The 'discovery' of the categorical imperative as the form of the moral law, right or wrong, was a marvellously creative inspiration which unsettled not just Kant's thinking about the place of reason, but also much of his earlier philosophy. How was he to reconcile it with the "transcendental deduction" of the first critique? His attempt to reconcile it was via *The Critique of Practical Reason*. Here he conducts a critique of reason as pure practical reason and not just pure speculative reason alone. The cornerstone of the critique becomes transcendental freedom rather than the transcendental deduction with the intuitions of space and time. In this critique of practical reason, it is not intuition that is fundamental to rational beings, but rather their freedom. The notion of freedom here becomes transcendental because the process of critical reflection on the comprehension of the moral law, the categorical imperative, proves that the conditions for such comprehension necessarily imply that such a being is free in the direction of its own will. Kant is exceptionally, one might even say uncharacteristically, lucid on this point in a passage from the Preface to the *Critique of Practical Reason*.

The passage is worthy of quotation at length.

> Inasmuch as the reality of the concept of freedom is proved by an apodictic law of practical reason, it is the *keystone* of the whole system of pure reason, even the speculative, and all other concepts (those of God and immortality) which, as being mere ideas, remain in it unsupported, now attach themselves to this concept, and by it obtain consistence and objective reality; that is to say their *possibility* is *proved* by the fact that freedom actually exists, for this idea is revealed by the moral law.
>
> Freedom, however, is the only one of all the ideas of the speculative reason of which we *know* the possibility *á priori* (without, however understanding it), because it is the condition of the moral law which we know.[27]

This remarkable passage indicates a substantially different perspective to that of the first critique and, despite Kant's claims to the contrary, renders redundant or peripheral much of the first critique. Kant says that the purpose of the *Critique of Practical Reason* is to show that there is pure practical reason and by the process of critique show that pure reason can be practical, in that it can, and indeed if it can then must, determine the will by the moral law and thus it discloses the basis of transcendental freedom.

Two issues will now be discussed which relate to the issue of the development of an understanding of the self in the light of Kant's discussion. They are, what is the connection between transcendental freedom and autonomy, and what are the implications for the constitution of the self?

To take up the issue of the connection between transcendental freedom and autonomy it is necessary to go back to the *Groundwork* and particularly to the third section. Kant begins the third section of the *Groundwork* with a negative definition of freedom. He defines the will as a kind of causality belonging to rational beings and freedom as the property of determining the will of rational living beings.[28] This definition is negative in that it defines the will as being 'free of foreign causes' and whilst it does help to clarify the domain of freedom, it does not help to discover its essence. Kant then does offer a positive definition of freedom as the autonomy of the will. The positive definition of freedom reveals its essential elements and shows that, 'What else can freedom of the will be but autonomy, that is the property of the will to be a law unto itself?'.[29] And that, 'a free will and a will subject to moral laws are one and the same'.[30] The law that the free will recognises as a law unto itself is that every action should be on a maxim, that if willed could become a universal law, which is the formula of the categorical imperative, and thus an expression of the moral law itself. What Kant means by 'free will' might be somewhat misleading. He makes it clear that the will itself does not have the property of freedom; it is rather that in rational beings the will is freely directed by beings that are themselves autonomous. The freedom is in the determination of the maxims.

It is also in this sense that reason is free and is also why Kant, in the later writings, emphatically ties the notion of reason to judgement rather than being. Reason does not have the power to construct a *logos* but rather to judge principles with respect to a *logos;* a rational being is a being that is capable of conceptually grasping an idea, this is what Kant later in the *Critique of Practical Reason* calls 'a fact of reason'. This view is supported by Wellmer who says that, 'fact of reason' as Kant understands it is not reducible to [the] generalisation principle' which underlies the categorical imperative.[31] Reason as it were gives us, as rational beings, the power to stand at one remove from reality and consider it conceptually and construct ideas with respect to it. This power of rational beings also provides the ground for further development of the concept of imagination in regard to both freedom and reason which will be a focus of *The Critique of Judgement* and a key to understanding the self to be explored in later chapters.

The "practical reason" that Kant explores here, is a reason that 'has causality in reference to its objects'.[32] Practical reason changes the world, theoretical reason only describes it. But here an important insight from the first critique remains valid. That is; via the transcendental aesthetic with the employment of the imagination, we construct the world for rational human minds. It is, of course, possible that other rational beings, angels say, structure their manifold quite differently, and that for the Supreme Being there is no distinction between the noumenal and phenomenal worlds(universes); that is there is no difference between the structuring of the divine manifold and reality. In this way, it can be seen that practical reason, as proposed by Kant, is more powerful than theoretical reason because it has the power to determine the objects of theoretical reason. Thus, Kant claims, that with respect to the relation of cause and effect, Hume is correct; pure reason shows us no necessary connection, but that practical reason overcomes Hume's objection and does reveal such a connection.[33]

Again, in the moral philosophy, we find Kant's agenda largely set by the concerns expressed by Hume and Hutcheson.[34] Hume is famous for his pronouncement that 'Reason is, and only ought to be the slave of the passions',[35] although it is likely as J. B. Schneewind points out that Kant was reacting to the views of Francis Hutcheson in this regard, who also strongly influenced Hume.[36] Kant felt very strongly that such a view of human motivation was dangerously mistaken and could lead to the collapse of morality and the loss of the concept of the good or *summum bonum*. He certainly did not share Hume's faith in the moral sentiments. However, Kant did agree that if reason was narrowly considered merely as purely theoretical reason then it could not have the power to move the will. But, if pure reason could be considered as practical, then not only could it move the will, but jointly with the notion of autonomy, would necessitate action in accordance with the moral law.

Kant identifies both freedom of the will and transcendental freedom with autonomy and explains this conjunction in the *Groundwork*. But it is in the *Critique of Practical Reason* that he provides a more substantial definition of autonomy. In the Analytic of Pure Practical Reason he expounds his position in a number of places. Unfortunately, illuminating as they are, not all the expositions are entirely consistent. In section VIII

Theorem IV he states that, 'The autonomy of the will is the sole principle of all moral laws, and of all duties which conform to them'; and later in the same passage, 'Thus the moral law expresses nothing else than the *autonomy* of pure practical reason; that is, freedom;'.[37] Whilst there is a confusion here with respect to the role of autonomy, some clarification can be achieved if it is seen here that the emphasis is on the self-legislation of the pure practical will and its connection with freedom. The meaning of autonomy here is the freedom all rational beings; that is, self-legislating wills. The emphasis is on autonomy as the positive sense of freedom.

Later in a particularly intense passage which is worth quoting at length, he says:

> The moral law is *holy* (inviolable). Man is indeed unholy enough; but he must regard *humanity* in his own person as holy. In all creation everything one chooses, and over which one has any power, may be used *merely as a means;* man alone and with him every rational creature, is an *end in himself.* By virtue of the autonomy of his freedom he is the subject of the moral law, which is holy. Just for this reason every will, even every person's own individual will, in relation to itself, is restricted to the condition of agreement with the *autonomy* of the rational being, that is to say, that it is not to be subject to any purpose which cannot accord with a law which might arise from the will of the passive subject himself; the latter is therefore, never to be employed merely as a means, but as itself also, concurrently, an end. We justly contribute this condition even to the Divine will, with regard to the rational beings in the world, which are His creatures, since it rests on their *personality,* by which alone they are ends in themselves.[38]

A number of elements in this paragraph deserve close attention, the concept of autonomy here is more subtle and more complex than the earlier passage. Firstly, Kant is defining autonomy as a characteristic of rational beings; but also as something which is exercised by beings possessed of "personality", as it is, he claims, personality alone which makes them ends in themselves. The link between transcendental freedom, autonomy and personality is critical to understanding Kant's position and the importance of the "kingdom of ends". Kant is recognising that autonomy is only fully explainable when exercised by beings of a certain type. Here, merely to contrast autonomy with heteronomy and define it as the exercise of the rational will is insufficient; the concept of autonomy now cannot be explained without reference to personality. The term "personality" may be misleading to the contemporary reader and should now only be understood in a rather anachronistic sense, as the standard Abbott translation is now rather dated. Today the word "personhood" might be more appropriate. Kant continues in the following paragraph to refer to 'This respect-inspiring idea of personality which sets before our eyes the sublimity of our nature(in its higher aspect)...'.[39] So it is clear, that by the stage of writing the *Critique of Practical Reason,* Kant had come to the view that there was a uniquely important element to rational beings, which humans shared, this was their "personality" and this was then the basis of their autonomy. As Kant says it is 'by which alone they are ends in themselves'.

It would appear that Kant has reduced the notions of autonomy and free will to properties of rational beings, a notion which might seem reminiscent of Aristotle. Yet, Kant takes a position that is distinguishable from an Aristotelian position; although there are both similarities as well as significant differences. He almost certainly would have rejected any suggestion that his position on morals was close to Aristotle and certainly did not regard happiness in any form as itself the aim of life. He saw that happiness, resulting as a consequence of a good will obeying the moral law, was a position that superseded Aristotelian ethics. The strongest similarity to Aristotle resides with the notions of free will and practical reason. Here Kant may be close to the Aristotelian position on the way in which the will and reason are related, but the significant difference lies in Kant's conception of the way autonomous reason dictates to the will. Aristotle, whilst not holding such a rigid view as Plato, still maintained that reason was discovered by contemplation and was external to the powers of cognition.

Some commentators, such as MacIntyre, have drawn parallels between Kant and Aristotle on the notion of practical reason which attack Kant's view as a purely formalistic. There are some similarities between Kant and Aristotle, Kant was after all a good Aristotelian scholar, but the differences are significant.[40] Although Kant has come to his position by a rather different route to Aristotle it is interesting to see that he has arrived at something similar to Aristotle's 'divine element'.[41] However it cannot be concluded that because such similarities exist that Kant's position can be reduced to an Aristotelian position; Kant's claims are based on much stronger arguments and based on a radically different understanding of the relationship of the self to practical reason. The steps in Kant's argument are as follows. Humans are capable of formulating maxims which are subjective principles of individual actions. The fact that they formulate such maxims (rather than acting either instinctively or blindly) shows that they are capable of reflection on the maxim and possessed of reflexive consciousness. The act of reflection on maxims leads to the principle of universalisability and thus the categorical imperative. The act of universalisation necessarily involves the use of reason. The categorical imperative is an expression, for humans, of the moral law which must apply to all rational beings. Now pure reason can also be practical if we can act upon categorical imperatives, but if we can so act we must be free to will the act. The notion of freedom is not part of the empirical world, and can only come to us *a priori* and thus involves a transcendental element; which further demonstrates the universality of the moral law and establishes freedom as part of the "intelligible" world and links it to the noumena. A being that is free to act in accordance with the moral law must be self-ruling and is therefore an autonomous being. Any being thus able to act must be a being-in-itself and thus possessing "personality". Such a being is an end-in-itself and thus a member of the "kingdom of ends" and worthy of respect as such. This conclusion admits a substantive element in the formulation of the maxims and goes well beyond Aristotle in the establishment of autonomy.

Kant has here established that humans, as autonomous rational beings, are indeed independent and self-responsible. He has succeeded in reaching a position similar to the conclusion of the Cartesian argument for personhood but avoiding the pitfalls associated with Descartes introspective method. The transcendental self of the first critique has, in the Groundwork and the second *Critique* been developed into an independent being, whilst retaining transcendental character, that is able to act in both the sensible and intelligible worlds. The formal unity and identity of the first critique has been "fleshed out" into a substantial and comprehensive theory that incorporates both metaphysics and morals. However, whilst Kant has demonstrated an independence for the self at this point, it is in the *Critique of Judgement* that he takes the next step to demonstrate that such a being can only exist in a world of other similarly autonomous beings who share the characteristics of a common subjectivity in conjunction with the cognitive power of imagination.

Kant's theory of the categorical imperative contained the seeds of more radical positions, some of which he realised, in part at least, in later work and some that have been only followed through by succeeding generations and some yet to be developed. The more radical position leads to a political philosophy that was only partially developed by Kant himself.

In the *Groundwork* Kant ventures the supposition that there exists 'something whose existence has in itself an absolute worth',[42] that is, a being which could be an end in itself, and further as Kant says: 'and in this and this alone would lie the source of a possible categorical imperative', and that, man and generally any rational being *exists* as an end in himself'.[43] Such rational beings are persons, Kant says: 'rational beings ...are called *persons*, because their very nature points them out as ends in themselves'[44] and that '*rational nature exists as an end in itself*'.[45]

This leads Kant to the formulation of the practical imperative:

> *So act as to treat humanity, whether in thine own person or in that of any other, in every case as an end withal, never as a means only.*[46]

This statement of the categorical imperative is really a preliminary statement of the principle of "the kingdom of ends" which Kant amplifies in later statements. The essential element of the kingdom of ends is embodied in the third statement of the kingdom of ends where Kant claims that 'the will of every rational being [is] a *universally legislating will*'.[47] The notion of a kingdom of ends is clearly important to Kant's formulation of morality. Being a member of the kingdom of ends embodies the rest of the moral philosophy, as only rational autonomous beings qualify for membership. It also later becomes an important basis for Kant's political philosophy. Whilst the notion of a republic expressed in the essays *Universal History* and *Perpetual Peace* is not identical with the "kingdom of ends" which is an essentially moral notion, it is dependent on the same transcendental principles.[48] These principles require that each member of an ordered civil state be self-legislating in the way in which an ideal state would be self-legislating. Similar principles would govern the relations between states.

However, Kant's discussion of the kingdom of ends is rather perplexing and indeed has perplexed many commentators since. Whilst it is a key notion in Kant's moral philosophy and potentially important to the political philosophy, it is not developed after the *Groundwork* and surfaces only tangentially in his later work. It is hard to find a clear development of the notion and its implications. It would appear that he had not thought out the concept fully in relation to his other philosophy, or that he saw the notion as too much of a distraction from other lines of thought and therefore attempted to isolate it.

Kant commences in the *Groundwork* by defining kingdom: 'By *kingdom* I understand the union of different rational beings in a system by common laws'.[49] A kingdom of ends is a kingdom in which all rational beings are united by 'common objective laws'. The theory of the kingdom of ends is at once a theory about the harmony of ends chosen by rational beings and a claim about the supremacy of the moral law; there are also clear political considerations such as those referred to in *Perpetual Peace* and other political writings. In the brief discussion in the *Groundwork* Kant does not adequately distinguish between the elements of the theory, as his main intention is clearly to establish both the universality and primacy of the moral law. It is also within the kingdom of ends that the notion of duty arises. To a sovereign in the kingdom of ends duty does not apply, because such a being would have a perfectly free will and would not be subject to the will of others. However, that is not the state of humanity, or as Kant says "man" because humans have needs and wants and rely on the cooperation of others. As such there would be reciprocal duties to others who are ends-in-themselves, commencing with the duty not to treat them as means to an end. Here, may be the key to why Kant refers to the kingdom of ends as 'a very fruitful conception'.

A major problem for Kant is one of what we might term "moral solipsism". Kant has established, via the categorical imperative, that under the moral law, rational beings, including humans, are ends in themselves each necessarily, as moral beings, capable of comprehending the moral law, a priori. The question for Kant now is "What binds such beings into a single universe of morality"? The answer is that he has created in his moral universe beings who, by his description, are quasi-deities. Indeed the Deity itself is, according to Kant's account, a perfect rational being with a divine will. Humans can also aspire to this divine status by the exercise of rational discipline over the will. Thus, Kant could be seen as having created a morality in which the moral agents act each in isolation from the other. Kant runs the risk of having created a universe of autonomous rational beings capable of acting totally independently of each other, as sovereigns in their own kingdoms. If this were to be the case Kant would have created a universe of self contained monads, which was clearly not his intention, and it is a view he opposed. He needs a principle capable of uniting such beings in a single universe; this is the function of the kingdom of ends.

Kant makes it clear that the uniting factor is indeed the moral law itself. Each individual must be able to legislate for its own will and at the same time universally.

Morality consists then in the reference of all action to the legislation, which alone, can render a kingdom of ends possible. This legislation must be capable of existing in every rational being, and of emanating from his will, so that the principle of this will is, never to act on any maxim which could without contradiction become a universal law. Kant continues to explain that if the maxims (subjective principles) of rational beings do not coincide with this objective principle then the recognition for them to do so is called "duty", and each (imperfect) rational being must recognise their duty to obey the moral law.

There are a number of problems for Kant in the formulation of the "kingdom of ends". Not the least of these is an apparent circularity in the argument. Kant seems to be arguing back from the universality of the moral law to the necessity of the kingdom of ends, but at the same time claiming that it is the kingdom of ends that establishes the universality of the moral law. This is a serious problem for Kant and one which is not to be overcome merely by sympathetic interpretations. Lying behind the circularity are Kant's problems with the claimed objectivity of the moral law against the subjectivity of the individual's maxims. The circularity is generated by a number of factors. One is the complexity of the argument itself, which masks the circularity, another is Kant's inconsistency about the kingdom of ends.

But Kant does not see the argument as circular which might indicate that there some critical elements to the discussion which are not being given due account. One interpretation, which might in part at least, avoid the accusation of circularity, would rely on Kant's notion of "personality", discussed above, as an essential characteristic of all rational beings. "Personality" might well act as a basis for membership of the kingdom of ends, rather than mere recognition of the universality of the moral law. Thus there is a step in the argument from the premise referring to rational being, to "personality" referring to the whole being of which rationality is merely a part. In *The Critique of Practical Reason* Kant links personality to notions of duty and autonomy but not explicitly to the conception of the kingdom of ends. What the notion of personality does do is indicate an element of subjectivity which will later be incorporated into Kant's overall architectonic.

However, despite problems of explication and substantiation the notion of a kingdom of ends plays a crucial role in Kant's overall scheme and constitutes a very important grounding principle for further discussion. Without the notion of the kingdom of ends, or something similar, Kant is condemned to a moral solipsism.

Later, in the *Critique of Judgement* Kant comes to recognise that there is a further cognitive power, that of judgement, which in turn for its a priori basis rests on the capacity of communicability of subjective states. Here Kant has a powerful new perspective that overcomes the solipsism the moral law and allows the "kingdom of ends" to function under it as universalising principle. This may be why there is no further explicit discussion of the principle in later work.

From a contemporary perspective the role of "the kingdom of ends" takes on a particular importance. It provides part of the basis for later theories of communicative rationality and for the grounds of a democracy of all rational beings. Also, it indirectly contributed to the development of pragmatism via Peirce's interest in a semiotic interpretation of Kant's logic and thus the community of informed practitioners could have a transcendental ground. In the development of the kingdom of ends and the universalisation of practical reason via the moral law Kant proposes that it is the moral law that binds all rational beings. The use of the term "kingdom" strongly points to the notion of an ideal community not that dissimilar to the notion used later by Karl-Otto Apel, Jürgen Habermas and others.[50] It is at this point that Apel and Habermas propose not only 'an expansion of Kant's moral principles into discourse ethics',[51] as Wellmer claims, but also into a larger project of communicatively based reason.

Kant himself made it clear in a number of places, particularly in the later works, that both the achievement of the *summum bonum* and the practical employment of reason were communitarian and public activities.[52]

Notes

1 Habermas, Jurgen (1971), *Knowledge and Human Interests*, Beacon Press, Boston, p. 191ff.
2 Kant, Immanuel (1909), *Critique of Practical Reason and Other Works*, trans. Thomas Kingsmill Abbott, Longman, London.
3 Kant, Immanuel (1929), *The Critique of Pure Reason*, trans. Norman Kemp Smith, Macmillan, London, pp. 468 - 469.
4 Ibid., p. 469.
5 Ibid., p. 479.
6 Ibid.
7 Taylor, Charles (1989), *Sources of the Self*, Cambridge University Press, Cambridge, Chapter 20. See also Guyer, Paul (1993), *Kant and the Experience of Freedom*, Cambridge University Press, Cambridge.
8 See for example, O'Neill, Onora (1989), *Constructions of Reason*, Cambridge University Press, Cambridge.
9 See for example, Kant, Immanuel, *The Critique of Pure Reason*, B 766 and B 781.
10 Kant, Immanuel, *Critique of Practical Reason and Other Works*, p. 38.
11 Ibid., p. 35.
12 Ibid.
13 Ibid., p. 39.
14 Ibid., p. 37.
15 Ibid., p. 39.
16 Ibid., p. 46.
17 Schneewind, J. B. (1992), "Autonomy, obligation and virtue: An overview of Kant's moral philosophy" in *The Cambridge Companion to Kant*, ed. Paul Guyer, Cambridge University Press, Cambridge, p. 330.
18 O'Neill, Onora, *Constructions of Reason*, pp. 52 - 55.

19 Kant, Immanuel, *Critique of Practical Reason and Other Works*, p. 7.
20 O'Neill, Onora, *Constructions of Reason*, p. 53.
21 Kant, Immanuel, *Critique of Practical Reason and Other Works*, p. 67.
22 O'Neill, Onora, *Constructions of Reason*, p. 59.
23 Ibid, p. 64.
24 Kant, Immanuel, *Critique of Practical Reason and Other Works*, pp. 139 and 146.
25 Ibid., p. 239.
26 See for instance, Paton, H. J., *The Moral Law*.
27 Kant, Immanuel, *Critique of Practical Reason and Other Works*, p. 88.
28 Ibid., p. 65.
29 Ibid., p. 65 - 66.
30 Ibid.
31 Wellmer, Albrecht (1991), *The Persistence of Modernity*, Polity Press, Cambridge, p. 121.
32 Ibid., p. 67.
33 Ibid., p. 143.
34 Schneewind and Henrich point out that Kant was influenced by Hume's predecessor Francis Hutcheson who was better known than Hume at the time. Kant had read Hutcheson and Hume's earlier work but may not have read Hume's later and more mature, moral philosophy.
35 Hume, David (1978), *A Treatise of Human Nature*, ed. Selby-Bigge, L. A., ed., second edition, Oxford University Press, Oxford, p. 415.
36 Schneewind, J. B. (1992), "Autonomy, obligation and virtue: An overview of Kant's moral philosophy", in *The Cambridge Companion to Kant*, ed. Guyer, Paul, Cambridge University Press, Cambridge, p. 327.
37 Kant, Immanuel (1909), *Critique of Practical Reason*, trans. Thomas Kingsmill Abbott, Longman, London, p. 122.
38 Ibid., pp. 180-181.
39 Ibid.
40 See for instance, MacIntyre, Alasdair (1981), *After Virtue*, Duckworth, London, especially. p. 42ff. MacIntyre claims that Kant's formalism does not give us a substantive morality and that Aristotelian practical reason can be shown superior to Kantian. See also Charles Taylor on this point.
41 See Aristotle, *Nichomacean Ethics*, Bk. X Ch.7.
42 Kant, Immanuel, *Critique of Practical Reason and Other Works*, p. 49.
43 Ibid.
44 Ibid.
45 Ibid., p. 47.
46 Ibid.
47 Ibid., p. 50.

48 See Kant, Immanuel (1983),"To Perpetual Peace. A Philosophical Sketch", in *Perpetual Peace and Other Essays*, trans. Ted Humphrey, Hackett Publishing, Indianapolis, especially Appendix II.

49 Ibid., p. 51.

50 Habermas, Jurgen (1992), "Individuation Through Socialization: On George Herbert Mead's Theory of Subjectivity", in *Postmetaphysical Thinking*, trans. William Mark Hohengarten, Polity Press, Cambridge, p. 190.

51 Wellmer, Albrecht, *The Persistence of Modernity*, p. 139.

52 See for instance, "Religion within the Limits of Reason Alone", in *Perpetual Peace and Other Essays*, p. 97.

5 Transcendental Arguments and the Ideal Communication Community: Karl-Otto Apel

Karl-Otto Apel takes up the Kantian project to establish an objective transcendental philosophy based on clearly grounded categories of thought. Apel aims to retain the transcendental character of Kant's philosophy without the "idealism". He claims that the transcendental idealism of Kant can be transformed linguistically; not into a metaphysical idealism but into an "ideal communication community". It is this "ideal communication community", modelled on Kant's "kingdom of ends", that provides the grounding of a new transcendental philosophy.[1] He further claims that "ideal communication community" will lead to a 'real communication community' in which our 'real selves' will be constituted. This approach provides for a discursive basis for transcendental philosophy which overcomes the objections to Kant's apodictic approach and contributes significantly to the grounds for the establishment of intersubjectivity.

Apel's work is founded upon the central notion of "the transformation of philosophy". The "transformation" takes many aspects around a central theme of a linguistic transformation of Kantian philosophy. Apel takes up what Wellmer calls the "communicative substructure" in Kant's philosophy and particularly his ethics.[2] He believes that the project of transcendental philosophy can be achieved by a joint linguistic, hermeneutic and pragmatic transformation of traditional philosophy. The transformation can be applied across the philosophical spectrum and Apel systematically applies it to, ethics, the philosophies of social and physical science, linguistic philosophy and philosophical psychology. Apel also derives from his transformational method the grounds for a theory of the, similarly transformed, "transcendental" constitution of the self. He posits a self which in many ways resembles Kant's 'transcendental consciousness as such' from the first *Critique*, but transformed by a critique emphasising the transcendental importance of language as a ground for self-constitution.

Equally important as the notion of the transformation of philosophy for Apel is the notion that both follows from and underpins it, of the "ideal communication community". This notion Apel develops from Peirce's formulation of the 'indefinite community of (informed) investigators'.[3] The presupposition of an ideal communication community undergirds Apel's philosophy and supports his other important notion of "transcendental pragmatics".

It should be pointed out here that Apel uses the term "transcendental" in a way common in recent German philosophy but not so familiar in Anglo-American philosophy. The term has its origins in Kant's notion of the "transcendental aesthetic" and in more recent times has come to mean something like "the constitutive conditions of..." or "the conditions for the possibility of". It is especially used where a set of normative conditions is presupposed. "Transcendental" in Apel's work is not necessarily meant to carry any strong "super real" or other worldly connotation but is meant to establish a framework of interpretation that transcends individual consciousness.

Apel's philosophical roots lie with Kant, with Anglo-American analytic philosophy, with Charles Sanders Peirce and pragmatism, and with hermeneutics, in particular with Gadamer and Wittgenstein.[4] Whilst operating in close parallel with Habermas, Apel does not, like Habermas, rely heavily on critical theory and the "Frankfurt School" for his philosophical lineage and discussion of critical theory plays no part in theory.[5]

The philosophical position adopted by Apel is a strongly objectivist position. He sees himself as re-establishing a set of categories similar to those of both Kant's first and second critiques.[6] The path to such categories is rather different and their form literally "transformed" but their status and reality as categories of thought is intended to be every bit as firm as that proposed Kant.

An exposition and discussion of the thematic development of Apel's work presents some difficulties. Firstly, much of the published work, has been published in the form of articles in journals or as collections of papers, with some of the earlier work difficult to access. *Understanding and Explanation* is the only fully developed thematic text of Apel's original philosophy. This work is primarily concerned with questions of meaning and explanation but has some relevance to the question of philosophical foundations and thus the foundation of the self. Also there is the issue of style. Apel's prose is, by any account, dense and prolix, which makes for great difficulties of interpretation.

Apel is responsible for introducing the work of Charles Sanders Peirce to a German speaking audience through a major work on Peirce published in two volumes in 1967 and 1970.[7] Through this work the philosophy of Peirce became better known in Germany than in English speaking philosophy at the time. It generated a great deal of interest in the extension of philosophical ideas of truth, and a development of new methods in the philosophy of science and philosophy of social science in a post-Kantian context that were alternatives to both the phenomenological and empirical/analytic traditions. Apel devotes a large section of the in the first volume of work to the Peirce's study of Kant. Apel in his later work takes up many of the themes initiated by Peirce and Peirce's study of Kant.

Peirce rejected Kant's notion of 'incognizable things-in-themselves' but retained Kantianism in the form of 'regulative principles to which nothing empirical can correspond'.[8] Peirce attempted to establish, in his disordered and piecemeal fashion, that Kantian philosophy could be semiotically transformed. Murphey, quoted by Apel, sums up Peirce's program as follows: 'Its foundation was to have been mathematics and formal logic which would supply a priori the possible formal categories that would come from phenomenology. Upon this base would be built the normative theory of inquiry, which would supply the aim and methods of investigation in all areas of knowledge. Then should have come the metaphysics'.[9] This summation could well serve as a rough summary of Apel's own work. However Apel is more of an orthodox Kantian than Peirce. One of the main ideas that Peirce took over from Kant was the principle of the "architectonic".[10] By an "architectonic" Peirce meant something further than Kant's principle; he proposed a dynamic framework which would embody the sort of logic of inquiry and deliver the sort of outcomes that the pragmatic program proposed. It is a concept that Apel also employs although in a mode more in line with Kant than Peirce.

It was the model of a critical reconstruction of Kant, semiotically transformed in the mode of Peirce, that provides the starting point for an entry into the work of Apel. Apel incorporates into the Kantian scheme the late Peircian concept of pragmatics and the insights of the "linguistic turn", particularly Wittgenstein and the speech act theory of Austin and Searle to which he adds a structural element from Chomsky.[11]

Apel uses the Wittgensteinian concepts of "language game" and "form of life" as a basis for his development of transcendental theory. He takes the view that the grounding of the social sciences lies in the "transcendental language game"; he is claiming that there has to be a set of conditions of some sort in order for there to be any language games at all.[12] These conditions require both, the irreducibility of the a priori of argument and the existence of an ideal communication community. The communication community provides the forum as it were for the "playing" of language games and the a priori element is necessary for the horizon of meaning. It is significant that Wittgenstein himself would not have been at all comfortable with the notion of "language game" being used in this way. Wittgenstein in his total opposition to metaphysics was adamant that there should be nothing "behind" language games. They should be essentially local and each different in many dimensions. Apel's appropriation of the concept of language game is not necessarily inappropriate and he runs the risk of diluting the notion by using it in a different framework to that in which it was generated.

Apel wishes to tie the idea of a language game rather tightly to the Wittgensteinian idea of a "form of life" as a means of grounding meaning in language in a process of pre-linguistic action. The term, "form of life" first appears in the *Philosophical Investigations* and appears only rarely in various other places in Wittgenstein's posthumous works.[13] Of course, for Wittgenstein, it was not meant as a technical term, let alone a term indicating anything like "transcendental conditions". The notion of "form of life" was not a notion to which Wittgenstein gave any central importance. He uses it only to support the far more significant notion of "language game". The notion of "form of life" connects language to the activities, the business of human communities. He says: '...the *speaking* of a language is part of an activity, or of a form of life'.[14] All Wittgenstein wants to convey by reference to "form of life" is that language games have a non-linguistic dimension and that they are connected to human communities. Many commentators, including Apel have given much greater significance to the notion of "form of life". This is because they see in it the opportunity to ground both Wittgenstein's linguistification of philosophy and the implied relativism that goes with it.

Wittgenstein would, no doubt, have had a deep aversion to any such talk.[15] He seems, and one must speculate here, only to invoke "form of life" to show that language games must stand in relation to some form of human activity; that they are cannot be just word games. They have many varieties and forms and must essentially involve activity; or a doing connected with the world.

However the more technical interpretation is precisely the way in which Apel wishes to adopt the term. Indeed, if transcendental conditions for the existence of language games can thus be established, then, by further argumentation, there would be a grounding for the human sciences in a transcendental form of life/language game. The problems associated with, for instance the Winchean relativism of language games would thus be overcome.[16]

Apel is using the term "language game", not so much in a different sense to its use in Anglo-American philosophy, but in a rather different context. He is assuming that Wittgenstein can be viewed in the context of philosophical hermeneutics. This is in contrast to the Anglo-American tradition that locates Wittgenstein in the analytic tradition of Russell and Whitehead or later in the "ordinary language" tradition of G.E. Moore and J.L. Austin. Apel is interpreting Wittgenstein largely as part of the European tradition and reading him against a background of Dilthey, Husserl and Gadamer (and perhaps, Schopenauer). He maintains that Wittgenstein's ideas can be evaluated fully only against an interpretive, rather than a merely analytic, background; indeed against the broadly self-reflective philosophical tradition that originates with Kant. Apel also sees a strong affinity between Wittgensteinian notions of both "language game" and "form of life" and some of the central notions of Pragmatism, particularly Peirce's ideas of an informed community of practitioners.[17]

It is against this interpretive theoretical perspective that Apel proposes an integrated theory of philosophical foundations based on the notion of the "transcendental language game". Claims for the transcendence of language games or similar linguistic structures, have been made by a number of philosophers including Peirce, Royce and Husserl.[18] What is required in Apel's framework is a philosophical foundation which grounds language games or similar structures in a more transparent way. If this can be done then there is a basis for grounding the human sciences and an understanding of the self in the world in such a way that establishes a framework of interpretation.

Wittgenstein indicated that language games were to be grounded in action and Peirce related sign use to the sign user as an actor in the community of interpretation. This view has also been recently espoused by Habermas as part of the theory of communicative action.[19] The problem with grounding intersubjective meaning in action is that action itself does not speak; it must be subject to interpretation. And any interpretation involves, at least in part the actor as interpreter. Thus there remains the irreducible hermeneutic component.

The Austinian speech act theory and indeed the theories of meaning of Dummet, Davidson and Chomsky seek to address the issue of the grounding of language. But they attempt to ground language in either meaning, cognition or structure (or all three) and fail to ground meaning in social action. They do not, so Apel claims, take into account that irreducible hermeneutic component that any attempt to ground language for a theory of the human sciences, must incorporate. The meaning of action, including social action, can only be determined by a process of contextual interpretation. The actor, including his intentions, does not constitute the full content of meaning. The full meaning includes a reflexive understanding of the context of action. This Apel seeks to achieve in his understanding of the grounding of the social sciences. He illustrates this in relation to the critique of ideology where critique must, he says, 'lay claim to the synthetic unity of the transcendental language-game and thereby assumes that this unity can, in principle, be realized for any language-game by reflexive self-transcendence of the actual rules...'.[20]

In the positive thesis offered here it will be argued that a thorough explication of the notion of intersubjectivity is a precondition of both language and meaning and also provides a rational basis for the foundation of the human sciences. There is also the reflexive element which, it will be shown in later chapters, depends on the essential element of imagination. Such a notion of intersubjectivity is also a condition for the understanding of the self.

As previously noted, Apel's primary concern throughout is with the issue of philosophical grounding, particularly the grounding of ethics, the social and the physical sciences. He is a passionate campaigner for objectivity and the Kantian project, but also with a concern for the defence of philosophy in the twentieth century, which he sees as under attack from a number of quarters, in attempts to reduce it to positivism, "historicism" or contingency of various forms.[21]

In "The Communication Community and the Social Sciences"[22] Apel provides a clear statement of his program for the transformation of philosophy. He discusses Kant, Peirce and Wittgenstein, amongst others and strongly reinforces their contributions to the foundation of the physical sciences, social sciences and ethics. He claims that any "logic of science" including social science, must meet the, 'Kantian question for the transcendental presuppositions for the possibility and validity of science'.[23] He also claims that the 'transcendental subject of science must be mediated by, ... the insight into the transcendental importance of language and, thereby of the language community'.[24] The argument that he constructs is based on is the elevation of personal intuitive evidence to 'a 'paradigm' of the language game'.[25] Personal evidence can then be secured as 'a priori binding knowledge' via a consensus theory of truth. Apel says:

> By means of the - implicit or explicit - elevation of personal evidence for consciousness to a paradigm of the language-game, the *argumentative sense* of the intuitive certainty of each consciousness for the community of communication and interpretation is, to some extent, secured.[26]

This move is a critical step towards the establishment of intersubjectivity and language as a transcendental ground. Whilst Apel goes much of the way towards providing a ground for communicative theory, he ultimately does not succeed because he fails to provide an adequate account of the relationship between language and intersubjectivity.

He takes the terms "language game" and "form of life" and "indefinite community of investigators" in a fairly formal sense agreeing with Peirce that such notions as his "indefinite community of investigators" can be a form of semiotic transformation of Kant's "transcendental logic".

The terms "form of life", "language game" and "community of investigators" are metaphors or quasi-metaphors. It is not clear that either Wittgenstein or Peirce meant them as metaphors, yet they tell us more of what it is like to participate in a certain society of discourse than what it is to *be* in it. What Apel seeks to do is to "literalise" the metaphysical content of these metaphors in such a way that they form not just a illuminating function but an explanatory function as well. It is significant that at times Apel shifts to the terms "life-forms" or "habits" when discussing Wittgenstein's "forms-of-life", which tends to concretise the notion as extra-linguistic in a way that is at odds with Wittgenstein's use.

Apel's is clearly not primarily concerned to develop a theory of the self. His views on the constitution of the self are contained within his discussions of other philosophical issues concerning mainly physical science, social science and ethics. This is because his theoretical structure, not unlike Kant's, is developed as an interconnected whole. However as later discussion will show he, like Habermas, requires a theory which relates human subjectivity to his broader theory.

In a late statement which reflects his position Apel says:

> Human beings, as *linguistic beings* who must share *meaning and truth with fellow beings* in order to be able think in a valid form, must at all times *anticipate counterfactually* an *ideal form of communication and hence of social interaction.* This "assumption" is constitutive for the institution of argumentative discourse.[27]

This statement clearly indicates Apel's Kantian structure; Apel is still working within a Kantian architectonic. However he does not sufficiently clarify what he means by "linguistic beings". He does not make it clear whether or not language constitutes being or whether humans are beings who use language in a linguistic community. The latter interpretation remains consistent with his overall discussion.

Apel also explicitly takes up the issue of the assertion of the "fact of reason" to support his case for philosophical grounding. He provides a critical reconstruction of the use of "fact of reason" to support the universality of the moral law and his foundational position. Commentators on the *Critique of Practical Reason* have considered Kant's appeal to "fact of reason" to be a crucial weakness in the exposition, as Kant has to rely on assertion rather than argument.[28] Apel believes that his principle can deduce a superior version of the "moral law" where Kant was doomed to fail. He argues that if one tries to *deduce* a priori foundations then one will, with Kant, inevitably be caught in the foundationalist trilemma.[29] However, Apel proposes an ingenious, if somewhat prolix, argument for fundamental justification, he says: 'The fact that the normative principle which is necessarily presupposed in all argumentation cannot be *logically proven* without a *logical circle*, in this case takes on a completely new and unusual significance'.[30] The special significance, he claims, is that the very fact that the ground cannot be (deductively) proven, proves that the ground is unavoidable and that this unavoidability follows from the, '*transcendental pragmatic* (i.e., reflexively observable for the subject of argumentation) necessity of the presupposition of the principle in question'. He continues with the assertion that the principle cannot be disputed without '*pragmatic self-contradiction*' by those participating in the argument.[31]

A number of examples follow, perhaps the most illuminating is this:

> I hereby assert as true that I am not obliged *in principle* to recognise all possible members of the unlimited community of argumentation as having equal rights.[32]

Thus the speaker would of course deny, as a pragmatic contradiction, his/her 'equal right' to make the statement. This is without question a contemporary version of Kant's categorical imperative.

The questions have to be asked as to whether Apel's argument stands up and if so, what advance, if any, is there on Kant.

The argument is ingenious and is a development of an earlier discussion of the "Munchausen trilemma". "In The Problem of Philosophical Foundations" Apel starts by analysing Hans Albert's statement of the Munchhausen trilemma.[33] The principle of the Munchhausen trilemma is that when it comes to philosophical foundations one is forced to choose between three unacceptable alternatives.

The trilemma forces one to choose between the following alternatives: (1) an infinite regress that appears to be required by the necessity of always going further back in the search for reasons, but that is not feasible and therefore yields no solid foundation. (2) A logical circle in the deduction that results from the fact that in the process of giving reasons one has to resort to statements that have already shown themselves to be in need of justification - a process that because it is logically faulty, likewise leads to no firm foundation. (3) Breaking off giving reasons at a particular point, which, while in principle feasible would involve an arbitrary suspension of the principle of sufficient reason.[34]

Apel however thinks that it is possible to provide a foundation for philosophical discourse that avoids the binds of the trilemma. His method is to mount a critical reconstruction of the trilemma. This reconstruction of the trilemma is at once a reconstruction of the question of philosophical foundations and, by a further reconstructive process, an attempt to answer part three of the trilemma through a critical examination of the type of reasons that can be provided for philosophical foundations. The reasons are to be different to those involved in an apodeictic-deductive train of argument in conventional foundational arguments.

In his critical reconstruction of the trilemma Apel does not wish to defend the position of classical rationalism because that reduces a theory of knowledge to a theory of consciousness. And a theory of consciousness, so he argues, cannot provide for the 'validity of linguistically formulated statements'.[35] It will be argued later that a communicative theory requires a radically reconstructed theory of consciousness and that the failure to do so is one of the major shortcommings of Apel's theory.

The argument for philosophical foundations in "Ethics, Utopia, and the Critique of Utopia", incorporates an insight beyond the earlier discussion where, Apel was really challenging and attempting to reconstruct the third arm of the trilemma.[36] Now Apel is using the trilemma against itself by employing the critical-reflexive mode to it. He accepts that it is an impasse but now asks the question: 'What conditions must pertain in order that it be such an impasse?' The form of argument used by Apel here is reminiscent of Kant's move in the first critique where he challenged Hume's sceptical position, where Kant looked at the conditions necessary for perception rather than the content of the perception. Here Apel is saying that certain conditions must be fulfilled in order for the trilemma, and particularly its third arm, to be intelligible. The demonstration that such conditions must exist overcomes the trilemma opens the way for philosophical grounding.

Here is to be found Apel's equivalent of the transformation, conjointly, of the "transcendental unity of apperception" from the *Critique of Pure Reason* and the notion of transcendental freedom from *The Critique of Practical Reason.* Apel's position with respect to subjectivity, and his reading of Kant's view of subjectivity, is revealed in an earlier passage where he refers to the, 'insight of Kant into the necessity of the presupposition of "I think" for all objectively valid knowledge'.[37]

In support of his position Apel says:

> It now first becomes clear - due to the necessity of the unlimited sharing of linguistic meaning and truth in the sense of intersubjective validity - the presupposition of the "I think," which is inavoidable for theoretical arguments, is not to be separated from the ethical-practical presupposition of recognition of the norms of an ideal community of argumentation.[38]

Apel is clearly extending the notions contained in Kant's program via his transcendental-pragmatic transformation of philosophy. Apel elaborates his claim by drawing a distinction between consensual-argumentative and strategic rationality, further claiming that anyone who enters into a context in which they are seeking or expressing an interest in 'a rational redemption of justified claims', is necessarily committed to, indeed 'is presupposing a priori', an ideal community of communication and is committed to discourse as the means of establishing the justification and legitimation of disputed validity claims. As Apel has claimed, human beings as linguistic beings, must share meaning and truth with their fellow beings in order to be able to think in a valid form. And elsewhere Apel claims: '... it follows that all human communication - and thus also human *thought*, which is dependent on communication - must always have participated in the *principle of trans-subjectivity*'.[39]

If Apel's position can be justified he will have succeeded in making a significant advance in the application of transcendental-pragmatic reasoning to a broad range of philosophical issues and providing a foundation for communicative theory. In order to establish the degree of success achieved by Apel it is necessary to make a closer examination of some of his key ideas and arguments.

Firstly, it is appropriate to make an examination of the idea an "ideal communication community". Apel, as previously stated, takes this notion from Peirce's "community of inquirers". This notion, like so many one finds in Peirce, seems to be incompletely developed, yet it forms an essential foundation of his theory of pragmatism. For instance Peirce claims:

> Modern science accepts no proposition as self-evident but rests on the consensus of the community of scientific investigators as to what premises one may adopt for the sake of inquiry.[40]

Peirce indicates that the notion of the "community of investigators" is foundational to his philosophical "architectonic". It replaces the notion of objective truth, and also in part, that of formal rationality, with a notion that is at once non-subjective but capable of taking account of the subjectivity of understanding. It can also accommodate a public process of hypothesis testing not locked into, what he regarded as, the impossible requirements of objectivity. Peirce was concerned to oppose Cartesian subjective foundationalism and at the same time to update and transform the Kantian transcendental deduction into a form suitable for a modern philosophy of science. It is precisely these elements of Peirce's philosophy that are adopted by Apel. However, Apel uses the idea in a rather different context to Peirce. The context differs in a number of ways. Apel is addressing a world context, in a post-linguistic turn period, with different values and ethical orientations and also different pressing human and policy problems.

Apel's move to establish the "communication community" is based on a number of moves. Firstly, there is the rejection of the, 'evidence of consciousness in Descartes', Kant's and Husserl's 'sense',[41] as a sufficient ground for knowledge. Next, he claims that it is necessary to invoke, in a fairly formal sense, the late Wittgensteinian notion of a "language-game" to transpose, by means of linguistic agreement, the personal evidence of consciousness by way of an a priori validity of meaningful statements for us. The personal evidence of consciousness becomes possible only under the "paradigm of language" and it is under this paradigm that a communication community is operative.[42] Then, Apel claims that the two concepts of "language-game" and "the indefinite community of investigators," taken together, provide a "*communicative synthesis of interpretation*" which functions as the equivalent of Kant's "highest point" in 'a semiotically transformed transcendental philosophy'.[43]

Indeed, both the Wittgensteinian concept of the 'language-game' and Peirce's concept of the "community" can be interpreted in such a manner that, on the one hand, the functional point of Kant's transcendental idealism is retained (i.e. an equivalent can be established for the "highest point" of Kant's transcendental deduction and for the, 'highest maxim of synthetic judgements' according to which the preconditions for the possibility of experience are at the same time the preconditions for the possibility of the objects of experience); whilst on the other, a mediation of Kant's transcendental idealism with a realism, and even historical materialism of society that has indeed always been presupposed (as the subject-object of science), is implied.[44]

Anyone who enters into an argument aimed at establishing claims is necessarily presupposing the existence of a communication community wherein the acknowledgment of the validity of such claims could occur. Such entering into argumentative claims implies an a priori of the 'communicative synthesis of interpretation'.

There is yet another element, not extensively discussed in Apel's exposition, which is nevertheless important for Apel's thesis, it is the "private language argument". Wittgenstein's discussion of the impossibility of a private language will be discussed in more detail in a later chapter. The "private language argument" will be discussed in more detail in a later chapter in relation to Kant's views on privacy, but it is necessary to provide some discussion here of its importance for Apel. The importance of the private language argument for Apel is that it does two things. Firstly it supports the logical requirement for a linguistic community and secondly it provides the grounds for a transition from an "ideal" to a "real" language community.

Wittgenstein's so called "argument" is difficult and somewhat inconclusive. This is because he had difficulty imagining what a private language would be like. He argues that a private language of sorts was not absolutely impossible, as a set of sounds or signs and objects could be put together, but such a "language" would not go anywhere; it would have no use and not be a language in any accepted sense. It would, no matter how elaborate, be no more than a private list correlating sensations with signs or events.

In *Philosophical Investigations* the discussion of private language continues over some sixty or so sections from §241 to about §309 and spasmodically to §363.[45] It is mixed with a discussion of the privacy of experience and the experience of pain. Wittgenstein is as much concerned to show that we cannot know that we have private sensations as he is to make a more general point about the language game of referring to what is private. Part of the significance of Wittgenstein's position, as noted by Kenny[46] is that it undermines the basis of empiricist positions which require that we have immediate knowledge of our own experiences. Wittgenstein's point is not so much that it is strictly impossible to invent, in some elaborate set of circumstances, what could be a private language but that it would be useless or purposeless to do so. He insists that language is like an instrument that is used for communication; the problem with a private language is that it does not do anything. As soon as it does anything, like communicate an instruction or a sensation for instance, it becomes public. Words cannot acquire meaning merely by being linked to private experiences in a form of private ostensive definition.

In §265 he discusses how even a fairly primitive private language would fail. If we were to associate a mental table with a word or any sign the success of the meaning would rely remembering the mental table correctly. The same would be true of using a sign eg "S" for a sensation. It requires recognising the same sensation from one occurrence to another. As soon as one uses a justification for the use of this sign "S" to refer to a certain sensation the process is necessarily accessible to others and therefore public.

Interwoven with this discussion is the implied claim that there is really no such thing as "privileged access" to our own mental states; at least not in the sense required for a justification of empiricism. All such access is mediated via the language game. In this sense the argument is radically anti-Platonic in showing that experience arises outside subjective reflection.

There are many difficulties in dealing with Wittgenstein at this point in his discussion, many of which will be taken up in more detail later; here it is sufficient to point to those difficulties that have significance for Apel. One is his refusal to locate his discussion within the context of an historical philosophical debate. Another is his refusal to advance theses in philosophy. He saw the role of philosophy as entirely descriptive; its role was to clear up confusions arising from the way in which we use or mis-use language. Thus, Wittgenstein does not advance the thesis that a private language is impossible, nor that empiricism is based on an incorrect view about the way in which words refer to experience. Rather, he shows how a private language is senseless; it does not work, it merely misleads. Apel in taking up Wittgenstein's apparent views on private language uses him to support the program of the linguistic transformation of the Kantian project.

Apel takes the view, rather too definitively, that Wittgenstein had established that a private language was impossible: '...[For Wittgenstein] the truly revolutionary insight for all philosophical thinking [is] that a private language is, in principle, impossible'.[47] A private language is impossible for Apel because there could be no criteria, other than self-defeating subjective criteria, for the successful use of such a "language". This being the case any use of language is necessarily a public use presupposing the existence, or the real possibility of existence, of other users of the language.[48] Apel implicitly adopts this insight of Wittgenstein and incorporates it into his concept of the "ideal communication community". He believes that the impossibility of a private language supports the a priori element of the ideal communication community and thus further proves that all argumentation, indeed all communication whether linguistic or gestural, presupposes the existence of such a community. It follows that any beings, whether human or not are capable of forming such a community according to their own form of communication and own language games. This is, in Apel's philosophy, the equivalent of Kant's concept of the categorical imperative applying to all rational beings even though others might structure the manifold of apperception differently to our own.

The acceptance of Apel's concept of the ideal communication community depends upon the acceptance of a number of assumptions regarding transcendental philosophy. These assumptions can either be denied or challenged. For instance, Richard Rorty in *Philosophy and the Mirror of Nature* would simply deny outright the existence of any such transcendental assumptions.[49] Rorty says that Kant confused predication with synthesis, and that had he not done so, the problematic of the transcendental deduction would not have misled us to the extent it has. It is probable that Wittgenstein would have taken a similar view, as indeed have his followers such as Malcolm and Winch.[50] These philosophers would claim that such assumptions were merely an extension of outmoded metaphysics, and along with such metaphysical notions should be discarded. Arguments of this kind claim that no matter how radically 'transformed', any transcendental type argument happens to be it assumes the existence of some sort of other level of reality, or other world, which simply cannot be proven. They amount to sort of philosophical "phlogiston" theory that confuses rather than clarifies the truth. It would also be claimed, in a more Wittgensteinian mode, that such transcendental assumptions do not help our understanding of philosophical problems, but rather get in the way because, even if they were true, then there would be a further transcendental reality to be accounted for; an even more difficult challenge than the original problem. In short we would be back to the objections to Kantian notions of "things-in-themselves" and of a "noumena" somehow supporting reality or realities.

Apel's method of dealing with such objections is to rebut them by emphasising the need for transcendental-pragmatic foundations in order to mount such an objection. We could be faced here with an impasse of assertion and counter assertion based on mutually incompatible ways of viewing the world unless there is some move which can break such and impasse. Such a move can be successfully made using the method of reflexive transcendental-pragmatic critique.

In denying the possibility of transcendental foundations in a communication community, post-Wittgensteinians such as Winch or post-Pragmatists such as Rorty, are asserting an incoherent position, that does not differ in essentials from certain forms of crude empiricism. Their position entails the same fundamental flaw of leading to a 'methodological solipsism'. Any person who engages in a communication situation, especially an argument situation where the outcome matters in terms of their interests, must make certain assumptions. There must be the assumption that they can form the intention to communicate, then, that their choice of signs represents their intention, and then that those signs will be similarly, but possibly not precisely, understood by others who are capable of engaging in a similar process. There must also be implicit criteria for determining the success or failure of the communication. The signs here are independent of the individual's consciousness and are part of a public lexicon. If this were not so, we would not meaningfully be able to correct a speaker by saying, "Oh, you really mean 'x'", nor perhaps accuse anyone of self-deception. A closely related position is adopted by Apel in his discussion of Habermas where he claims that a person who refuses to enter into discourse constitutes a case of a pathological sceptic who refuses self-understanding.[51] We would be rather like Swift's philosophers who refuse to use words and carry sacks full of objects that they can show to each other in order to communicate.

To deny the necessity for transcendental foundations would be to deny the possibility of grounding argumentation as a form of discourse. Those who would deny transcendental foundations are in fact presupposing exactly what they seek to reject by mounting their objection. It would seem that those who deny such a grounding are faced with the sort of unpalatable options contained in the "Munchhausen Trilemma". Specifically, the post-Wittgensteinians must rely on assertion as a foundation. The post-pragmatists are not in a totally dissimilar position but with an added element of relativism such that all grounding is only 'local'. The problem here is not that their limited claims cannot be sustained, but rather that their claims do not recognise the reality of the genuine scope of philosophy. There are both moral and epistemological reasons for resisting such a position. On moral grounds the situation of humanity is denied; it would be hard to find reasons for doing anything about issues that were not 'local', such as global pollution or famine.

The hermenueticists in this situation are clearly faced with the possibility of an infinite regress as any interpretation must rely on a prior interpretation, and a context of interpretation. But is not Apel in the same situation here in presupposing "communication community" which entails as part of its conception Peirce's community of "interpretation"?

Apel is not in precisely this position because he relies on two underpinning notions. The first is 'the *a priori* of the communication community', the second is the employment of the Kantian notion of the "fact of reason". Firstly he contends that any person who enters into a communication situation, that is one in which claims to truth and validity are made and redeemed, is already presupposing the existence of an "ideal communication community" and thus acknowledging a (synthetic) a priori equivalent to Kant's "synthesis of apperception". Secondly, Apel believes he has overcome the problems associated with Kant's notion of a "fact of reason". Apel would be inclined to agree with Ilting[52] and Kant scholars such as Schneewind[53] that the reliance on "fact of reason" as a justification for the categorical imperative presents a major problem. In fact, it leaves Kant little better placed than Hume, with an assertoric basis for ethics and also knowledge.[54] However Apel believes that the Kantian notion of "fact of reason", never fully resolved by Kant himself, can be resolved in a transcendental-pragmatic context. He believes that, 'we can interpret Kant's reference to the 'fact of reason' *qua* uncontestable *fact* of moral self-determination (through a self-imposed law of self-transcendence) as a result of transcendental self-contemplation, that can be reconstructed in the sense in which we have indicated, namely, as an implication of the *a priori* argumentation'.[55] The fact of reason is the ground for reflective judgement in Kant's theory and this can be seen by regarding it as the ground for transcendental-pragmatic reflection in Apel's "transformed" theory.

Whilst these moves go a long way towards establishing Apel's theory for philosophical grounding and a critical transcendental-pragmatics Apel does not securely establish the ideal communication community as a basis. What his theory lacks is a theory of (intersubjective) consciousness.

The weakness of Apel's theory is that it only seems to work within a broad Kantian context; that is on untransformed Kantian assumptions. Despite Apel's strong claims to the contrary, he has not conclusively demonstrated that anyone who enters into a argumentative discourse situation must accept, 'the a priori of the communication community', or the 'universal language game'. This is where Rorty, and in a more constructive context Habermas,[56] have a point. One simply does not have to play the game of philosophical foundations. It may be the case that other positions "go nowhere" or even undermine the "justificatory role of philosophy" but that of itself does not compel those who hold alternative positions to adopt the necessity of establishing universal foundations. This is recognised to a degree by Apel but it is a position he just cannot accept, because of his commitment to a Kantian architectonic, and a basic belief that communication would not be possible without a fundamental objective ground.[57]

A different, but related criticism, is made by Wellmer. In an exhaustive discussion of Apel, and also Habermas in "Ethics and Dialogue", Wellmer attacks the notion of an "idealizing communication community" as unable to supply the ground for a consensus theory of truth and, largely as a consequence, unable to support discourse ethics.[58] His objection is that the idea of an ultimate communication community rests on a 'profound ambiguity',[59] that the ideal communication community presupposes the idea of an ultimate language.

He says:

> The ideal communication community would have passed beyond error, dissent, non-understanding and conflict, but only at the price of freezing language, of the extinction of its productive energies, and thus of suspending the very life-form of humanity.[60]

Wellmer also says that this objection applies to Habermas' weaker version of philosophical grounding of consensus, as the notion of the "ideal speech situation" also involves an "idealizing consensus".

Wellmer succeeds in his criticisms of the idealizing elements of consensus theory, yet concedes that if a discourse ethics, which he supports, is to succeed and avoid a trivialising relativism, then some means of grounding discourse is essential. He opts for a reconstructed Kantianism that is capable of distinguishing between legal and moral norms as a way of arguing that moral discourse succeeds when agreement is reached in complex, concrete moral situations. He says on this point: 'Moral discourse, however, would above all be a discourse about the correct way of understanding reality from a moral point of view'.[61]

What Wellmer fails to adequately recognise in his sympathetic critique of Apel and communicative theory, is the question of the subject of understanding in ideal communication situations is crucial to their success. Communication is communication amongst subjects who also speak and act. Further radical reflection on the subject is necessary to support communicative theory.

Despite the problems and rigidities of Apel's complex theory, it constitutes the most powerful contribution to philosophical reconstruction via transformation of the "linguistic turn" to date. What the theory lacks is an intersubjective theory of consciousness. Indeed the lack of such a theory is at present the greatest impediment to the advancement of a reconstructed philosophy, not just for Apel, but for Habermas and others. Until such a theory is developed any philosophical theory, no matter how "transformed" will continue to carry the burden of a post-Cartesian theory subjectivity, with its well documented shortcomings.

In the following chapters Apel's contributions to a theory of consciousness will be reviewed in a discussion of the intersubjective pragmatism of G. H. Mead. In following sections there will be a discussion of the contributions of Ludwig Wittgenstein and the later work of Kant. Then an outline of an intersubjective theory will be offered that would complete a revised project of "philosophical transformation".

Notes

1 Apel, Karl-Otto (1980), "The Problem of Philosophical Foundations", in *After Philosophy: End or Transformation?* eds. Kenneth Baynes, James Bohman and Thomas McCarthy, MIT Press, p. 281.

2 Wellmer, Albrecht (1991), *The Persistence of Modernity*, Cambridge, Polity Press, p. 143.

3 Apel, Karl-Otto (1981), *Charles Sanders Peirce; From Pragmatism to Pragmaticism*, trans. John Michael Krois, University of Massachusetts Press, Amherst, p. 7.

4 Apel argues that Wittgenstein is best understood in the context of German Hermeneutics, see for instance Apel, Karl-Otto in *Towards a Transformation of Philosophy*, Chapter 1.

5 See Wiggershaus, Rolf (1994), *The Frankfurt School*, trans. Michael Robertson, MIT Press, Cambridge, Mass., especially p. 537ff for more background detail.

6 See Apel, Karl-Otto (1980), in *Towards a Transformation of Philosophy*, pp. 136 - 139.

7 Apel, Karl-Otto (1967), *Der Denkweg von Charles S Peirce: Eine Einführung in den amerikanischen Pragmatismus*, Suhurkamp Verlag, Frankfurt am Main.

8 Apel, Karl-Otto, *Charles Sanders Peirce; From Pragmatism to Pragmaticism*, p. 11.

9 Ibid., p. 13.
10 See Immanuel Kant, *Critique of Pure Reason*, B 860-61.
11 Apel, Karl-Otto (1980), "Noam Chomsky's theory of language and contemporary philosophy: a case study in the philosophy of "science", in *Towards a Transformation of Philosophy*, trans. G. Adey and D. Frisby, Routledge and Kegan Paul, London, see especially pp. 201 - 212.
12 Apel, Karl-Otto, op. cit., Towards a Transformation of Philosophy, p. 157.
13 Wittgenstein, Ludwig (1958), *Philosophical Investigations*, Basil Blackwell, Oxford, see Part I, sections 1 and 23.
14 Ibid., p. 11e.
15 See, Pears, David (1971), *Wittgenstein*, Fontana, Glasgow, Introduction.
16 Critical comment by Habermas and others of Peter Winch's *Idea of a Social Science* and "Understanding a Primitive Society" have sustained accusations of a relativistic interpretation of language games.
17 Peirce, C.S. (1931), *Collected Papers*, eds. C. Hartshorne and P. Weiss, Cambridge, Mass., Vol. 1, Chapters 2 and 3.
18 See Apel, Karl-Otto, *Towards a Transformation of Philosophy*, Chapter 4.
19 Habermas, Jurgen (1984), *The Theory of Communicative Action, Vol. 1*, Beacon Press, Boston, Mass., pp. 95-101.
20 Apel, Karl-Otto, "The Communication community and the social sciences", in *Towards a Transformation of Philosophy*, p. 170.
21 Apel, Karl-Otto (1992), "Normatively Grounding Critical Theory" in *Philosophical Interventions in the Unfinished Project of the Enlightenment*, eds. A. Honneth et al., MIT Press, Cambridge, Mass., p. 150.
22 See Apel, Karl-Otto, *Towards a Transformation of Philosophy*, Chapter 5.
23 Ibid., p. 136.
24 Ibid.
25 Ibid., p. 137.
26 Ibid.
27 Apel, Karl-Otto (1990),"Ethics, Utopia and the Critique of Utopia" in *The Communicative Ethics Controversy*, eds. Seyla Benhabib and Fred Dallmayr, The MIT Press, Cambridge, Mass, pp. 46-47.
28 See Schneewind, J. B. (1992), "Autonomy, obligation and virtue: An overview of Kant's moral philosophy", in *The Cambridge Companion to Kant*, ed. Paul Guyer, Cambridge University Press, Cambridge, p. 327.
29 See Apel, Karl-Otto, "The Problem of Philosophical Foundations", in *After Philosophy: End or Transformation.*
30 Ibid., p 42.
31 Ibid.
32 Ibid.
33 Albert, Hans (1985), *Treatise on Critical Reason*, trans. Mary Varney Rorty, Princeton University Press, Princeton.
34 Ibid, p. 18.

35 Apel, Karl-Otto, "The Problem of Philosophical Foundations", in *After Philosophy: End or Transformation*, p.254.
36 Apel, Karl-Otto, "Ethics, Utopia and the Critique of Utopia", in *The Communicative Ethics Controversy*, pp. 46-47.
37 Ibid., pp. 44-45.
38 Ibid.
39 Apel, Karl-Otto (1984),"The Situation of Humanity as an Ethical Problem", *Praxis*, Vol. 4, No. 3, Basil Blackwell, Oxford.
40 Peirce, Charles Sanders (1966), "Questions Concerning Certain Faculties Claimed for Man", in *Charles S. Peirce: Selected Writings*, ed. Phillip P. Wiener, Dover, New York, p. 17.
41 Apel, Karl-Otto, "The Communication Community as the Transcendental Presupposition for the Social Sciences", in *Towards a Transformation of Philosophy*, op. cit., p. 137.
42 Ibid.
43 Ibid., p. 138.
44 Ibid., p. 138.
45 See Wittgenstein, Ludwig, *Philosophical Investigations*, §243, Also see Apel " Wittgenstein and Hermeneutic Understanding", op. cit., p. 32.
46 Kenny, Anthony (1973), *Wittgenstein*, Penguin Books, Harmondsworth, p.178.
47 Apel, Karl-Otto, *Towards a Transformation of Philosophy*, p. 32.
48 The case recently came to my attention of an Australian Aboriginal woman who is the only speaker left of her tribal language. Whilst there are no other actual speakers of the language, this is clearly not a case of a private language in that she is the last speaker of a public language. The woman expressed a great sense of loss and personal anguish at the loss of the language and said that she felt that " the whole world was lost and that she was desperately alone".
49 Rorty, Richard (1970), *Philosophy and the Mirror of Nature*, Princeton University Press, Princeton, pp. 151 - 154.
50 See Winch, Peter (1958),*The Idea of a Social Science*, Routledge and Kegan Paul, London.
51 Apel, Karl-Otto (1992), "Normatively Grounding Critical Theory", in *Philosophical Interventions in the Unfinished Project of the Enlightenment*, eds. A. Honneth et al., MIT Press, Cambridge, Mass., p.156.
52 See Ilting, Karl-Heinz (1990)," The Basis for the Validity of Moral Norms", in *The Communicative Ethics Controversy*, eds. Seyla Benhabib and Fred Dallmayr, MIT Press, Cambridge, Mass., pp. 220 - 226.
53 Schneewind, J. B. (1992), "Autonomy, obligation and virtue: An overview of Kant's moral philosophy" in *The Cambridge Companion to Kant*, ed., Paul Guyer, Cambridge, Cambridge University Press, p. 325.
54 Apel, Karl-Otto, *Towards a Transformation of Philosophy*, p. 271.
55 Ibid., pp. 272-3.
56 See for instance a recent statement of Habermas' position in "A return to Metaphysics", Jurgen Habermas, *Postmetaphysical Thinking*, Pt IV.

57 See Apel, Karl-Otto, "Normatively Grounding Critical Theory", in *Philosophical Interventions in the Unfinished Project of the Enlightenment.*
58 Wellmer, Albrecht (1991), *The Persistence of Modernity*, p. 181.
59 Ibid., p. 176.
60 Ibid.
61 Ibid., p. 202.

6 Apel, Mead and Intersubjectivity

Apel recognises that the transformation of transcendental philosophy requires a transformation of the transcendental subject. The clearest statement of this necessity is found in the final chapter of *Understanding and Explanation.*

He characterises the transformation of philosophy thus:

> ...in order to conceptualize this synthesis of understanding as an a priori mediation between empirical subjects of knowledge and forms of life in the synchronic and diachronic dimension, we must radically transform the classic concept of the transcendental subject. It can no longer be grounded in the pre-lingual and precommunicative synthetic unity of the consciousness of objects and self-consciousness.[1]

Apel's position on the self and self-consciousness opposes the idea of an unengaged ego outside the world and asserts a progressive transformation of the Kantian approach to the determination of a form of subjectivity. Apel believes that the actual content of the Kantian system is incorrect, because the notion of "things in themselves", which are available only via the transcendental deduction, marks a retreat back to a form of Cartesianism, of an ego disengaged from the world of reality. However, Apel also believes that, 'the critical and metaphysical deep meaning of the Kantian system', must be respected.[2]

Whilst Apel's account differs with respect to the content, his view is consistent with the full implications of Kant's statement that every thought is accompanied by "I think" and not just the "cogito". Apel's transformation of this observation by Kant establishes, via the notion of the "ideal communication community", intersubjectivity as a precondition for meaning and thus a precondition for self-consciousness. Apel uses the device of a critical re-appraisal of a hermeneutic position to, in part, establish his claim by appealing to a 'hermeneutic synthesis of understanding' to establish the unity of intersubjective consciousness, where Kant would have appealed to the synthesis of apperception to establish the unity of individual consciousness.

Apel further argues that scientific (and social scientific) actions must be able to be articulated in order to be comprehensible to the individual subject of knowledge; which, in turn, shows that reflexive and subjective understanding presupposes intersubjective communicative understanding and a model of communicative interaction that cannot be reduced to purposive-rational action.[3] Thus, the human interest in hermeneutic understanding can be complementary to the interest of scientific-cognitive understanding. As an aside at this point, Apel makes the interesting observation that the complementarity of these positions can serve to unify the apparent oppositions within the social sciences between the quasi-natural scientific explanatory and descriptive modes.[4] In place of the unity of the transcendental subject, Apel has developed a theory of the transcendental unity of consciousness, which must accommodate 'the thought of the communication community as the subject of processes of coming to an understanding about meaning'.[5]

Unfortunately Apel does not expand to any great extent on his views regarding subjectivity and the self. This is clearly because his major philosophical directions, reflecting the major issues of his generation, lie elsewhere; namely with the issue of the grounding of philosophical discourse and the methods of science. There is, for Apel, in contrast to Kant, no transcendental "I", but there is however, in a certain sense, a transcendental "we".[6] The "we" is the subject of the intersubjective transcendental subject of knowledge. Yet it is an indisputable fact of experience that "we's" do not have consciousness only "I's" do. That is, that whilst intersubjectivity is intelligible, inter-consciousness is the stuff of science fiction.

How does Apel deal with this type of objection?

One must speculate to a degree on how Apel would cope with such objections. His way of dealing with the issue is embedded in much of his wide-ranging discussion. The response lies in the discussion of the transformation of the subject of consciousness. The unity and coherence of consciousness is now to be found in a post-linguistic 'hermeneutic synthesis of communication'. It is the case that it is only as members of the communication community, via the playing of language games, that we are able to differentiate self-consciousness and other consciousness. Non-linguistic animals, for instance, would not be able to do this. Apel, it would seem, is saying that we must first, by a priori reasoning, postulate the communication community as a "we" and then through the pragmatic-reflexive use of language establish an "I" as a point within the community. This pragmatic-reflexive move upon further reflection establishes the transcendental communication community as the conditions for the postulation of other "I's" within the community. Such other "I's" must necessarily exist, as transcendental-pragmatic subjects, on the same terms as the "I" of "this" subject. This view is captured in Apel's statement that, 'the purposive-rational understanding of subjective, nature-manipulating actions and their results must be linguistically articulatable even to be comprehensible to the individual subject of knowledge'.[7] And thus intersubjective understanding is presupposed.

The problem remains that if one does not share Apel's Kantian assumptions, then it seems that Apel offers no argument that compels the reader to agree with him. His case may be compelling, if one accepts that entering into communication presupposes the a priori of the communication community; or indeed the existence of the "a priori" at all. There are differing positions, for instance Habermas takes the position that is possible to sustain a defence of discourse ethics without maintaining Apel's insistence on 'ultimate justification'.[8] If Habermas is correct, then all one can conclude is that Apel has provided an ingenious and significant extension of the Kantian project, but that he is still subject to the full force of the significant objections that have been raised against Kant's "transcendental subject".

It is my view that Apel's development of the Kantian project constitutes a significant advance towards its completion and is the most substantial attempt, to date, to overcome the problems that Kant left unresolved. Of particular importance is the insight that meaning must be grounded in some framework that requires an intersubjective dimension. His arguments demonstrate the necessity for such an element, but his attempt to articulate such a position remain unsatisfactory for lack of a theory of subjectivity and linked intersubjectivity. His views on the communication community and intersubjectivity require much development if he is to overcome the problems of the Kantian position and to establish a basis for his own position.

An essential element for the completion of Apel's project and for communicative theory in general is a developed theory of subjectivity capable of supporting the sort of intersubjectivity required for an intersubjective communicative theory. Habermas' intersubjective communicative theory also requires a developed theory of the subject, however he unlike Apel, turns to Mead to offer the basis of such a theory.

George Herbert Mead provides a basis for the development of a theory of the self, which provides an intersubjective social basis of consciousness and self-consciousness. Mead's theory has the potential to support Apel in many important respects. Mead was a social psychologist strongly influenced by the philosophy of pragmatism. Mead and John

Dewey were close friends at the University of Michigan and at the University of Chicago, and at Michigan Mead studied under Josiah Royce. There was a further influence on Mead's intellectual development. He studied in Berlin where he came under the influence of Wundt, attending his lectures on philosophy. In Berlin he also came under the influence of Dilthey, one of his academic teachers, and of German Idealist philosophy in general.[9] Joas tells us that, 'Mead passed freely between philosophy, psychology, sociology, and the natural sciences at a time when the specialization and professionalization of these disciplines was just beginning and was still slight'.[10] Whilst Mead characterised himself as a scientific social psychologist with a penchant for philosophical issues, two factors in his work are of significance for our concerns here. Firstly, his interest in gesture derived from Wundt and post-Darwinianist pragmatism. Secondly, partially under the influence of Gestalt psychology, his interest developed in not just the act, but the social context of the act. In this Mead recognised that social actions required interpretation and that neither mere "mentalistic" intention, nor an objectivistic empirical description, could fully characterise the significance of social actions.

Joas succinctly summarises the guiding themes of Mead's intellectual labours.

> The fundamental themes that can be extracted from Mead's biography can be subsumed under three headings: confidence in the emancipatory prospects of scientific rationality; a striving to root 'mind' or 'spirit' in the organism; and the attempt to elaborate a theory of intersubjectivity that would conceive of the self as socially originated.[11]

It is the last of these fundamental themes that we shall be concerned with here, however it is important to always bear in mind when reading Mead that the previous two themes exist in the background. Of particular importance, and almost universally overlooked, is the emancipatory theme. It links with the other two but it helps us understand the force of Mead's theory of the social generation of the self. A socially formed self is one in which, 'one of the cornerstones of bourgeois ideology in the strict sense is eliminated, namely possessive individualism'.[12]

Dilthey was a further major influence on Mead's intellectual development. This was a critical influence on his philosophical development as Mead's study of German idealism was tempered by Dilthey's hermeneutic and psychologistic methodologies. He undertook, under Dilthey's supervision, to write a dissertation on the empiricist conception of space, which went beyond the Kantian conception of space as an intuition. The dissertation, which set out to show that space was a consequence of the fundamental constitution of the human species, was never completed, but the intellectual plan of the dissertation reveals the basis for the later development of symbolic interactionism.

A further influence of Dilthey on Mead relates to his psychological approach to ethics. Joas tells us that Mead attended Dilthey's lectures on ethics and developed a "developmental psychological approach" based on Dilthey's more conceptual psychological approach. It is also worth noting that at this time Mead was influenced by the German social democratic movement, an influence that he was to carry throughout his life.[13]

Mead's writings on nineteenth century philosophy reveal that he regarded Kant as the pivotal thinker, and that he saw his work as carrying on the Kantian project, albeit a century later and by what he took to be different means. Mead took a universalist orientation towards knowledge and freedom. He replaces Kant's transcendental subject with the community collaboratively seeking knowledge and emancipation though symbolically mediated activity. Here the influence of Fichte, pre-eminently amongst the post-Hegelians becomes of major importance to Mead, where he saw the transformation of transcendental consciousness as a critical step of development from both Kant and Hegel.

Mead was described by his student and editor Charles Morris as a "social behaviourist". This description is unfortunate and misleading. Mead was writing before reductionist or "Watsonian" behaviourism had become firmly established as the behaviourist orthodoxy. Joas tells us that Mead took steps to distance himself from Watsonianism and to establish his own "true" non-reductionist behaviourism.[14] The description by Morris is unfortunate in that it has unecessarily coloured interpretations of Mead. He is often seen as a "soft" behaviourist without the tough-mindedness of later reductionists. This is an inadequate interpretation, to say the least, and represents a distortion of Mead's true intellectual mission. He had in fact embarked on an intellectual agenda far broader than behaviourism. He was setting out to integrate both the "inner" interpretive dimensions of experience with the "outer" social dimension of community.

Unfortunately the "social behaviourist" label has stuck to interpretations of Mead with Habermas, for instance, claiming that Mead presented his theory under the rubric of "social behaviourism".[15] Habermas further claims that Mead's reason for this was to present a 'criticism of consciousness'. It is true that Mead wanted to criticise forms of Cartesian consciousness but he did not use behaviourism as the vehicle of this criticism. Habermas makes this apparent in subsequent discussion, where he makes it quite clear that Mead held a non-reductionist position. However Habermas' main interest in Mead is as a precursor to the theory of communicative action. Mead was attempting to build the links between the individual act and society through action which could generally be described as behaviour in a larger interpretive framework. It would be better to drop the description of Mead as a "social behaviourist", as Joas suggests, as it only serves to divert attention from his true intellectual purpose.

There is a further aspect of Mead's work which makes the task of the present day interpreter rather more difficult. This aspect is that most of Mead's writings were lecture notes prepared by him and later elaborated by his students, particularly Morris. This is true of his most widely read work *Mind, Self and Society*, which was composed posthumously from students' lecture notes. The problem for the contemporary reader is that this work has the lack of explanatory background and a degree of repetition that one frequently finds in such notes. One has little grasp of Mead's work as part of a larger system and it is difficult to discern the sophistication of his philosophical background.

A problem in dealing with Mead's ideas from a critical point of view is that it is often not clear what particular philosophical framework he is employing. Although Mead had studied in Germany and was very familiar with Kant and German Idealism, it can be somewhat frustrating in the analysis of his work to identify Kantian or other frameworks which Mead seems to be claiming arise *ab initio* from his own social-psychological reflections. At certain points Mead's work seems to be remarkably naive. Take, for instance, the following passage: 'We are continually changing our social system in some respects, and we are able to do that intelligently because we can think'.[16] Even by the standards of American sociology at the time this a rather superficial observation; however in the context a lecture presentation it is hard to judge the significance or otherwise of this observation. Yet we know that Mead was a sophisticated philosophical and political thinker and activist, advocating a rather radical social democracy.[17]

Joas asserts that Mead was unable to distance himself from being over influenced by the achievements of the science and technology of his day and was thus unable to realise fully the interpretive dimension of his thought.[18] Thus, Joas emphasises the functionalist and structuralist elements in Mead and claims that he is closer to Piaget than a critical philosophical position. Joas further claims that the key to interpreting the work of Mead can be grasped through the concept of "practical intersubjectivity". This was not a term used by Mead, but it does justice to the core of Mead's theory. It brings together the concept of action, including linguistically mediated action, with that of intersubjectivity. Joas points out that the concept emerges from the body of his work and offers a preliminary definition of "practical intersubjectivity" as 'a structure of communicative relations between subjects, a structure that is suited for transcending, on the theoretical plane, the opposition between the individualistic bias in the theory of action and a structural theory that does not recognise subjects or human action'.[19] This indeed encapsulates what Mead sets out to do and his success depends on the foundation of the concepts of "the subject", "the act" and "community".

Mead owes his recognition of the notion of "the community" as implicitly both a community of interpretation and a communication community to Royce.

Mead attended Harvard in 1887 as a postgraduate. His decision was influenced by two factors the relative intellectual freedom of Harvard and the opportunity to study under the Christian neo-Hegelian Josiah Royce. Mead fell under the strong influence of Royce and was to carry the greatest admiration for Royce throughout his life. The influence of Royce is of great importance in understanding Mead's philosophical system. Royce provides a link to Peirce who was known to, and respected by Royce, although the two men were worlds apart in their values and lifestyles.[20]

In his discussion of "community" and the "social act" he is not, of course, operating in Apel's (or Rorty's) "post linguistic turn" environment, but he is very consciously operating within the context of Peirce, Dewey and Royce. In The *Problem of Christianity* Josiah Royce gave prominence to the idea of the "community of interpreters" which is a clear development of Peirce's imprecise idea of the unlimited community of practitioners.[21] Mead's introduction to German idealism was no doubt permanently coloured by Royce who, 'transmitted to him the basic model of a philosophy of history that interpreted the kingdom of God as the historical realization of a community of all human beings brought about by universal communication'.[22] This concept both explicitly and implicitly forms an important part of the background of Mead's thought. For example:

> The organisation, then, of social responses makes it possible for the individual to call out in himself not simply a single response of the other but the response, so to speak, of the community as a whole.[23]

and similarly,

> A person who has in himself the universal response of the community toward that which he does, has in that sense the mind of the community. As a

scientist, we will say, one's community consists of all his colleagues, but this community consists of anyone who can understand what is said.[24]

These comments clearly reveal a close resemblance to the ideas of both Peirce and Apel.

However before exploring in more detail Mead's views on the community, society and communication it is necessary to examine more closely his central concept of the construction of the "self".[25]

Mead's discussion of the self commences with the discussion in *Mind, Self and Society.* This view, his substantial thesis, is somewhat qualified in the later published, *The Philosophy of the Act.* Mead proposes a number of phases in the development of the self; the development of generalised social attitudes, the development of the "I" and the "me" and the realisation of the self. He adopts a developmental perspective. In this perspective the self develops from the basis of a physiological organism in the milieu of society. The vehicle which permits the development of the self he terms, "the mind". For Mead, language is also an essential part of the development of the self. He is dogmatic on the point that pre-linguistic animals may have an animal intelligence but they do not develop a self. Organisms, as Mead calls them, including human beings have a basic awareness appropriate to their species, which allows them to have experience. But this experience does not necessarily, of itself, translate into either a mind or a self, or a form of social organisation that could be called a society. He points out that ants and bees have a complex form of social organisation which is not a society. In humans, Mead says, that the self is clearly distinguishable from the organism.[26] He takes some trouble to distinguish the self from the organism, which to the contemporary reader seems a rather obvious series of steps. However, it is important to remember that he was writing against a post-Darwinian background and directly in a context where behaviourism, particularly in psychology, was being established as a new paradigm. Against this paradigm, Mead claims that the self is separate from the body and can be an object to itself, in the way that the body cannot. This characteristic of the self, being an object to itself; both as subject and object, Mead claims to be very important, as it is the basis for the objective use of reason and also why we have *self*-consciousness and not just consciousness.[27] Mead distinguishes two senses of the term "consciousness", one which could be called basic awareness linked to physical states of the organism and another, 'that which we term thinking or reflective intelligence'.[28] In order to become a self one must be able to take an objective attitude towards oneself; Mead calls this taking the position of the 'generalised other' which becomes a key notion for Mead's position.[29] Mead claims: 'it is necessary to rational conduct that the individual should thus take an objective, impersonal attitude towards himself, that he should become an object to himself'.[30]

He continues in the following paragraph:

> The individual experiences himself as such, not directly, but only indirectly, from the particular standpoints of other individual members of the same group, ... he enters his own experience as a self or individual, not directly or immediately, not by becoming a subject to himself, but only in so far as he first becomes an object to himself ... and he becomes an object to himself only by taking the attitudes of other individuals towards himself within a social environment or context of experience and behaviour in which both he and they are involved.[31]

Thus it can be seen how radical a view Mead is developing of the self. In his theory we are social beings first, before we are either selves or individual beings. As Mead frequently reasserts, the self is a social process: 'The self, as that which can be an object to itself, is essentially a social structure, and it arises in social experience'.[32] We can only consider the concept of a solitary self after the formation of the self in social experience and it is, 'impossible to conceive of a self arising outside social experience'.[33]

Mead having discussed the generation of the self, continues to discuss the notion of the unity of the self. He says that a multiplicity of selves is in fact normal. One is a different self in different situations; 'we discuss politics with one self and religion with another'. [34] But there is, he claims, a unifying element to the self, which may in fact fail in certain psychopathologies. The unity of the self for Mead is also the consequence of a social process. The passage in which he puts his position on the unity of the self is one of his most incisive, if compressed, philosophical statements and is worth quoting in its entirety.

The unity and structure of the complete self reflects the unity and structure of the social process as a whole. Each of the elementary selves of which it is composed reflects the unity and structure of one of the various aspects of that process in which the individual is implicated. In other words, the various elementary selves which constitute, or are organised into, a complete self are the various aspects of the structure of that complete self, answering to the various aspects of the structure of the social process as a whole. The structure of the complete self is thus a reflection of the complete social process. The organisation and unification of the social group is identical with the organisation and unification of any one of the selves arising within the social process in which that group is engaged, or which it is carrying on.[35]

There are strong echoes here of a Kantian position approaching the transcendental unity of the self, but transformed into a social context. Mead, as read here, is saying that the unity of the self is the unity of the various selves that are generated by, and within, a social context. What gives unity to the self is the unity of the social context. There are clearly significant problems with this statement and unfortunately Mead's published lecture notes do not provide much support for elucidation or interpretation. For instance a fractured social context does not necessarily lead to a similarly fractured self, although it may do so in extreme situations. What Mead here needs is support from his broader discussion allowing for an account based on the dynamics of the structuring of the social process as a whole.

Notwithstanding the problems of Mead's position here he does offer a very radical theory of self formation which leads to a basis for recent communicative theory. It would seem clear that he is appealing to a principle very similar to that which Kant or Apel would call a transcendental principle. However, Mead on this point, is not very forthcoming about the principle of the unity of the "self of selves" and does not take it further.

Mead has put forward a crucial new argument for the advancement of our understanding of the self. He has provided an important step towards formulating a framework for grounding an intersubjective theory of the self which would complete the project of the "transformation of philosophy". Here is, in part, the grounds for the transformation of the transcendental subject that Apel's theory lacks.

There are many important aspects of Mead's theory that need to be sketched in before amplifying and critically assessing the argument above. These relate particularly to his treatment of language, communication, including gesture, action, and their particular relation to the self.

Mead traces the origin of communication from the gesture. Gesture can be a feature of communication between all animals, including humans. Organisms are capable of reacting to gestures which will generate gestures in return. In the human case, indeed in the case of all rational organisms, the gesture can become a symbol. A symbol can be expressed by one person and understood by another. In the case of speech; there are first of all, vocal gestures which can be transformed into language when certain vocal gestures become symbols as words.[36] In order for such communication to succeed it is necessary that the vocal gesture call out the same response in the hearer as it does in the speaker.

Here we should call out in ourselves the type of response we are calling out in others; we must know what we are saying, and the attitude of the other which we arouse in ourselves should control what we do say. Rationality means that the type of response which we call out in others should be so called out in ourselves, and that this response should in turn take its place in determining what further thing we are going to say and do. What is essential is that the symbol should arouse in one's self what it arouses in the other individual. It must have that sort of universality to any person who finds himself in the same situation.[37]

Here Mead is giving us a theory of the intersubjective genesis of language as essentially located in a speaker/hearer situation. The influence of Wundt is clear here, there are elements of Wundt's ideas on both parallelism and imitation. But there is more than merely the influence of Wundt, there is the treatment of the symbol which clearly reflects Peirce. The important characteristic of the symbol is its universality, as Mead says: 'it has to mean the same thing to all individuals involved'.[38] Mead then maintains that it is the social process that generates meaning. 'Meaning', he says: 'is thus a development of something objectively there as a relation between certain phases of the social act; it is not a psychical addition to that act and it is not an "idea" as traditionally conceived'.[39] But Mead goes on to make an even more audacious claim for language.

He says:

> Symbolization constitutes objects not constituted before, objects which would not exist except for the context of social relationships wherein the symbolization occurs. Language does not simply symbolize a situation or object which is already there in advance; it makes possible the existence or the appearance of that situation or object, for it is a part of the mechanism whereby that situation or object is created.[40]

Mead is here making a claim very similar to Kant's transcendental apperception but attributing the power to constitute objects, not to the transcendental aesthetic within the dimensions of space and time, but to language employed in the social process or the social act. It is, he claims the ability to use symbols consciously, and not just unconsciously as the higher animals might, which constitutes mind.

It appears that Mead is saying here that it is the ability to "symbolize" situations in language, presumably by meaningful words, or to put it another way, words in ordinary language, that creates, for us, the object or situation. We have to be able to represent to ourselves, in language, via words of the public language that we understand, those objects and situations from the point of view of the other in order to create those things for us. This is a very radical position, particularly for Mead's time. Whilst Mead provides a detailed discussion of the processes that he sees as responsible for the development of these capacities from the point of view of a social psychologist, he does not readily provide substantial philosophical argument to support the theoretical structure necessary for such a view. This could well be a consequence of the fact that we must work from Mead's lecture notes, but unfortunately the sort of close argumentation required to establish such a radical position is not given. One needs to read Mead sympathetically in order to provide the support for his radical stance in support of communicative theory.

Mead is presaging, in an almost eerie fashion, many of the positions taken in Wittgenstein's later philosophy; on things like mind, the necessary publicity of language, the importance of gesture, a discussion of pain, the nature of the act and the seeming irrelevance of the will and many other topics. His discussion of play, the game and rules also has a close similarity to Wittgenstein and a similar importance.

Habermas alludes to relationship between Mead and Wittgenstein, especially in respect to responses of the other and following a rule but does not develop the discussion beyond showing that a rule cannot be followed privately.[41]

One example of this is found Mead's discussion of the role of play and games in the development of the self. In many ways Mead's discussion resembles the positions taken by Wittgenstein in the *Philosophical Investigations* where he discusses the generation of the "language game" and the form of life that supports them.[42] Mead says that the child learns to adopt the attitude of the generalised other through the stages, first of play, then of the game. Mead says: 'In the game we get an organized other, a generalized other, which is found in the nature of the child itself...'.[43] It is thus via the game that the child learns to take the roles of others towards itself and thus, in conjunction with the 'inner conversation of gesture', develop a self as the first stage of the reflected generalised other. The child is thus adopting various social roles, derived from the community as parts of the proto-self, out of which it will, with a mature self-consciousness, become a full self-conscious being.

There are elements in Mead's theory of the development of self-consciousness at this point which are of significance in a theoretical sense, which he does not fully expound; although a contextual reading is of assistance. Mead touches on the significance by saying that the child liked to get into 'organisations that come into existence and pass out of existence'.[44] What is implied here and throughout the following section is that the person, in the form of the child, is developing a self by a form of social experimentation. He or she is not just mimicking the roles observed in others in the community, he or she is taking over those roles in the evolution of each self. He or she is learning "what it is like" from the inside by becoming progressively each of the roles, and not just performing them. This is an ontological theory not an epistemological position.

> The structure, then, on which the self is built is this response which is common to all, for one has to be a member of a community to be a self. ...He is putting himself in the place of the generalized other, which represents the organized response of all other members of the group.[45]

Mead also provides some remarks to the effect that the self is composed of a 'structure of attitudes'. Attitudes are built on habits. Habits are unreflected expressions, whereas attitudes are self-consciously derived from the community and in turn reflect the values of the community. As Mead here again points out: 'Selves can only exist in definite relationships to other selves'.[46]

Whilst the attitudes that we each develop are derived from the community and also serve to constitute that community it is also true, so Mead claims, that we can take the attitude of a generalised other that goes beyond (transcends) the immediate community. Mead says that this involves setting up a, 'higher sort of community which in a certain sense out votes the one we find'.[47] Mead continues here in *Mind, Self and Society* in a particularly interesting passage:

> A person may reach a point of going against the whole world about him; he may stand out by himself over against it. But to do that he has to speak with the voice of reason to himself. He has to comprehend the voices of the past and the future. That is the only way in which the self can get a voice which is more than the voice of the community.[48]

The interest in this passage is that Mead is here proposing something very similar to Apel's "ideal communication community". Apel would of course give the ideal communication community transcendental status in his transformed philosophy and link it to a Kantian framework. Mead is here making an important move to show that the individual's particular consciousness is more than the reflected consciousness of the community. Again as in passages quoted earlier it is "reason" or the "voice of reason" that is critical in that individuation process. Once again it is not spelled out what he understands reason to be in this context. If it is some transcendental constitutive element of the communication community then his position becomes close to an earlier version of Apel and would lend weight to Habermas' position. The process of conversation is one in which the individual has not only the right but the duty of talking to the community of which he is a part, and bringing about those changes which take place through the interaction of individuals.[49]

Mead develops around this insight a theory incorporating many precursive aspects of later communicative theories, theories of communicative rationality and communicative action, which are capable of spanning the gap between the subjective and the public spheres of consciousness.

Mead, of course, makes no such explicit connection and his roots in Pragmatism would not support such a claim; yet, nevertheless, there is here a clear recognition that the necessity for a larger framework exists. Mead also outlines a process of dialogue by which we may seek to change the attitudes of the community. This is clearly an approach to a transcendence of the self. The self and self-consciousness first developing in the community and then reaching beyond the immediate to some ideal or universal "community". Further weight is given to Mead's "transcendental theory" in his rejection of the basis of the self being in 'reflexive affective experiences' as proposed by Cooley and James.[50] The self, Mead claims, is not to be found in a "self-feeling", the essence of the self is cognitive.

> The essence of the self, as we have said, is cognitive: it lies in the internalised conversation of gestures which constitutes thinking, or in terms of which thought or reflection proceeds. And hence the origins and foundations of the self, like those of thinking are social.[51]

If the self is essentially social and arises only by reflection in a community, Mead recognises that he must account for the differing modes of subjective dispositions. He must distinguish between the "I" and the "me" as he puts it. Certainly the "I" and the "me" are not identical. A more simple theory of a socially reflected self could run the risk of failing to distinguish between the two first person modes of subjectivity as each would be a reflection of existing social attitudes. Mead needs to give sense not just to the idea of a self-consciousness but also to the idea of identity. A world where there were only "I's" and no "me's" would be a solipsistic world. And a world in which there were only "me's" would be a world in which there were no distinguishable individuals; a world in which there were acts but no authors of those acts. Mead claims that although the "I" and the "me" are both reflections of the community they are not identical. First there is an element of soliloquy in the "I" that is lacking in the "me". The "I" thus relies, in part on memory, and it is by memory that we are able to hold conversations with ourselves. The "me" is the public persona of subjectivity reflecting the attitudes of the community.

Mead says by way of definition:

> The "I" is the response of the organism to the attitudes of others; the "me" is the organized set of attitudes of others which one himself assumes. The attitudes of the others constitute the organized "me" and then one reacts towards that as an "I".[52]

Whilst this distinction certainly has an intuitive validity it requires a more methodical account.

Mead says that the "I" does not appear in the same sense in experience as the "me". In a sense it is the "I" that acts and the "me" that reflects and adopts attitudes including the attitudes of the community. Mead accepts that the "I" is never fully knowable to itself; or as he says, 'the "I" is something that is never entirely calculable'.[53] This "unknowable" aspect of the "I" is something that Mead never fully reconciles and something that he uses in an ambiguous way. He says:

> Taken together they [the "I" and the "me"] constitute a personality as it appears in social experience. The self is essentially a social process going on with these two distinguishable phases. If it did not have these two phases there could not be conscious responsibility, and there would be nothing novel in experience.[54]

Yet this process depends on the "I" being hidden from the "me". The "I" here has not fully freed itself from Descartes. It still carries both a self-aware and a non-self aware aspect. It is this rather than the tension between the "I" and the "me" that energises or "constitutes" the personality. This point is conceded by Habermas who observes that Mead's elucidations, 'remain tied to the model of the philosophy of consciousness'.[55]

The influence of Peirce and Royce is clear, but the influences on them, of Kant in the case of Peirce and both Kant and Hegel in the case of Royce is also clear. Mead was not directly influenced by Peirce but via William James and Royce was strongly influenced by pragmatism and thus indirectly by Peirce.[56] Mead would seem to be reflecting a foundational framework; either without acknowledgment, or more likely given his psychological interest, without full awareness of the metaphysical 'baggage' he is importing. Clearly, there is a very strong influence of the Kantian mode in Mead. There are a series of unarticulated transcendental assumptions concerning the unity and identity of consciousness. Mead is addressing not just the epistemological issue of the relationship between the "I" and the world but also the ontological issue of the identity of the self. He is addressing the problem that Kant's philosophy of the self posed but could not resolve. The problem of how the self can at the one time be both the transcendental unity of apperception or rational autonomy, and yet stand outside itself in a way that allows it to have both self knowledge and self determination.

A further major problem for Mead is that he is using a Cartesian concept of the ego identity within the Kantian framework. He uses this conception in an uncritical fashion, proposing a private self referring "I" and a public socially constructed "me" to form a composite which is the "self".

Habermas engages Mead in two major discussions, the earlier discussion is in volume two of *The Theory of Communicative Action* and the later in *Postmetaphysical Thinking*.[57] In *The Theory of Communicative Action* Habermas sees Mead's social psychology as preparing a paradigm shift to a communicative concept of rationality.[58] Habermas commences his discussion of Mead with an explanation of how Mead approached the problem of a socially generated self. He observes that Mead used an approach already employed by Augustine; that of the internal dialogue. This dialogue presupposes the existence of the other and is based on 'taking the attitude of the other' in the internal dialogue.

His discussion here has complex aims that are not always clearly differentiated. On the one hand he is seeking to show that the only credible form of individuation is social individuation, on the other he is attacking the notions of self-referential individuation that support modern notions of an atomised division of labour. Habermas attempts to situate Mead in the historical mainstream of late modern thinkers. He is placed in the contexts of symbolic interactionism, the linguistic turn and speech act theory and the debt to Dewey and pragmatism is also acknowledged. However, Habermas appropriates Mead rather too fully to suit his own purposes and sidesteps some of Mead's central concerns; for instance the explanation of behaviour and the complexity of the "I" - "me" relationship.

Habermas claims that Mead has superseded the Cartesian position and established the sort of basis required by communicative theory. Habermas claims:

> For this reason [Mead's "me" to "I" construction], original self-consciousness is not a phenomenon inherent in the subject one that is communicatively generated.[59]

Habermas continues to enlist Mead in the cause of communicative theory:

> The turn to an intersubjectivistic way of looking at things leads in the matter of "subjectivity" to a surprising result: the consciousness that is centered, as it seems in the ego is not something immediate or purely inward. Rather self-consciousness forms itself on the path from without to within, through the symbolically mediated relationship to a partner in interaction. To this extent it possesses an intersubjective core; its eccentric position attests to the tenacious dependence of subjectivity upon language as the medium through which one recognises oneself in the other in a non-objectifying manner.[60]

This is the essential element for supporting Habermas theoretical stance, and indeed an intersubjective basis of self required for communicative theory, yet it is, as it stands, not sufficient. The key element lacking in Mead, and not recognised by Habermas, is the lack of an explanation of a substantive subjectivity sufficient to support intersubjective theory. There is nothing here that the intersubjectivity hangs on. In Mead's defence it must be said that he was not looking to establish a proof of self in first philosophy but rather, as a sophisticated social psychologist, to give an explanation of social experience. A philosophical proof for the intersubjective basis of consciousness is still required. Mead attempts a number of configurations of a proof of the social foundation of the self, but without conclusive success; Habermas is satisfied with a critical account; a sort of critical reality test that leaves the philosophical basis wanting.

To draw a parallel with Descartes. The strength and enduring quality of the Cartesian position has not been just that it supports certain social structures and value systems but that the *Cogito* remains a strong and, still to some a convincing, proof. Of course the problem with the *Cogito* is that it begs the question. The "I" of the "am" is assumed in "I" of the "think". Our puzzlement these days is why this was not obvious to philosophical commentators for so long.

A problem with providing a proof for intersubjectivity is that of avoiding the Cartesian assumptions that are now built into the very language of consciousness. Words in both common usage and in the scholarly literature have an implicit ego reference that does not stand the test of a reflective critique. Mead does not fare well in this respect as he always discusses the condition of intersubjectivity from an "I" - "me" standpoint which leaves the reflexive step suspended. In this he leaves himself open to an infinite regress of there always being a self aware consciousness, a subject, that identifies the "me" in the other; which would in turn locate a reflexive "I" that would identify a further "me" and so on. Wittgenstein is the only thinker who to date has grappled with this dilemma. His account of language and its relation consciousness avoids making such assumptions about language.

Interestingly, Habermas shows awareness of this problem for Mead, where he examines the reasons why Mead could not simply collapse the "me" into the "I". In response Habermas asserts that the "me" has primacy as 'the bearer of moral consciousness'.[61]

Habermas then moves on to a discussion of the moral dimensions and implications of Mead's theory. His reason for doing so is that it becomes clear that individuation cannot occur successfully unless the self is related to society. Such a relation necessarily carries a moral dimension. It is most important for both Habermas and, indeed, Apel to assert the primacy of a normative dimension in the process of intersubjectively based individuation. Habermas relates Mead to Kant's "Kingdom of Ends" by taking up Mead's notion of being a member of the "commonwealth of rational beings". Mead argues that the moral attitude as a guide to initiating action arises from the attitude of the "me" to the "I"; the me taking on the attitude of the wider society. To avoid the accusation that this is simply a form of conservative conventionalism Mead picks up on the pragmatist idea of appeal to the concept of a wide community of informed participants and universalises the notion of community to the 'commonwealth of rational beings'.[62] Habermas continues:

> This wider commonwealth is not, however, an ideal in the Kantian sense, severed from the empirical world: " It is a *social* order, for its function is a common action on the basis of commonly recognised conditions of conduct and common ends". Kant's Kingdom of Ends must be *supposed* here and now as a context of interaction and as a communication community in which everyone is capable of taking up the perspective of everyone else and is willing to do so.[63]

There is significant conflation of views and attribution here. Firstly, Kant's Kingdom of Ends applies to all rational beings as total beings; Mead's notion applies to selves via the "me" component of the self. To "*suppose*" the Kingdom of Ends "here and now as a context of interaction and as a communication community" is a most audacious claim. It is the sort of claim that communicative theorists need to make to substantiate their theory. Whilst this claim is supported by Habermas, he fails to fully establish it in this discussion. One essential point that Habermas does not acknowledge here is that Kant's concern was with an essential definition of freedom. The Kingdom of Ends is a union of beings who possess a free will and act autonomously as a consequence. Autonomy as a person is ultimately the key membership of the kingdom of ends. Kant says of the Kingdom of Ends: 'For all rational beings come under the *law* that each of them must treat itself and all others *never merely as means,* but in every case *at the same time as ends in themselves*'.[64]

Kant continues a little further on:

> A rational being belongs as a *member* to the kingdom of ends when, although giving universal laws in it, he is also himself subject to these laws.[65]

It further must be remembered that later Kant accounts for rationality in terms of the will and autonomy.

There is in fact little in Mead that Kant would have found surprising or interesting. He would probably have agreed with Habermas' version of Mead that, 'individualism [is] the flip side of universalism'.[66] Kant would have wanted to know what the ground for this was; what was equivalent to the "universal law" of the categorical imperative. He would certainly and justifiably not have been satisfied with the answer that the individual must be capable of taking the attitude of every other individual as the basis for a universalism. The issue here is what precisely is meant by "universal". Mead mistakes the generality of experience for universality. The universality, however, must stem from a principle not from the fact that the performative attitude of the personal pronoun makes it possible for each person to put themselves in the place of the "me" of the other.

Seyla Benhabib makes a related point:

> Consent alone can never be a criterion of any thing, neither of truth nor of moral validity; rather, it is always the rationality of the procedure for attaining agreement which is of philosophical interest.[67]

However, I would contend that whilst Benhabib, along with Apel is in large part correct there is still more to the issue. It is surely more than the "rationality of the procedure" that is required for a communicative ethics and communicative theory in general. What is required is a communicative basis for rationality. If such a basis cannot be found then communicative ethics relies for its basis on conceptions of rationality which must be separately defined.

The key of course is language and the linguistic turn. If one looks to language rather than either behaviour or the organism then Mead's project can be underpinned with language providing, in large part the ground for the theory.

Notes

1 Apel, Karl-Otto (1984), *Understanding and Explanation*, trans. Georgia Warnke, MIT Press, Cambridge, Mass., p. 238.
2 Ibid., p. 233.
3 Ibid., p. 236.
4 Ibid.
5 Ibid., p. 239.
6 Ibid., p. 238.
7 Ibid., p. 235.
8 See Habermas, Jurgen (1990), *Moral Consciousness and Communicative Action*, trans. Christian Lenhardt and Shierry Weber Nicholsen, The MIT Press, Cambridge, Mass., pp. 77-81.
9 Morris, Charles (1962), Introduction to Mead, George Herbert, *Mind, Self and Society*, University of Chicago Press, Chicago, Introduction, pp. xi-xiii.
10 Joas, Hans (1985), *G. H. Mead: A Contemporary Re-examination of his Thought*, trans. Raymond Meyer, Polity Press, Cambridge, p. 4.
11 Ibid., p. 33.
12 Ibid., p. 34.
13 Ibid., p. 21.
14 Ibid., p. 5.
15 Habermas, Jurgen (1987), *The Theory of Communicative Action, Vol. 2*, trans. Thomas McCarthy, Polity Press, Cambridge, p. 4.
16 Ibid., p. 168.
17 Joas notes that Mead was a constant critic of policy at the University of Chicago and was active in the political debates of his day taking a consistent, if at times somewhat naive, anti-bourgeois line. See G. H. Mead: *A Contemporary Re-examination of his Thought*, pp. 25 -27.
18 Ibid., see ch. 9.
19 Ibid., p. 13.
20 Royce was Christian whereas Mead, although from a Christian background, had given up his belief.
21 Apel, Karl-Otto (1981), *Charles S. Peirce: From Pragmatism to Pragmaticism*, trans. John Michael Krois, University of Massachusetts Press, Amherst, p. 135.
22 Joas, Hans, *G. H. Mead: A Contemporary Re-examination of his Thought*, p. 17.
23 Mead, George Herbert (1934), *Mind, Self and Society*, ed. Charles Morris, University of Chicago Press, Chicago, p. 267.
24 Ibid., p. 268.
25 It was about this time, 1888, that Mead decided that philosophical problems could not be solved merely at the idealist or theoretical level and he decided to specialise in physiological psychology.
26 Ibid., pp. 136-7.

27 Ibid., p. 138.
28 Ibid., p. 165.
29 Ibid., see pp. 155-157.
30 Ibid., p. 138.
31 Ibid.
32 Ibid., p. 140.
33 Ibid.
34 Ibid., p. 142.
35 Ibid., p. 144.
36 Ibid., p. 149.
37 Ibid.
38 Ibid., p. 54.
39 Ibid., p. 76.
40 Ibid.
41 Habermas, Jurgen, *The Theory of Communicative Action, Vol. 2*, p. 17.
42 See Wittgenstein, Ludwig (1963), *Philosophical Investigations*, trans. G. E. M. Anscombe, Basil Blackwell, Oxford, pp.63-67, 71. There is a more detailed discussion of these issues in later chapters.
43 Mead, George Herbert, *Mind, Self and Society*, p.160.
44 Ibid., p. 160.
45 Ibid., p. 162.
46 Ibid., p. 164.
47 Ibid., pp. 167-8.
48 Ibid., p. 168.
49 Ibid.
50 Ibid., p. 172.
51 Ibid., p. 173.
52 Ibid., p. 178.
53 Ibid.
54 Ibid.
55 Habermas, Jurgen, *The Theory of Communicative Action, Vol. 2*, p. 9.
56 Joas, Hans, *G. H. Mead: A Contemporary Reexamination of his Thought*, p. 37.
57 Habermas, Jurgen (1992), *Postmetaphysical Thinking*, trans. William Mark Hohengarten, Polity Press, Cambridge, chapter 7.
58 Habermas, Jurgen, *The Theory of Communicative Action, Vol.2*, p.5.
59 Ibid., p. 177.
60 Ibid., pp. 177 - 178.
61 Ibid., p. 182.
62 Mead, George Herbert (1934), *Mind, Self and Society*, "The Community and the Institution", see also "Philanthropy from the Point of View of Ethics", ed. Charles Morris, University of Chicago Press, Chicago.
63 Habermas, Jurgen, *Postmetaphysical Thinking*, p. 185.
64 Kant, Immanuel (1909), *The Fundamental Principles of the Metaphysic of Ethics*, trans. Thomas Kingsmill Abbott, Longmans, London, pp. 51-52.

65 Ibid., p. 52.
66 Habermas, Jurgen, *Postmetaphysical Thinking*, p. 186.
67 Benhabib, Seyla (1992), *Situating the Self*, Polity Press, Cambridge, p.37.

7 Charles Taylor and Expressivist Views of the Self

To go beyond the enlightenment conception of the self as an individuated consciousness with certain capacities, including reason, judgement and perception, it is necessary to return to Kant and reconstruct a theory with a critique parallel to the transcendental syntheses of apperception as it applies to the transcendental unity of the self.

It will be argued here for a form of transcendental unity of the self based on the notion that self is a transcendental unity of many possible selves. These selves are generated by the "imaginative" capacities of free autonomous beings. They require expression as a way of creating the world of their experience but are not just expressive in the sense used, by Taylor. They require a framework for their generation akin to Apel's transcendental framework. The understanding of "transcendental" will be based in language and be a development of the previous critique of Apel's form of the transcendental as a "the language game of language games". Kant says:

> A *person* is a subject whose actions can be *imputed* to him. *Moral* personality is thus the freedom of a rational being under moral laws. (Psychological personality is merely the power to become conscious of one's self-identity at different times and under the different conditions of one's existence.) From this it follows that a person is subject to no other laws than those which he (either alone or at least along with others) gives himself.[1]

The essential element in building an intersubjective theory of the self is recognition of Kant's radical assertion of freedom. Kant stated in the first critique that it was the power of perception according to intuition that synthesised the manifold and gave form, together with meaning, to experience. Much of the *Critique of Pure Reason* is devoted to an attempt to derive the rules (laws) by which this process occurs. The attempt is of questionable success because Kant is left with an unsatisfactory account of "things in themselves"; he must propose the existence of the noumenal world to underpin phenomena but he is precluded, by his own theory, from offering an account of them. It is of more than passing interest, however, that Kant does later offer a path to at least partial insight into the noumenal via aesthetic judgement.

In *The Critique of Practical Reason* Kant sees that there is a critical next step to be taken in his account if he is to explain practical reason and morals. The next step relates to the pivotal role of freedom. If humans are to be able to synthesise the manifold to be able to have experience, they must be essentially free to do so. Freedom here becomes the basis of rationality; the pure theoretical reason of the first critique is superseded by pure practical reason of the second critique. Freedom is the essence of being, not reason. Kant was daunted by such a conclusion, and indeed it is daunting. He spent much of his later philosophy attempting to reconcile the "reason" of his earlier thought with the "reason" of his later thought, without final success. He was not prepared to give up the transcendental form of reason as a grounding for a transcendent freedom. He was, it seems, terrified by the clear conclusion that freedom determines reason, because of the introduction of an apparently capricious element which was anathema to Kant's entire project. Yet he had the intellectual honesty and courage to face this conclusion in its own terms. Rather than overcome the radical scepticism of 'the esteemed Hume' he had in fact led himself to the edge of far deeper intellectual chasm. The chasm that beings are, in essence, free to structure reason. At this point it might seem that reason was in danger of becoming merely subjective, which would mean that it would in fact dissolve altogether. That rather than becoming an instinct based on "constant conjunction" of experience, as it was for Hume, it would become the instrument of the will at best and caprice at worst.

Kant was then as a consequence of this alarming "discovery", required to expand his program and found it necessary to prepare the third critique *The Critique of Judgement* to assign a role to reason that was not merely instrumental but essential to aesthetic judgement. In the third *Critique* he was then able to recognise the full force of freedom in conjunction with imagination and assign to reason a proper place amongst the mental powers. He characterises this as follows:

> Man is the only natural creature whose peculiar objective characterisation is such as to enable us to recognise in him a supersensible faculty - his *freedom* - and to perceive both the law of causality and the object of freedom which that faculty is able to set before itself as the highest end - the supreme good in the world.[2]

However, there is here a confusion about the force or priority of freedom and that of the moral law. Benhabib notes that there is a fundamental confusion in Kant's discussion of freedom and actions falling under the moral law. She claims that Kant conflates two distinct issues, the issue of, 'the epistemology of human actions', and actions falling under natural laws.[3] The problem for Kant, in her view, stems from his 'metaphysics of two worlds', the phenomenal and noumenal world. The problem for Kant is his belief that what holds as law, as absolute in the noumenal world, ought also to hold for the phenomenal world of experience, manifested of course in different ways, but nevertheless, fundamentally law determined. A manifestation of this was the strongly implicit view that all actions once performed must fall under natural laws as events; seemingly ruling out freedom in the performance of action. Freedom in Benhabib's view, becomes restricted to the realm of judgement rather than action. Her view is reinforced in a later passage: 'Kant's error was to assume that I, as a pure rational agent reasoning for myself, could reach a conclusion that would be acceptable for all at all times and places'.[4] This interpretation contains a misreading of Kant. The difference in interpretation is subtle but significant. Kant's view is not that 'I as pure rational agent' can reach a conclusion that is universally valid, although that is a consequence, it is that each person reasoning for themselves can equally, because of their humanity impose upon themselves a universally valid maxim.

Benhabib does not take adequate stock of the radical nature of Kant's statement of freedom. She has not come to terms with the later somewhat reluctant discovery by Kant that in fact his theoretical structure dictates that freedom is the essential quality of a rational being and not reason. Kant clearly says: 'An *end* is an *object* of free choice, the thought of which determines the power of choice to an action by which the object is produced'.[5] Kant continues, '...the adoption of any end of action whatsoever is an act of *freedom* on the agent's part and not an operation of *nature'*.[6] Kant then attempts to deal with the issue of the selection of the "end" in a somewhat less than convincing manner. Either the end is noumenally determined or Kant has a circular argument again; free choice leads us to choose the end and reason, a consequence of freedom, determines the end to be chosen. However Kant is in this later work aware of this dilemma and attempts to disengage the argument from circularity. The ends which we can rationally choose from duty are, human perfection and the happiness of others. Kant says, obviously with Aristotle in mind, that of course every person desires to be happy, but to seek it as an end in itself is self defeating, as it is not a duty which we can impose upon ourselves.[7] Self perfection, properly understood as seeking to manifest our full potential humanity is a duty which we can so impose; for instance, according to Kant, 'it is [a person's] duty to diminish his ignorance by education and to correct his errors.'[8] Kant's explanation here is far from complete, but nevertheless he states clearly enough that it is the aim to perfect humanity which is at the heart of morally practical reason, and that perfection is something we must be free to pursue; otherwise we would be less than the human we seek to perfect. Practical reason does allow choice in the sense of preferring appetite to duty in Kant's world, but to do so is a denial of human perfection and therefore a lesser duty and a lesser humanity. The limiting case is of course a form of non-humanity.

It is important to notice the achievement of human perfection is the reason behind the establishment of the categorical and thence hypothetical imperatives. Whilst the moral law is sublime in its authority, and worthy of respect for its' own sake the purposiveness in our respect is the seeking of human perfection. This is an aspect not given full consideration by Benhabib, nor by many other commentators. What emerges in Kant's later philosophy, particularly the normative and political works, as key are the concepts of personality and humanity. It is these qualities of beings that emerge as fundamental to the way in which we human beings "synthesise the manifold" rather than through transcendental apperception alone.

Charles Taylor provides a more accurate interpretation of Kant's position, he says: '...Kant shares the modern stress on freedom as self-determination. He insists on seeing the moral law as one which emanates from our will'.[9] Taylor continues to point out that Kantianism mixed with naturalism leads to a very limited concept of human agency so familiar in modern life; a concept which regards the good as procedural rather than substantive. Quoting from Iris Murdoch, 'Stripped of the exiguous metaphysical background which Kant was prepared to allow him, this man is with us still, free, independent, lonely, powerful, rational, responsible, brave, the hero of so many novels and books on moral philosophy'.[10]

Kant was definitely strongly wedded to the notion of a universal ethics based on a metaphysics that was axiomatically universal. However, once he recognised that freedom was the key to both pure and practical reason he struggled to defend a prescriptive universality in a consistent way. It is also important to recognise that in discussions of Kant it is not possible, as Iris Murdoch suggests, to do away with the 'exiguous metaphysical background'. Mere logical universality is not a Kantian position; for Kant, the metaphysical ground is the foreground, never the background. Kant, until his dying day, wanted to know what it was that made the universe as it is. The discovery that rational beings must be essentially free in order to conceptualise that universe presented Kant with a daunting challenge, yet it was also the cardinal clue to the completion of his project. Taylor continues to argue that Kant's procedural ethics leaves a "perplexing gap" because it informs us about how we should act but, not what we should do. Various philosophers operating broadly in the Kantian tradition have moved to fill this gap, most notably of recent times Jurgen Habermas and Taylor himself.

Habermas takes an intersubjective approach to ethics and the self, which is still a proceduralist approach. Habermas through his discussion of Kohlberg and communicative ethics provides an illuminating discussion of the development of a normative structure but it is not a theory that offers a substantive view of the good. Taylor follows a broadly expressivist view of the self and a substantialist view of ethics.

Taylor in *Sources of the Self,* in the most painstaking, scholarly and illuminating fashion, sketches out the sources of and his version of the modern identity. The purpose of the book is to reveal the sources and complexities that underlie the development of the contemporary identity. In the course of the development of the work Taylor also expounds his own view which, in itself, is not very modern. It is basically that the self is a good-bearing and good-doing being. To that extent it offers an alternative to the Kantian perspective which retains some transcendental elements. Taylor's view is elaborately drawn, inspiring and intricately woven through many themes but in the end it remains unconvincing. Not because it is necessarily wrong, but because he fails to make out a case for it which is more than suggestive. In the face of his genealogy, or "schematic map", of the modern identity he simply has not produced the weight of convincing grounds to establish his view. [11]

For Taylor the self is complex and intricate; it is not something which can be reduced to formula, an essence or a definition. It is part biology, part socially and historically constructed and part divine. He takes the view that there is a subjective particular identification, although not strictly Cartesian, and that there is something irreducibly spiritual about human selves which can only be denied with loss and a real sense of loss. The self is irreducible and located in really existing beings in Taylor's discussion. He explicitly seeks to demonstrate that the self cannot be in Plato's sense "dominated by reason", nor can the self be reduced to various forms of nature, either by traditional scientific method or by recent sociobiology. Neither can the self be simply a social construct in either of the forms generated by Weber or Mead. There is an expressive sense in which the self is a free self-creation. Taylor is attracted to this view, which he calls the 'expressivist turn',[12] and claims that has its origins with Hegel and Schiller and that it underpins the romantic movement. His account is expressivist in that it endorses the enlightenment philosophy of nature which can be known 'through articulating what we find within us'.[13] His endorsement of "expressivism" is the endorsement of, 'a new and fuller individuation',[14] in which what is hidden within becomes manifest for myself and others. This presents the elements of both autonomy and imagination as the discovery of "nature within" through expression, and to this extent is a further development of his conception of the self as a "good doing" being. He also acknowledges the importance of language and the linguistic turn in constituting the self.

Taylor starts building the core of his theory through a discussion of Augustine. It is hardly an exaggeration to say that it was Augustine who introduced the inwardness of radical reflexivity and bequeathed it to the Western tradition of thought.[15]

For Augustine, as interpreted by Taylor, God was to be found in the world of reflection not in the outward world of knowledge of external objects. The radical turn of reflection taken by Augustine was not just reflection or, 'care for one's self' but the adoption of the 'first person standpoint'.[16] Taylor says that for Augustine the turn to the self was a turn to radical reflexivity; that 'it made the language of inwardness irresistible'.[17] Clearly not all reflexivity is radical in this sense, although Taylor claims Western thought often treats it so. He is strong in his praise of Augustine's achievement, and believes it is time for a just re-appraisal.

> [The change] that he wrought was to make a turn to the self in the first person dimension crucial to our access to a higher condition - because it is a step on our road back to God - and hence to inaugurate a new line of development in our understanding of moral sources, one which has been formative of our entire western culture.[18]

Taylor is adamant that we cannot blame Augustine for Cartesianism nor Platonism; he cannot be held responsible for the interpretations of either his predecessor or his successor. Augustine, independently of Plato and in a different sense to Descartes, developed a form of "proto-cogito". It has the self-reflective element of Descartes but does not claim to be a logically indubitable proof. Augustine is concerned to establish an argument for a self-presence and not an indubitable logical proof of the existence of a self-reflexively identified ego. His reason is that he is concerned not so much to establish the irrefutable existence of the self but a reflective proof for the existence and presence of God. Augustine's proof for the existence of God is a proof from subjectivity which seeks to establish that no matter how certain we are of our own subjectivity there must be a higher truth that guarantees the veracity of that subjectivity.

Here is the core of Taylor's view of the self; it is both his strength and his weakness. The following passage is instructive:

> The reasons Augustine took this path seem to me to be rather that his concern was to show that God is to be found not just in the world but also and more importantly at the very foundations of the person (to use the modern language); God is to found in the intimacy of self-presence. God as Truth gives us the standards, the principles of right judgement. But he gives them to us not just through the spectacle of a world organized by the Ideas but more basically by that "incorporeal light ... by which our minds are somehow irradiated, so that we may judge rightly of all things.[19]

This view is in fact the essence of Taylor's own complex view of the self and accounts, to some extent, for it being difficult at times to discern his true position. He reveals this by asserting that Augustine's insights are in fact essential to understanding the subsequent more developed understandings of the self. Taylor's treatment of the exposition of Augustine merits some close attention as it reveals not only the elements of Cartesianism but also elements of the treatment of the will by Kant and others. It also constructs a ground for the uniqueness of the self or the element of "personality" referred to in Kant's later critiques. In order to make Taylor's theory of the self credible he needs to establish just what it is that this "God within" does for the existence of the self that another "interior" theory could not do.

The essence of Augustine's theory of the self, in Taylor's version, which goes beyond Plato, is to recognise that there has to be something higher than reason. If, indeed, it were to be reason that judges what is true or good there must be a fundamental principle of judgement that is higher than reason. What could such a principle be? As reason is the highest element of human being then there must be another element beyond mere human capacities of which there can be none higher; and that is God, whom Augustine still closely identifies with Plato's Idea of the Good. This is Augustine's version of the ontological proof for the existence of God. Yet we humans are capable of the employment of reason based on the principles of right judgement, therefore there must be some of the divine element within each person. It is indeed this element which, for both Augustine and Taylor, give personhood and identity to each human. Much of the balance of Taylor's book is occupied with a critique of modern versions of the self against this ground.

Taylor's position, with or without God, is actually a form of non-Kantian transcendental argument for a substantive self. He is arguing, certainly, that method is not a sufficient ground either in ethics or metaphysics. He is also arguing that there must be grounds for reason and these grounds must constitute some substantive good. A form of ontological argument is being used for the existence of an individual self. That is, there must be a higher element in the self than reason, otherwise reason could not be employed in judgement. The transcendental element comes from the God within and finds expression through acts in the world which are motivated by love and by self-love, a self-love which however maintains a respect for the divine element of being. Yet Taylor's position is not, as was Augustine's, merely an extension and development of the Platonic mode. Taylor adds an expressive dimension. It is not sufficient to merely know the good, one must act reflexively on the good and for the good. And so to the discovery which dissipates the perversity of the will, and which the rectifying of this perversity makes possible, is that of our dependence on God in the very intimacy of our own presence to ourselves, at the roots of those powers which are most our own.[20]

Expressivism is one of Taylor's three main sources of the good, or goods, that underpin the self; the other two being theistic grounds and disengaged reason. It is the philosophy of nature as a source of the good and of the self. In the expressive act we not only make something manifest but bring something to be.[21] In this making manifest, Taylor says, I am 'realizing my nature' and giving my life some formulation and definition.[22] In this way I am realising myself by giving expression to the sources of nature within. Expressivism also gives rise to the modern sense of fuller individuation; to the idea that each individual is unique, different and original. This is a more radical sense of individuation than any that has gone before in that each person and their life is self-creating from the 'realizing of our deep nature'.[23] Expressivism also brought with it a new understanding of art and its place in human life. Art comes to be the dimension through which we express and realise our full humanity. As Taylor puts it:

> The awe we feel before artistic originality and creativity places art on the border of the numinous, and reflects the crucial place that creation/expression has in our understanding of human life.[24]

This expressive dimension is a development of Taylor's version of Augustinian inwardness. Augustine uses not only the ontological argument but also an adaptation of Plato's argument from "memory" of the *Meno* to support his notion of the God within. In Augustine's case it is not recollection of a previous existence but access to something higher or superior which is found within by self-reflection. The truths gained by such reflections are not truths recollected from a previous existence in the world of the Forms, but truths which are planted within by the presence of God within. Augustine does not deny the necessity of experience and the created world for experience but does not see this as a route to enduring knowledge or to God. But our principal route to God is not through the object domain but "in" ourselves. This is because God is not just the transcendent object or just principle of order of the nearer objects, which we strain to see.[25]

Here both Taylor and Augustine recognise the divine presence within as a transcendent element. Taylor amplifies this view of the transcendent: 'God is not just what we long to see, but what powers the eye that sees -the underlying principle of our knowing activity'.[26] There is for Augustine a light within that enables us to see the things of the world, not because as for Plato the form of the Good enlightens perception but because God within empowers the self to take a reflexive stance to the external world of experience. Blumenberg puts it thus, for Augustine: 'The man who knows is not himself the light to which he owes the intelligibility of his objects, but himself stands in the light'.[27]

There are echoes of Kant's world of transcendental apperception here but the modality is quite different. For Kant the reflexive critique of experience is transcendent in that it sets out to determine that there must be conditions necessary for that experience to have the nature it does. For Augustine, the transcendental element is a substantive element that determines the way we perceive the elements of experience. Clearly Kant's argument is the more significant and the more challenging in a post-enlightenment context, yet Taylor's Augustinian position cannot be too readily dismissed.

The apparent move to counter Augustine is very simple. To counter his position one might simply deny the existence of God or the immanent divine presence by denying it the burden of proof. The argument is countered by means of the well known refutations of ontological arguments in general, that the existence of God is not necessitated as the result of the existence of certain ideas about a divine being. Unless certain metaphysical assumptions, to the effect, that there must be something that ideas represent, are accepted, ontological arguments don't work and Augustine's position simply collapses. However were one to do this the problem of the inwardness of the self, the "interiore homine" of the modern self, still has to be dealt with. The denial of the immanence of God does not solve the issues of reflexive inwardness but rather deprives us a more straightforward metaphysical solution.

The problem has to be reconceptualised and recontextualised to see the full significance of Taylor's account and to do justice to the significance of the Augustinian position. The issue for this discussion centres on the validity of the discourse of inwardness; it is not just a question of whether or not there are true 'selves' or whether the self is an elaborately constructed text, but a question of the legitimacy of whole discourse of inwardness.

Some clearer contextualisation can be taken from Taylor's recent article "Inwardness and the Culture of Modernity" which is, in some respects, a summary and clarification of the position developed in *Sources of the Self.*[28] Here he makes it clear that the transcendental element of the Augustinian position is expressed by asserting that there must be an inner self that is the experiencer and judge. It is through the process, Taylor claims, that took root in the eighteenth century that we come to think of ourselves as "selves". The origins of inwardness stem from Augustine who introduced the notion of inwardness into the Christian tradition, but the secularisation of this way of thinking about ourselves really comes from Descartes and Locke. For both Descartes and Locke, and to the greater degree Locke, the self becomes something quality-less within. Such an understanding of the self is generative of instrumental rationality and modern Western scientific method as it allows for a self to stand outside of or behind experienced reality. Such an approach to the self Taylor calls an acultural theory in contrast to his preferred substantive theory based on a notion of the Good.

Taylor notes his dissatisfaction with the way the acultural theory, arising out of the enlightenment, tends to blank the various understandings of the self that have arisen in pre-enlightenment Western thought and those which have during and since the enlightenment expressed different theoretical positions. Taylor says:

> In short, exclusive reliance on acultural theory unfits us for what is perhaps the most important task of social sciences in our day: understanding the full gamut of alternative modernities that are in the making in different parts of the world. It locks us into an ethnocentric prison, condemned to project our own forms onto everyone else, and blissfully unaware of what we are doing.[29]

The "standard" modern view, as Taylor calls it, is the detached pointilistic self of capitalism and scientific rationalism; it is the reflexive inwardness of method rather than the reflexive inwardness of a substantive self. Such a reflexiveness permits the self to be stripped of any characteristics to a Lockean extensionless point of consciousness. Such a concept of the self can, according to Taylor, lead to all the sterility and amorality of modern societies, with the dominance of instrumental reason and contingent values. Rationality becomes 'a property of subjective thinking, rather than consisting in its vision of reality'.[30]

Taylor rejects this concept of the self, for good reasons, as finally incoherent. A quality-less self, defined solely by its experiences, becomes quite trivial, lacking definition and any heuristic power at all. Considered by itself each self is indistinguishable; perhaps put more damagingly, each self is interchangeable; each being only a point of view. This is a problem for all modern theories of the self based on the Lockean model. It is also a problem for more critical modern theories such as those of Mead, Habermas and communicative theories in general in that the self as subject needs to be more fully expounded. However, these theories have the advantage over physicalist and functionalist theories in that they do not critically turn on the "qualityless subject". Taylor points to this problem by drawing attention to the fact that no matter how far the reductionist position goes it is just not possible to list selves as part of the natural order alongside other things such as tables and chairs or electric charges. The paradox which shows the basic untenability of the position, is that objectivity and disengagement in the end rely on extreme subjectivity; an unchallengeable first person stance. It is the very apodeictic unchallengability of the stance which betrays the untenability of the position. It leaves us with no ground for a critical perspective; there is no place to stand where we could see things differently. Each perspective is equally valid (or invalid) and at the time of taking each stance it is, as it were, as absolute as any other.

What this shows is that the punctual self is a myth, a metaphor for outer experience. Taylor, as indicated above, believes that there are two paths that lead from Augustine's reflexive examination, the path that leads to the rationalistic self with disengaged self-control, and the path that leads jointly to self-exploration and self-expression. The former path taken alone leads to the sterility of modern rationalism, the latter to a "cultural" self with the sort of radical reflexivity and the type of self-objectification, that is a self capable of being for the Good. Taylor's view is that each path is not in opposition. In fact they are complementary, although the latter is clearly of prior importance in his view.[31] However, Taylor still depends on the Augustinian transcendental position for the grounding of his position. Taylor's position, although elusive, it is actually much more like that of a cognitive realist with a transcendental basis.

Taylor sums up his "cultural" account of the dimensions of inwardness and the self as part of the modern identity thus:

> I have connected their development to a skein of particular conceptions of the human good and the corresponding notions of human agency. In a nutshell, I have been arguing that our modern ideas of inwardness and the self are connected with views of human excellence and fulfilment which privilege activities inseparable from radical reflexivity, specifically those of disengaged self-objectification and self-control on one hand and the range of forms of self exploration on the other, which have ramified thought the Romantic period and beyond and have become deeply intricated with our notions of personal fulfilment, of artistic originality, and of the creative imagination.[32]

Taylor endorses the Schillerian ideal, derived from Kant, of the unity of truth, good and beauty, found in artistic expression. In this vein he says that in the Christian dimension of Schillerian romanticism: 'What we have in this new issue of affirming the goodness of things is the development of a human analogue to God's seeing things as good; a seeing that also effects what it sees'.[33] Taylor admits that there can be a purely atheist version of this doctrine, as articulated by Nietzsche; but Taylor sees the Christian version associated with the idea of grace as the more powerful.

Taylor summarises this view in a particularly strong passage:

> In fact the notion of a transformation of our stance towards the world whereby our vision of it is changed has been traditionally connected with the notion of grace. Augustine holds that in relation to God love has to precede knowledge. With the right direction of love, things become evident which are hidden otherwise. What is new is the place and power of the creative imagination. This is now an integral part of the goodness of things, and hence the transformation of our stance and thus our outlook helps to bring about the truth it reveals.[34]

This is a strongly Kantian passage except for the fact that Taylor has also asserted the importance of a substantive self, potentially oriented to the good. However, Taylor does not fully represent the Kantian position. He is often, although not always, inclined to represent Kant as the Kant of only the first critique and the *Groundwork* as, '...picturing ourselves as pure rational agents', this is an inaccurate representation of the full richness of Kant's later position.[35] For the later Kant the synthesis of reason with autonomy and expression become equally important and supersede the notion of the pure good will as the expression of reason. Yet to complete Taylor's theory there is also the expressive element. This is not just an historic perspective but also a logical and moral compliment to Augustinian inwardness. Following Schiller, Taylor emphasises the importance "epiphanic" art[36] and expression in general, taking us beyond the rational control of the eighteenth century to the, 'harmonized, free being ... who would spontaneously want to be good'.[37]

It is in Taylor's discussion of epiphanic art and the role of expressivism that both the Kantian and Augustinian transcendentalism, in part, combine. The origin of this convergence is the Kantian influence on Schiller. Taylor subscribes to this convergence without fully articulating it. He says:

> The germ was there in the new aesthetic which developed in the eighteen century. It defined the beautiful in terms of a certain kind of feeling or subjective reaction. Kant gave a new and powerful articulation to this in his third critique.[38]

Taylor points out that the Romantic movement was both a development of, and a reaction to, enlightenment rationalism. We see in Rousseau and Montaigne a new romantic naturalism which is an extension of Kantian ideas of autonomy to nature and, at the same time, a reaction against the totalising aspects of instrumental rationality. There is, though, a critical dimension here, nature is not just "out there" but also within; there is a naturalised inwardness, and thus a harmony of the inwardness and outwardness. However the roots of Romanticism, and what Taylor calls "the expressivist turn" remain beyond precise definition. Romanticism arose in the late eighteenth century as a generalised movement in which philosophy played a mixed role; sometimes pivotal, sometimes insignificant and irrelevant. Wordsworth, Herder and William Blake are just as significant as Hegel or Rousseau. There was also the important political element in pre-revolutionary movements and currents of thought particularly in France and England, which is not fully recognised in Taylor's discussion. His discussion of revolution is in the context of expressivism and the radical enlightenment is in the context millenarianism. In this discussion millenarianism is seen as a transition from the age of conflict between good and evil, reason and nature, to the spiritual age of harmony, freedom, reason and reconciliation. However there is more guiding the ideas behind revolution than millenarianism. The guiding forces include the secular instrumentalism of Hobbes and Newton, for instance, as well as the new humanism of the "Philosophes".

There is a further element in the development of Romanticism that Taylor does not adequately develop, although he well might have, and that is the major impact of the reformation. Since Martin Luther, the path to salvation became an inward path via conscience and not the outward path of the established church. On matters of belief and authority and critically the interpretation of the Scriptures, it was one's own conscience that became the final court. After all it was the individual who was saved or damned and the individual must have the freedom to determine the worth of his or her life. The consequences of Luther's turn were momentous. It meant not only that the personal political authority of Rome was deeply subverted, as Taylor points out, but that the locus of truth, love and grace, as religious and later secular virtues, shifted from the public to the interior domain. Truth became an intuition rather than a correspondence with, or acceptance of, the revealed. Grace became an inner light bestowed directly by God rather than a reward bestowed sacramentally through the agency of the Church. These developments of course took place in the sixteenth and seventeenth centuries rather than the eighteenth century. However the importance of the influence of the Reformation on the Enlightenment cannot be underestimated. The turn to the authority of reason, then to inwardness and expressivism through the Romantic movement was a secular working through of ideas which had their generation in a very different context with Luther, Calvin, Wesley and Baxter. It was the religious thinkers of the reformation who laid the ground for the legitimation of the inwardness that led to the legitimation of reason as an authority and expression as a mode of being. Certainly Hobbes, Descartes, Locke, Hume, Kant and finally Hegel gave expression to the philosophical ideas of the enlightenment but the religious reformers must be given credit for unfettering the form of thinking which gave legitimacy to those ideas.

Taylor quotes with approval Novalis: 'Das Herz ist der Schlüssel der Welt und des Lebens' (The heart is the key to the world and life.) as embodying the spirit of the new Romanticism as the source of life and immanent truth.[39]

The Aristotelian version of the good life as the willing exercise of perfect virtue and as an objective encounter with the universal virtues, is replaced by the exercise of the virtue to be found within. A virtue based on the sentiments and the idea that the highest virtue is truth to oneself replaces the classical paradigm. Taylor comments that: 'The good life comes to consist in a perfect fusion of the sensual and the spiritual, where our sensual fulfilments are experienced as having higher significance'.[40] The consequence of this theme of the Romantic movement was to dissolve the distinction between the ethical and the aesthetic, again not in the classical mode deriving from Plato where the Form of the Good was perceived as superordinate to the Form of the Beautiful, but that the good and the beautiful in nature are aspects of the one experience and incomplete without each other within experience. They are also seen to inspiring of the will and to motivate each person to right action.

Taylor says that expressivism arises in Germany in the diffuse movement known as *Sturm and Drang* although it continues well beyond the demise of that movement. It was also a movement of reaction, 'against the mainstream Enlightenment view of man - as both subject and object of an objectifying scientific analysis'.[41] In the movement the split between the objective and the subjective was opposed and human persons were seen as an expressive unity, similar to a work of art. Each life was to be lived as a work of art in which our own inner nature was expressed as not just a self-exploration but also a self-revelation. Early modern religious theories, and secular theories related to Descartes, embodied the notion of self exploration but not the expressivist idea of "articulating our inner nature". The crucial factor here introduced by Herder and others is the idea of "inner depths". In later expressivist and "post-expressivist" developments the notion of inner depths is extended to that of an 'inexhaustible inner domain'.[42] Taylor continues:

> The inescapable feeling of depth comes from the realization that whatever we bring up, there is always more down there. Depth lies in there being always, inescapably, something beyond our articulative power. This notion of inner depths is therefore intrinsically linked to our understanding of ourselves as expressive, as articulating an inner source.[43]

The notion of "inner depths" poses some serious metaphysical questions which would be unanswerable without resort to something equivalent to Augustine's "God within" if taken head on. It is here that the "linguistic turn" takes us on a totally new and more fruitful path that leaves us in a position to start to unpack the daunting metaphysics of "inexhaustible inner depths".

An intimation can be found in Rilke:

Nicht daß du Gottes ertrügest
die Stimme, bei weitem. Aber das Wehende höre,
die ununterbrochene Nachricht, die aus Stille sich bildet.[44]

(Not that you could endure
the voice of God- far from it. But hark the suspiration,
the uninterrupted news that grows out of silence.)

I suggest that the impression of inner depths is that of the language speaking through us, but this is a theme I will take up elsewhere.

Taylor has offered an account of the self, which must ultimately draw its inner and expressive qualities from a divine element. For a theist, and particularly a Christian such as Taylor the element can be drawn from the Augustinian notion of the "God within". For the non-theist Taylor would still claim an undeniable unique "inner", which is the human essence and which powers the expressive capacities of self formation. Whilst on Taylor's account the development of the self remains a continuing story combining a plurality of historical themes, the essential elements of a preferred immanent self are clear. Taylor agrees with Habermas that: the 'self is constituted through exchange in language', but disagrees that this, 'in any way guarantees us against loss of meaning, fragmentation, the loss of substance in our human environment and our affiliations'.[45] What Taylor believes is required are moral sources outside the self which "resonate" within. However inspiring this view may be, the problem remains that Taylor is still proposing a noumenal self, a proto-self, which lies beyond this world. It seems that there are still Platonic elements here, with all their attendant difficulties, which Taylor is not willing to relinquish.

Taylor has offered a transcendental theory which still retains metaphysical elements. He acknowledges the contribution of the linguistic turn and communicative theory but does not accept the transformed transcendentalism such theoretical developments offer. Kant's account combining the elements of freedom and imagination in the *Critique of Judgement* remain clearly the major source of the modern view of the self and require further close analysis and development.

Notes

1 Kant, Immanuel (1964), *Introduction to the Metaphysic of Morals*, trans. Mary J. Gregor, Harper and Row, New York, p. 24.
2 Kant, Immanuel (1952), *The Critique of Judgement*, trans. James Creed Meredith, Oxford University Press, Oxford, p. 99.
3 Benhabib, Seyla (1992), *Situating the Self*, Polity Press, Cambridge, p. 131.
4 Ibid., p. 164.
5 Kant, Immanuel, *The Doctrine of Virtue*, p. 43.
6 Ibid.
7 I think Kant along with most other commentators misunderstands Aristotle on this point. This is probably in part due to difficulties of translation. Aristotle's version of "happiness" as being found in the exercise of perfect virtue, or of the highest virtue is closer to Kant's notion of self-perfection than more current meanings of "happiness".
8 Kant, Immanuel, *The Doctrine of Virtue*, p. 46.

9 Taylor, Charles (1989), *Sources of the Self*, Cambridge University Press, Cambridge, p. 83.
10 Ibid., p. 84. Quoted from Murdoch, Iris (1970), *The Sovereignty of the Good*, Routledge, London, p. 80.
11 Ibid., p. 495.
12 Ibid., see p. 368ff.
13 Ibid., p. 374.
14 Ibid., p. 375.
15 Ibid., p. 131.
16 Ibid., p. 130.
17 Ibid., p. 131.
18 Ibid., p. 132.
19 Ibid., p. 134.
20 Ibid., p. 139.
21 Ibid., p. 374.
22 Ibid., p. 375.
23 Ibid., p. 377.
24 Ibid., p. 376.
25 Ibid., p. 129.
26 Ibid.
27 Blumenberg, Hans (1983), *The Legitimacy of the Modern* Age, trans. Robert M. Wallace, MIT University Press, Cambridge, Mass., p. 310.
28 Taylor, Charles (1992), "Inwardness and the Culture of Modernity", in *Philosophical Interventions in the Unfinished Project of the Enlightenment*, ed. Honneth et al. MIT Press, Cambridge, Mass.
29 Ibid., p. 93.
30 Ibid., p. 98.
31 Ibid., p. 108.
32 Ibid., p. 107.
33 Taylor, Charles, *Sources of the Self*, Cambridge University Press, Cambridge, p. 449.
34 Ibid.
35 Ibid., p. 12.
36 By epiphanic art Taylor means an art which carries a particular transformation of the romantic vision. That transformation takes art out of its natural or realist frame into a spiritual dimension of spirituality; it takes on a "translucence".
37 Taylor, Charles, *Sources of the Self*, p. 423.
38 Ibid.
39 Ibid., p. 371.
40 Ibid., p. 373.
41 Taylor, Charles (1979), *Hegel and Modern Society*, Cambridge University Press, Cambridge, p. 1.
42 Taylor, Charles, *Sources of the Self*, p. 390.
43 Ibid.

44 Rilke, Rainer Maria (1939), Duino Elegies, Norton, New York, First Elegy 60.
45 Taylor, Charles, *Sources of the Self*, pp. 510-511.

8 Kant's Critique of Judgement and Communicability

In order to draw together a more complete treatment of a transcendental theory of the self it is necessary to discuss Kant's later philosophy, particularly the *Critique of Judgement* and the political writings. It is also illuminating to link this discussion to Wittgenstein, particularly the later writings on private language and the question of the priority of experience. In this discussion Wittgenstein is treated in the context of providing a critique of transcendental idealism, yet at the same time, assuming an implicit transcendental framework. It is only against such an implicit background that his "atheoretical" approach amounts to more than a collection of observations on language and experience.

There are also many intriguing parallels between Wittgenstein's later work and Kant's later works. These can be found in parallels between the *Lectures on Aesthetics, Psychology and Religious Belief,* and parts of *The Critique of Judgement*, where it would seem that the two philosophers have very similar views about the uniqueness of the faculty of judgement. Another striking correspondence concerns Kant's discussion of the necessity for a *sensus communis* for communicability and Wittgenstein's discussion of the impossibility of private language. There are many further resonances, some of which will emerge in the following discussion.

The key notion for developing the theme of the self is that of imagination. It is this that takes the notion of the subject as the originator of experience, freedom and judgement to the limit. The presence of imagination as a key to self and subjectivity implies, transcendentally, that the imaginer as a being capable of reflective experience can only be so in a community of similar beings. It is also via this discussion that many of the elements of Taylor's expressivist view can be incorporated in a wider post-Kantian theoretical framework.

First it is necessary to turn to an analysis of *The Critique of Judgement.* As many have commented this is a difficult work to approach.[1] Yet it is clear that a complete understanding of Kant's system of philosophy cannot be achieved without a reading of the critique and to a lesser extent of the late political works. This is because it is only in these works that he completes a discussion of the human faculties.

In the introduction to the *Critique of Judgement* Kant presents a summary of his philosophical project to that point. He states that he has dealt with thought in general by dividing it into *theoretical* and *practical.* The subject of the first critique being theoretical thought and that of the second critique, practical thought. The principle of the first critique was the critique of reason, purely applied to concepts and dependent on the establishment of the synthetic a priori. The principle of the second critique was the critique of practical reason, applied via the categorical imperative and resulting in the establishment, both of the autonomy of the will, and to an extent contrary to Kant's anticipated result, the establishment of freedom as a radical principle; even to the extent of a principle presupposing reason. Kant here is for the first time clear about separation of the concepts referred to nature and those referred to freedom. However, it is here also that Kant recognises that his program is incomplete. He recognises that he has established freedom and reason in a way which establishes them as operating in domains that are capable of operating quite separately. Yet, he also recognises that human experience has a completeness that each domain cannot encompass. The element that unites the domains, judgement, adds what Kant refers to as, 'the finality of nature for our cognitive faculties and their employment'.[2]

Kant lays out the necessity for a third critique and its rationale in the Introduction:

> Hence an immense gulf is fixed between the domain of the concept of nature, the sensible, and the domain of the concept of freedom, the supersensible, so that no transition from the sensible to the supersensible (and hence by means of the theoretical use of reason) is possible, just as if they were two different worlds, the first of which cannot have any influence on the second; and yet the second *is* to have an influence on the first, i.e., the concept of freedom is to actualize in the world of sense the purpose enjoined by its laws. Hence it must be possible to think nature as being such that the lawfulness in its form will harmonise with at least the possibility of [achieving] the purposes that we are to achieve in nature according to the laws of freedom. So there must after all be a basis *uniting* the supersensible that underlies nature and the supersensible that the concept of freedom contains practically, even though the concept of this basis does not reach cognition of either theoretically or practically and hence does not have a domain of its own though it does make possible the transition from our way of thinking in terms of principles of nature to our way of thinking in terms of principles of freedom.[3]

It is worth quoting this passage in its entirety, both for its succinctness, not a quality often associated with Kant, and for the definition which it gives to the project of the third *Critique.* It is also worth noting, even at this preliminary stage that one of the key 'failures' of the work has been set up.

Kant claims that judgement has no realm of its own, yet his methodology of critique immediately begins to examine it as if it did have such a realm which of itself proves to be empty. This is perhaps why Castoriadis says, 'Kant's third *Critique* in fact presents a description of rather than a "solution" to the problem of judging. Significant as this description is, it offers no help in the search for "foundations"'.[4] Yet it is the search for a priori foundations which is of interest here, in that those foundations, as it were, lie "within". However, it is rather the domain or realm of taste that is the primary subject of the critique. As Hannah Arendt notes as late as 1787 Kant was calling the work we know as *The Critique of Judgement* the "Critique of Taste".[5] But whilst taste is the avowed focus of the work, Kant himself, via the critique of teleological judgement, soon broadens the scope to include all mental processes that require judgement.

The work follows a consistent theme in the development of Kant's thought, but appears to be superficially disjointed, as the principles of aesthetic judgement and teleological judgement differ. Scholars have differed over the years as to whether or not the third critique can be read as a single unified work or whether it is a work of two distinct parts, the latter of less importance than the critique of aesthetic judgement.[6] It would seem that how the work is viewed is a matter of approach. If the interest is in art and the sublime on one hand and questions of causation on the other then there is a separation to be made between the two parts. However if the interest is in the human capacity for judgement then the work can be read as a unified whole. Kant wrote two introductions to the work the latter, shorter introduction being published with the work -the first introduction was later published separately. Both are complex and seek to justify the necessity for the work to complete Kant's critical scheme. Kant indicates in both introductions that he regarded the work as a unity thus lending support to a unified reading.

Although it is true that the work has many problems, including spiralling and inconclusive arguments, especially in the deduction, the apparent disjunction of the work can be answered when it is seen that, for Kant, judgements of taste about both art and nature and teleological judgements share the same faculty, although the judgements are usually, but not exclusively, about different things. A teleological judgement can also be an artistic judgement even though it is more likely to be a judgement about the purpose of natural processes. There is a further deeper dimension alluded to by both Schaper[7] and Pluhar[8] and clearly of interest to us here that unites the work. It is Kant's assertion in the "Aesthetic Deduction" that there are certain conditions necessary for experience in general that are revealed in judgement. Thus the two critiques, that of Aesthetic Judgement and that of Teleological Judgement can be read as complementary aspects of a single work.

Parallels will later be drawn between Wittgenstein and Kant which will reveal Wittgenstein as offering a critique of transcendental idealism. But it is sufficient to point out at this stage that there is a close parallel between Wittgenstein's view, that making aesthetic judgements is playing a certain distinct type of language game, or language games, and Kant's theory of aesthetic judgement as a distinct human capacity. In the *Lectures and Conversations on Aesthetics, Psychology and Religious Belief,* Wittgenstein elaborates a view of aesthetic judgement that emphasises the uniqueness of such judgements, setting out to show that they are not reducible to logic, psychology or a "science" of aesthetics.[9]

The focus here is on the self and the interpersonal presupposition that have to be made in order for a self to exist and be referred to. It is, in the third critique, that Kant offers the outline of such a theory centred around the notion of communicability. Kant set out to answer the problem, as stated by Pluhar, 'How, if at all, is it possible to judge something in nature (or in art) as beautiful on the basis of something very subjective, a feeling of pleasure, and yet demand for our judgement a universal assent?'[10] A more general version of Kant's problem can be put in both communicative theory and a post-Wittgensteinian context, as to how subjective states are communicable at all. Kant was motivated in his response by an opposition to the empiricists and, once again David Hume in particular, and also, according to Pluhar, in opposition to the dogmatic rationalists of his era, especially Leibniz and Wolff. He opposed Hume's view that taste, that is the pleasure taken in nature or art was merely an internal sensation of pleasure, as was ugliness a contrary sensation. A judgment that something was beautiful was simply the association of pleasure with the impression of that object. Hume refers to it as a 'a sentiment of delight'.[11] Yet there is a strong parallel, unrecognised by Kant, between Hume here and the position taken in the third *Critique.* Hume says, 'Now it is evident that this sentiment (of delight) must depend upon the particular fabric or structure of the mind, which enables such particular forms to operate in such a particular manner and produces a sympathy or conformity between the mind and its objects'.[12] This view is remarkably similar to Kant's view that imagination as the reflective capacity, and intuition of an object, are required to justify the pleasure taken by the apprehending subject when an object is judged as beautiful. Indeed this constitutes Kant's basic argument for the universalisabilty of judgements of beauty and thus the definition of taste.[13]

A similar position holds with regard to teleological judgements. Hume also took the view that teleology was the expectation, conditioned by habit, that impressions would continue to be constantly conjoined in the way conditioning had led us to expect. He maintained the view that the mind is disposed to construct a purposive expectation in "causes" that reads them as tending to an end. This end is in the faculty of association rather than nature. Kant strongly rejected Hume's sceptical conclusions, but seems not to have grasped, or perhaps been aware of Hume's more subtle understanding. He seems to have read Hume as asserting that taste was merely subjective and that teleology was entirely psychological and did not relate to any purpose in nature or the human species. He may not have read some of Hume's later essays or may simply have attributed to Hume a more vulgar version of empiricism than Hume actually held. It is quite clear that Hume held that certain powers of the mind did shape experience and that Hume and Kant are closer on these matters than Kant would concede. However, the critical factor that divides the two was the status of the a priori element; Kant asserting its centrality, whilst Hume either denied it, or at best, offered an embryonic version.

Equally, Kant could not accept the rationalist position, as he asserted that taste and aesthetic judgement were always involved in perception. No matter how much the mind might contribute there was still an object of judgement; an object perceived and judged as beautiful or otherwise. It is worth noting that Kant's rejection of the rationalist position of his day is based not on a rejection of the clarity of thought. He accepted the notion of clear and distinct ideas. What he rejected was the perfectibility of thought via concepts. He says, '... a judgement about beauty [cannot] be determined by an a priori proof, in accordance with determinate rules'.[14] If this were the case, he goes on to say, then aesthetic judgements made by rules, or maxims derived from reason would be logical rather than aesthetic judgements.

Kant makes the point with some feeling:

> I shall stop my ears, shall refuse to listen to reasons and arguments, and shall sooner assume that those rules of the critics are false, or at least do not apply in the present case, than allow my judgement to be determined by a priori bases of proof; for it is meant to be a judgement of taste, and not one of the understanding or of reason.[15]

Judgement, and in this case particularly aesthetic judgement, can be universally valid, 'extend its claim to all subjects', and be subjective but not on 'a cognitive base that can be compelled by proof'. The judgement, according to Kant's example, that this tulip is beautiful is a judgement of taste, it is universal but not of the form that all tulips are beautiful, therefore this particular tulip must have the quality of beauty. Beauty, he insists, is not a property to be derived in this way.

Kant saw that in judgement, as with the other faculties, there must be a synthetic a priori element. However, here there were more complications about that element due to the subjective dimension of taste, and for teleological judgements, the subjective dimension of purposiveness.

For the purposes of this discussion which focuses on the interpersonal basis of the self as subject the discussion of teleological judgement is of less importance as it concerns itself with 'scientific' judgement, as understood by Kant. There is one element of the discussion that relates to aesthetic judgement and judgement generally. It is the idea of "purposiveness", both objective and subjective and its relation to the "supersensible".

In the *Critique of Judgement* Kant establishes that the faculty of judgement is a distinct human capacity. It judges as to the beautiful or the sublime in art and nature and also judges the purposiveness in nature in teleological judgement. There is in the third *Critique* a very definite break, of the greatest importance, with the view of *The Critique of Pure Reason.* In the earlier work Kant regards judgement, in a manner orthodox for his time as a matter of applying a concept or a rule to particulars. Kant says in the "Transcendental Analytic":

> If understanding in general is to be viewed as the faculty of rules, judgement will be the faculty of subsuming under rules; that is, of distinguishing whether something does or does not stand under a given rule.[16]

This is the form of "determinate" judgement. To be distinguished from the form of "reflective" judgement of the third critique, where the particular is given and rule under which it falls has to be discovered, or in some cases invented by the imagination. This is somewhat more complex in its presentation than determinate judgement, for instance Kant says in §37:

> ...all judgements of taste are singular judgements, because they do not connect their predicate, the liking, with a concept but connect it with a singular empirical presentation that is given.
>
> Hence it is not the pleasure but *the universal validity of this pleasure,* perceived as connected in the mind with our mere judging of an object, that we present a priori as [a] universal rule for the power of judgement, valid for everyone.[17]

The deduction of judgements of taste is recognised as highly problematic,[18] however it is abundantly clear from this passage that the form of reasoning from a particular to a rule is totally different from that of the first *Critique.* It also needs to be pointed out here that aesthetic judgements, being reflective judgements, are not "determinative" judgements in the sense of determining what an intuition is, but are rather indeterminate reflecting the "subjective purposiveness of nature" and are thus truly aesthetic.

In the *Critique of Judgement* Kant demonstrates that beauty is not a quality of an object as the empiricists such as Burke or Hutcheson supposed.

So in his example: 'The rose at which I am looking is beautiful',[19] "beautiful" is not a property of the rose as this judgement is not made using the concept of a rose but rather with the mere intuition of the rose. The beauty is the subject's feeling. Another way of putting this insight of Kant's is to say that one does not have to know this is a rose to know it is beautiful; one does not have to understand the rose as an expert horticulturalist might in order to appreciate it. We could be confronted with a completely foreign object, say from an unknown culture or even a completely unknown object from another planet and still find it beautiful. Nor, importantly, does the agreement of others that an object is beautiful depend on their understanding the concept of it. It turns out to be the case that it is subjective agreement, in conjunction with imagination, that constitutes the basis of judgement. It is here that the role of the imagination, not only for aesthetic judgements, but for all cognition becomes important.

The notion of imagination is first introduced in detail in the "Transcendental Deduction" of *The Critique of Pure Reason:*

> There are three subjective sources of knowledge upon which rests the possibility of experience in general and the knowledge of objects- *sense, imagination,* and *apperception.*[20]

Here imagination is used very much in the sense of the power of the mind to bring before it what is not present. This is an essential element for without the power of imagination the synthetic a priori would not be possible. But only the *productive* synthesis of the imagination can take place *a priori;* the reproductive rests on empirical conditions. Thus the principle of the necessary unity of pure (productive) synthesis of imagination, prior to apperception, is the ground of the possibility of all knowledge, especially of experience.

He continues the exposition in the following paragraph to say: '...the transcendental unity of the synthesis of imagination is the pure form of all possible knowledge';[21] This treatment of imagination is continued in the third *Critique* where it becomes essential not just for knowledge but also for the faculty of judgement. The treatment of imagination is a development from the earlier discussion and is a continuous development rather than a revision of the earlier view. An important element that is retained is that it is imagination that provides the a priori, and thus part of the transcendental, element in judgement. In knowledge an empirical judgement, an intuition, matches a determinate concept. It is the active power to structure the intuition in accordance with a concept that is for Kant imagination, '...it requires that there be a harmony between two presentational powers, imagination (for the intuition and the combination of its manifold) and understanding (for the concept that is the presentation of the unity of this combination)'.[22] In aesthetic and teleological judgements a similar process occurs but without a determinate concept because aesthetic judgements do not attribute properties to objects.[23] This is because reflective judgements do not have a universal under which to predicate a particular. There must however be an indeterminate concept under which to make a judgement and this would be nature's "subjective purposiveness". Kant, as is so often the case, particularly in the third *Critique,* is both prolix and, to a degree, obscure. But the sense of this point can be illustrated by the following passage where he says:

> When an object is given in experience, there are two ways in which we can present purposiveness in it. We can present it on a merely formal subjective basis: as the harmony of the form of the object (the form that is [manifested] in the *apprehension* of the object prior to any concept) with the cognitive powers.- i.e., the harmony required in general to unite an intuition with concepts so as to produce a cognition.

Kant continues in relation to aesthetic judgement:

> But we can also present it on an objective basis: as the harmony of the form of the object with the possibility of the thing itself according to a prior concept of the thing that contains the basis of that form.

And in relation to teleological judgement:

> We have seen that the presentation of the first kind of purposeness rests on the pleasure we take directly on the form of the object when we merely reflect on it.[24]

The notion of a "subjective purposeness" in nature is important to Kant's account but can be rather perplexing. At one level it seems somewhat straightforward as a subjective attribution of a purposeness in nature to render nature understandable by us. In this way it is similar to the schemata or pure intuitions of the transcendental aesthetic such as those of the dimensions of space and time. Kant says: 'Hence we may regard *natural beauty* as the *exhibition* of the concept of formal (merely subjective) purposeness, ...which we judge by taste (aesthetically, by means of the feeling of pleasure)'.[25] There is however another "deeper" meaning of "subjective purposeness" used by Kant. In it our attribution of subjective purposiveness in art or nature becomes aligned with, or as Kant says, in harmony with, the supersensible. It seems, that Kant is saying in the solution to the antinomy of teleological judgement, that our intuition of a subjective purposeness in nature is the subjective presentation of the same supersensible that lies in nature. Thus the a priori understanding of a particular can at once be contingent, with respect to say effective causation, yet necessitated in the concept of an object. Kant then proposes that the supersensible "within us" is the same as the supersensible that underlies an object. This shows that there can be harmony between imagination and understanding in aesthetic judgement and also suggests, how there can be harmony between imagination and perception in knowledge.[26] On this point Pluhar says:

> Kant considers the supersensible basis of nature's subjective purposiveness to be *the same* supersensible as the supersensible substrate of both objects and subjects and the supersensible that "the concept of freedom contains practically"; this "same" supersensible is referred to in all these ways in the context of the solution to the antinomy of aesthetic judgement.[27]

But what does Kant mean by "supersensible"?

He is referring to the noumenal world and particularly those objects within it. They are things which cannot be experienced as phenomena, nor known in an empirical mode. They are the things in themselves which underlie, and ultimately unify, experience. They can only be thought. If it were not for the existence of the supersensibles, a priori understanding would not be possible; this is particularly true for the synthetic a priori principles. With the supersensible the world of particulars would be utterly contingent and thus random, the world of experience would not be unified but chaotic. To understand the role that supersensibles play here it is illuminating to compare Kant's discussion with that in the first *Critique.* There is a small but significant development between the *Critique of Pure Reason* (2nd edition) and the *Critique of Judgement.* The difference relates to acknowledgment in the *Critique of Judgement* of the supersensible "within". In the *Critique of Pure Reason* the supersensible is not knowable in any sense; it is beyond the bounds of cognition. The structure of our cognition leads to the conclusion that there must be a substrate in transcendental metaphysics, but to no more than that. In the *Critique of Judgement* reflective judgement leads us to conclude that there is a supersensible within us which forms the basis for our (univeralisable) judgements. In the solution to the antinomy of taste Kant refers to this supersensible within which he provides the indeterminate concept of judgement as '...the concept of what may be considered the supersensible substrate of humanity'.[28]

This brings discussion to the question of the basis of univeralisable, yet subjective, reflective judgements. It is through the exploration of this element of Kant's exposition that the basis for the self is formed; from a combination of an interpersonal and a reflective transcendental position.

The relevant section of the *Critique of Judgement* is the "Deduction of Pure Aesthetic Judgements" and in particular sections 37 to 40. It must be recalled that Kant's starting point in this discussion is with the question, as posed by Pluhar: 'How, if at all, is it possible to judge something in nature (or in art) as beautiful on the basis of something very subjective, a feeling of pleasure and yet demand for our judgement a universal assent?'[29] In order for this to be so such judgements must have a degree of necessity and a synthetic a priori element. They are not judgements of sense but judgements of reflection. In the previous two critiques Kant had discovered that each cognitive faculty had its a priori principles. Now in the third *Critique* he claims to have discovered that feeling, especially the feeling of pleasure taken in the beautiful as having its own, a priori principles. In the third critique there comes an important break with the a priori principles as expressed in the first two critiques where they relate firstly to reason and secondly to freedom, which are both accessible by individual mental powers, here they relate to communicability which presupposes other reflexively aware beings. In answer to the general question as to how synthetic a priori judgements of taste are possible, Kant's transcendental reply, for that is what is required, involves the communicability of subjective feelings, presupposing the reflexive communicability of other subjective cognitions.

Dealing with the "Aesthetic Deduction" is not a easy task, not only are the ideas and arguments very difficult, Kant's presentation leaves much to be desired. Schaper comments, 'It [the Aesthetic Deduction] does not present one unified argument, nor does it impress by cogency or coherence. And there is no agreement among scholars as to where the deduction begins and where it ends...'.[30] Notwithstanding these difficulties, the major lines of argument are central, not just to the *Critique of Judgement,* but to an understanding of Kant's entire work. His claim is not just that communicability is necessary for aesthetic judgements, because of the subjective element, but that communicability is necessary for cognition, and therefore knowledge, in general.[31] He is generally thought to have failed to support this claim, but the fact that he made it bears close attention in the light of later communicative theory, such as that proposed by Apel and Habermas, which may complete the argument.[32]

In his exposition of the deduction Kant asks the question how a judgement is possible based only on ones own feelings which is valid for all other subjects and 'does so a priori, i.e. without being allowed to wait for other peoples assent'.[33] He gives the short answer in the next section, section 37, where he says:

> Hence it is not the pleasure, but *the universal validity of this pleasure,* perceived as connected in the mind with our mere judging of an object, that we present a priori as [a] universal rule for the power of judgement, valid for everyone.[34]

Kant next makes the notorious remark that the deduction is "so easy", seemingly because '...we are justified in presupposing universally in all people the same subjective conditions that of the power of judgement that we find in ourselves'.[35] Critics are in agreement that Kant needs to do more here to demonstrate that the same subjective conditions exist in all people. Kant himself admits "unavoidable difficulties" and later goes on to propose a *sensus communis* as justification for the same subjective conditions. However, rather infuriatingly, he does not directly relate his short section "Comment" on the deduction to this issue. The footnote to section 38 does elucidate Kant's position a little. Schaper claims that it merely 'seems to bear out' the view that Kant makes only the simple assumption of sameness.[36] But it actually does more than this. What the footnote reveals is that there is a transcendental argument buried in here. It may seem easy to Kant after the labours of the transcendental deductions in the earlier two critiques, but here in the third *Critique* is an argument of the same form.

In the footnote Kant makes the major point that, 'in all people the subjective conditions of this power are the same as concerns the relation required for cognition as such between the cognitive powers that are activated and the power of judgement'.[37] The power referred to is the aesthetic power of judgement. Whilst it is not spelled out here in any detail it is notable that Kant refers to the "conditions", and specifically the "subjective conditions" of this power. He continues in the second part of the footnote, to draw attention to the "*formal conditions*" of the faculty of judgement, it being "pure", that is free from confusion with a concept. Kant is claiming that it is a transcendental prerequisite for aesthetic judgements to be made that humans must possess the same subjective cognitive conditions. They would not be able to make (human) aesthetic judgements if they did not. What makes the deduction "easy" is simply the lack of a determinate concept. This means that we are dealing with the powers of apperception and not with the apperceived. Notwithstanding this qualification the deduction is far from easy. Not, paradoxically perhaps, because the deduction is hard but because what it implies about the subjective conditions of all people is far from easy. Here the transcendental conditions are related to communicability in dealing with reflective judgement, but the implications of this move are far wider. As Schaper says: 'Communicability has now moved into a central position. It is shown to be a necessary requirement for all cognition'.[38] In fact it has been claimed more than "shown". It is only shown if one accepts as transparent the claim that the same subjective conditions must exist in all people.

In order to establish and demonstrate the sameness of subjective conditions Kant uses arguments for both a "common sense" and a *sensus communis* although having distinguished them he later, somewhat confusingly, runs them together.[39] These distinct, but related, notions are first introduced in sections 20 and 21 and then later amplified in section 40. Kant is constructing here his central argument for answering the fundamental question of the *Critique of Judgement* i.e. how can it be possible to judge something as demanding universal assent when it is based on a subjective feeling. It is a matter of acknowledging the principle of communicability as a transcendental principle. Kant expresses it thus: 'Hence taste is our ability to judge a priori the communicability of the feelings that (without mediation of a concept) are connected with a given presentation'.[40] In this passage Kant goes on to say that if we assume 'mere universal communicability' we are in a position to see how we can "require as a duty" assent of our judgement of taste based on a subjective feeling.

Kant has previously stated the clear transcendental case at the conclusion to section 37, where he says:

> Hence it is not the pleasure, but the *universal validity of this pleasure* perceived as connected in the mind with our mere judgement of an object, that we present a priori as [a] universal rule for the power of judgement, valid for everyone. That I am perceiving and judging an object with pleasure is an empirical judgement. That I find the object beautiful, i. e., that I am entitled to require that liking from everyone as necessary, is an a priori judgement.[41]

The capacity within us, and within each person, is identified as the *sensus communis*. It is distinguished from common sense as being not just a sense which is shared but a sense which "men" (sic) have as being part of humanity. Arendt calls it the specifically human sense and claims that human communication, and thus communicability depends on it.[42] It is she says, '...-like an extra mental capability-that fits us into a community'.[43] Whilst Arendt is primarily concerned with judgement as a political faculty, it must also be viewed as Benhabib claims, in a wider context as 'a moral faculty'.[44] Indeed there are indications in Arendt's discussion of imagination and aesthetic judgement that she may have been prepared to broaden the application of treatment of judgement in a more complete discussion of the topic than that which we have from the lecture notes of 1970. She continues to quote Kant from *Anthropology from a Pragmatic Point of View* as saying that: 'The only general symptom of insanity is the loss of the *sensus communis*, and the logical stubbornness in insisting on one's own sense (*sensus privatus*), which [in an insane person] is substituted for it'.[45]

Kant is not entirely clear just what he means by sense here. On the one hand he says that it is a sense because it involves feeling, but then he also says it 'is the power to judge'. As a power it would be akin to a sense of justice or a sense of decency and as such is not strictly a sense but more a capacity which is loosely called a sense. Kant waivers between the two meanings but seems to settle for an interpretation that would have humans with the capacity to feel pleasure at the result of a judgement that a particular is beautiful. It is a fundamental fact about the human species that they have this sense, and as such it cannot stand in need of justification; it simply is so. Yet this is ultimately unsatisfactory, not because one would deny the capacity that Kant calls a "sense" exists, but because it is opaque and does not satisfy as an explanation as to how we can claim universal assent for private states. Clearly it is not a sense such as a sense of smell or sensation in general. At best it is akin to Hume's "moral sense" but then it is not clear that it has any direct feeling of pleasure or displeasure as Hume claims for his moral sense. Rather here we have a second order pleasure taken in the power of reflection.

We see through this discussion that Kant has come a long way from his starting point in the *Critique of Pure Reason* where he set out to define human cognitive powers in terms of reason and to overcome what he saw to be the corrosive scepticism of Hume. In the *Critique of Practical Reason,* read in conjunction with the *Groundwork,* he has moved to the position of accepting that freedom, along with reason is also a basic human capacity and that reason without freedom is impotent. The will could not act to bring about any purpose, including the "final purpose" without reason.

In the *Critique of Judgement* Kant recognises that there must be the further distinct cognitive power of judgement. This not only unites reason and freedom but is a domain of synthetic a priori understanding in its own right. The third critique recognises the fundamental importance of judgement for all cognition and not just aesthetic or teleological propositions. The achievement of the critique goes even further in recognising the importance of communicability as a transcendental condition for all cognition not just judgement. The argument shows that in order for subjective cognitions to be had they must be in principle communicable to all humanity. Kant has therefore developed an argument for the non privacy of subjective conditions. The argument is incomplete as it stands, in that it does not articulate the case fully, but it establishes a *prima facie* case for non-privacy. The argument, however, can now be fully developed in a context post the linguistic turn, in which the self can be seen to be a particular of an interpersonal universality.

Notes

1 Hannah Arendt, Werner Pluhar and Cornelius Castoriadis are among recent commentators who comment on the difficulty of approaching the third critique.
2 Kant, Immanuel (1952), *The Critique of Judgement*, trans. James Creed Meredith, Oxford University Press, Oxford, p. 23.
3 Kant, Immanuel (1987), *The Critique of Judgement*, trans. Werner S. Pluhar, Hackett, Indianapolis, pp. 14-15.
4 Castoriadis, Cornelius (1991), *Philosophy, Politics, Autonomy*, ed. David Curtis Ames, Oxford University Press, Oxford, p. 91.
5 Arendt, Hannah (1982), *Lectures on Kant's Political Philosophy*, ed. Ronald Beiner, University of Chicago Press, Chicago, p. 66.
6 See Schaper, Eva (1992) "Taste sublimity and genius: The aesthetics of nature and art", in *The Cambridge Companion to Kant*, ed. Guyer, Paul, Cambridge University Press, Cambridge.
7 See Schaper, Eva, op cit., p. 369.
8 See Kant, Immanuel (1987), *The Critique of Judgement*, trans. Werner S. Pluhar, Hackett Indianapolis, Introduction.
9 Wittgenstein, Ludwig (1966), *Lectures and Conversations on Aesthetics, Psychology and Religious Belief*, ed. Cyril Barrett, Basil Blackwell, Oxford.
10 Kant, Immanuel, *The Critique of Judgement*, p. xlvii.
11 Hume, David (1948), *Hume's Moral and Political Philosophy*, ed. Henry D. Aiken, Hafner Press, New York, p. 342.
12 Ibid., p. 342.
13 See Kant, Immanuel, *The Critique of Judgement*, p. 30.
14 Ibid., p. 148.
15 Ibid.
16 Kant, Immanuel (1964), *The Critique of Pure Reason*, trans. Norman Kemp Smith, Macmillan, London, p. 177.
17 Kant, Immanuel, *The Critique of Judgement*, p. 154.
18 See Pluhar's Introduction to *The Critique of Judgement*, p. lix, for a discussion of the variety of critical opinion.
19 Kant, Immanuel, *The Critique of Judgement*, p. 59.
20 Kant, Immanuel, *The Critique of Pure Reason*, trans. Norman Kemp Smith, p. 141.
21 Ibid., p. 143.
22 Kant, Immanuel *The Critique of Judgement*, p. 151.
23 Ibid., p. 66.
24 Ibid., p. 32.
25 Ibid., p. 33.
26 Ibid., p. 214. See also Pluhar's informative footnote # 101 in the introduction, p. xciv.
27 Ibid., p. xcvi.
28 Ibid., p. 213.

29 Ibid., p. xlvii.
30 Schaper, Eva, "Taste sublimity and genius: The aesthetics of nature and art", op. cit., p. 376.
31 See Kant, Immanuel *The Critique of Judgement*, p.153. Kant claims the problem of critique of judgement is part of the general problem of transcendental philosophy.
32 See Eva Schaper, op. cit., p. 378.
33 Kant, Immanuel, *The Critique of Judgement*, p. 153.
34 Ibid., p. 154.
35 Ibid., p. 156.
36 Schaper, Eva, "Taste sublimity and genius: The aesthetics of nature and art", p. 376.
37 Kant, Immanuel, *The Critique of Judgement*, p. 155.
38 Schaper, Eva "Taste sublimity and genius: The aesthetics of nature and art", op. cit., p. 377.
39 This can be seen by comparing the distinction made in section 20 with that in section 40. In the former there are two distinct "senses", whilst in the latter it seems it is the ambiguity of "common" in common sense that leads to a more formal sensus communis.
40 Kant, Immanuel, *The Critique of Judgement*, p. 162.
41 Ibid., p. 154.
42 Arendt, Hannah (1982), *Lectures on Kant's Political Philosophy*, ed. Ronald Beiner, University of Chicago Press, Chicago, p. 70.
43 Ibid.
44 Benhabib, Seyla, *Situating the Self* (1992), Polity Press, Cambridge, p. 141.
45 Ibid.

9 Kant and Later Wittgenstein

Kant's argument for non-privacy bears a striking resemblance to Wittgenstein's "private language argument". Although at first sight the two philosophers might seem poles apart, there are in fact striking parallels between the development of the thought of Kant and Wittgenstein. Wittgenstein of course was working within a context where the importance of logic and formal language had recently developed, whilst Kant was in the mould of critical metaphysics opposing both Hume's empiricism and the rationalist metaphysics of Wolf and Leibniz.

The early work of Wittgenstein parallels Kant's first *Critique* by taking a view that the world can be exhaustively described within a logical framework of formal language and that it is not possible to have any understanding outside that framework. The later work, post the *Blue and Brown Books,* slowly comes to recognise that natural language is part of the world and cannot be formalised to define a limit of the world, although in many complex respects language still limits the world. As such, he acknowledges the importance of the embeddedness of language in humanity and the importance of judgement, belief and culture to understanding, and indeed to the making of the world.

Wittgenstein returned to Cambridge full time in 1938. The *Anschluss* had made it impossible for him to return to Austria and his haven in Norway was becoming less secure.[1] He was reluctant to resume the academic life as he had always been deeply ambivalent about the artificiality and intellectual pretentiousness of it all. Indeed, Monk makes the point that Wittgenstein was an intellectual, a creative philosopher and possibly a genius, but he was definitely not an academic in the traditional sense. His method of philosophising, tolerated at Cambridge would definitely not have been acceptable at the then more conventionally scholarly Oxford.[2]

Wittgenstein is notorious for his unscholarly approach to philosophy. It would seem, therefore, that there is no direct connection between Kant and the development of Wittgenstein's thought. There is no evidence that Wittgenstein ever read Kant, although he was familiar with and influenced by the post-Kantian Arthur Schopenhauer.[3] It was via this path that he was influenced by the ideas and philosophical agenda of transcendental idealism and Kant modes of thought are present in Wittgenstein's formulations of problems.

What is quite certain, however, is that even though there was no systematic reading of Kant, or indeed of any philosophical tradition, by Wittgenstein there is a strong indirect Kantian influence. Schlick, for example, commented on Wittgenstein's "pseudo-Kantianism", as Wittgenstein agreed with Kant that mathematical propositions were at least synthetic, if not a priori in a conventional sense.[4] There is also evidence that Wittgenstein approved of the critical method adopted in Kant's later works as an appropriate way to do philosophy but it clearly was not the method he closely followed himself.[5]

One commentator who acknowledges a correspondence between the work of Kant and Wittgenstein is David Pears. He says for example:

> It is true that Wittgenstein's attitude to metaphysical thinking is not the same as Kant's... But they have this much in common: both regard it as a natural and inevitable transgressor, and both think that much can be learned from its excesses.[6]

And later:

> Wittgenstein wanted to plot the limits of language, just the way that Kant wanted to plot the limits of thought.[7]

And again in *The False Prison*:

> This [the impossibility of drawing a limit to phenomena] places his philosophy in a different tradition from Russell's: its line of descent is from Kant rather than from the British Empiricists,[8]

It is surprising however, that Pears whilst drawing quite close correspondences between the issues and approaches of the *Tractatus* and the *Critique of Pure Reason,* should not go on and continue similar discussion of the correspondences between Wittgenstein's *Investigations* and other later works and Kant's *Critique of Judgement* where the discussion of issues of privacy of experience and the distinct nature of judgement occurs.

Hilary Putnam in his recent book *Pragmatism* sketches out what he sees to be the path from Kant to Wittgenstein (and Rorty) via the pragmatists Peirce, James and Dewey.[9] Whilst Putnam is at pains to point out the differences between Kant and Wittgenstein, particularly the vast difference in philosophical style, he also acknowledges that: 'Wittgenstein could not have seen so far if he had not stood on the shoulders of that giant'.[10] Rorty makes the observation that:

> Academic philosophy in our day stands to Wittgenstein as intellectual life in Germany in the first decades of the last century stood to Kant. Kant had changed everything, but no one was sure what Kant had said - no one was sure what in Kant to take seriously and what to put aside.[11]

It might be added that, even in the later decades of this century, philosophers are still coming to terms with the legacy of Kant. The issue here alluded to by Rorty is the necessity, in the case of both Kant and Wittgenstein, to make the paradigm shift to a new way of conceiving the problematics of philosophy. In both cases the "old" problems have to be reconceptualised into a new scheme with a new way of thinking. In both cases philosophy, and indeed all intellectual activity, has to adjust to new landscape.

In following the course of the theory of an interpersonal self it is the "later Wittgenstein" that is of most relevance. Particular attention will be paid to the "private language argument" and the issue of awareness of and communicability of subjective states, with some comments on culture and judgement.

Wittgenstein had taken up philosophy again in 1929 and returned to Cambridge full time in 1938.[12] His mission at Cambridge was continuous with the earlier program of the *Tractatus* but by the early 1930s he had come to recognise that the earlier work was far too limited and treated language in only its descriptive dimension and not in its fuller dimensions as infusing life. Many commentators speak of the early and late Wittgenstein as if they were diametrically opposed or as if Wittgenstein had undergone some radical conversion. This is not so and can be rather misleading as the continuity of Wittgenstein's thought is essential to understanding the overall whole.

In the discussion of the self and inner states it is necessary to be clear about Wittgenstein's purposes in philosophy. This is no easy matter as he was such a complex, self-accusatory human being; the philosophical agenda cannot be separated from the personal struggles. The formative role of Schopenhauer, particularly *The World as Will and Representation* remains a clear influence. This work, one of the few philosophical texts Wittgenstein claimed to have read, set the agenda for the dialogue of the "inside" world of the self and its relation to the "outside" world of reality which is a predominant theme for both the *Tractatus* and the later work. It is also a reason why it is appropriate to view Wittgenstein in the broader Kantian tradition and view his philosophy as an attempt to come to terms with what he took to be the deeply misguided assumptions of transcendental idealism. There is also here a mix of the personal issues for Wittgenstein who was constantly, and somewhat unsuccessfully, seeking to define, together, both who he was and the philosophical domain, with an embedded view of language and such a close textured world view.[13]

There are three major themes that can be discerned in Wittgenstein's work.

The first theme is that of the resolution of transcendental idealism. This theme was never far below the surface in Wittgenstein, but it was mixed with a subjective and intensely personal idealism, that was both a source of philosophical reflection and an inhibition to philosophising. It is present as a silent sub-text in all his work and also as the source of the hermeneutic element referred to by Apel.[14] Indeed Apel is one of the few commentators who see Wittgenstein in this context.[15] Wittgenstein is, for example, often exploring the conditions for the use of the concepts of transcendental idealist thought such as exploring the concepts of "mind", "meaning" "appearance" etc. in their uses in both philosophical and everyday contexts. The Anglo-American commentators still tend to see him in the context of analytic philosophy, however Wittgenstein takes only the problematic from Russell and Moore; never the method.[16]

A second theme in Wittgenstein's philosophy was opposition to the scientific way of thinking and thus to the metaphysics that he saw as supporting such thinking. The theme, however, can be seen as part of the larger theme of resolution of, or escape from, transcendental idealism. As a theme it emerged more explicitly in his lectures than in his writings. Thus, we find statements in *Lectures and Conversations on Aesthetics, Psychology and Religious Belief* that explicitly condemn the reductionist "ideology" of science. For instance he saw the idea of treating aesthetics as a branch of psychology as 'exceedingly stupid'.[17] The theme of the opposition to science is seen by Monk as the major theme in Wittgenstein's thought, he says: 'it [Wittgenstein's target] was, more generally the wretched effect that the worship of science and the scientific method has had upon our whole culture'.[18] It can be conceded that the opposition to "scientific worship" was a major theme in Wittgenstein's thought but it should not be seen, as Monk is inclined to see it, as the sole or totally predominant theme. Wittgenstein certainly saw the application of scientific ways of thinking to non-scientific realms, especially in philosophy, as highly destructive, but the theme runs deeper than this; it is an opposition to the rationalisation of life itself that becomes a guiding passion. It should, however, be noted that Wittgenstein continued to have respect for science as an intellectual practice in its own right, and for the integrity of those he regarded as genuine scientists.

A third theme in Wittgenstein's thought is the relationship between language and experience generally, including the self and consciousness. This was for Wittgenstein both an obsession and lifelong struggle, philosophically and personally. This theme takes many turnings during the course of Wittgenstein's works. In the *Tractatus* he struggles to find the limit to language, as much to delineate what lies beyond language as to specify what is within the world of language. Firmly on Wittgenstein's agenda is the establishment of the transcendental ground of the self by defining it as the limit of the world, and the boundary of language. He also wanted to establish what lay beyond language and thus was not subject to argumentation, such as the existence of God and the fundamentals of ethics and aesthetics.[19] For instance:

> 6.421 It is clear that ethics cannot be put into words.
> Ethics is transcendental.
> (Ethics and aesthetics are one and the same.)

and:

> 6.4312 The solution to the riddle of life in space and time lies *outside* space and time.[20]

In the later work, from the *Blue and Brown Books* on, he did not so much abandon his earlier view of language as enlarge and transform it to see language part of experience and not merely the means by which facts get into experience. The transformative aspect was relatively simple. It was to see that the function of language was not just descriptive but many dimensional so that language could be as much a part of the world as things or facts. The discussion of the way words and experience merge in "inner" experience and "expression" permeates the later philosophy. Here the self cannot be defined as the limit of the world, because it, like language is in the world. This is his most radical move which really does shift the landscape. The task of dealing with the subject, meaning and the world becomes most problematic. It is this task towards which the whole of the later philosophy becomes directed.

Many passages from the later works would illustrate the point, but take for instance the following:

> 477. "So one must know that objects whose names one teaches a child by ostensive definition exist". -Why must one know they do? Isn't it enough that experience doesn't later show the opposite?
>
> For why should the language game rest on some kind of knowledge?[21]

The answers, or pointers to the answers, have become more subtle but the theme of questioning remains the same.

What was the cause of this major shift in Wittgenstein's thought that led to his return to philosophy and generated such a radical perspective?

An intriguing and very credible supposition has been put forward by Ingemund Gullvåg that it was the indirect influence of the work of Charles

Sanders Peirce.[22] Gullvåg speculates that the ideas of John Dewey through the Austrian school reform movement may have been an influence, but that the main influence came through Wittgenstein's discussions with Frank Ramsay during the 1920s. In the late 1920s Ramsay read Morris R. Cohen's edition of Peirce's writing's *Chance, Love and Logic* and discussed these with Wittgenstein during 1929. It seems that any direct evidence of influence ends there but there is indirect evidence of influence in Wittgenstein's writing at the time. In the manuscript *Philosophische Bemerkungen* many topics which were present in Peirce are to be found. According to Gullvåg, these include, infinity, continuity, problems of the relationship between language and reality, the actual and the possible, thoughts as signs, whether we ever "get out" of language or sign systems, belief and the readiness to act. Not only are there certain topics common to both, but there is also a similarity between the philosophical approaches. Both are concerned with clarity and simplicity. Peirce said that according to the pragmatic maxim, that if there was no difference in the effects of an expression or sign, then there was no difference in meaning, a view close to Wittgenstein's dictum that the meaning of a word is its use.

Peirce also had his own version of the "private language argument" as he held that thoughts are signs and that signs are, necessarily, external and communicable. Both Wittgenstein and Peirce sought to avoid metaphysics and stressed the medium of communication as the true ground for understanding.

Perhaps not too much can be made of the supposed connection between Peirce and Wittgenstein but Gullvåg has performed a service in allowing us to see a little more clearly the formative context of the Wittgensteinian problematic. As Gullvåg says: 'It is tempting to say that Wittgenstein *does* what Peirce *says*, practices what he preaches in his expositions of pragmatism'.[23]

Wittgenstein's work is difficult to deal with on a number of counts. It is a reflection of this difficulty that many commentaries tend to be rather partial in their accounts. The task is not made any simpler by Wittgenstein's approach to philosophising. In his approach there are no clearly defined themes or programs; they are all within the epigrammatic text. The closer one gets to Wittgenstein's text the harder it becomes to deal with. One feels that either nothing much can be said or everything needs to be said. It is extremely difficult to maintain a critical thread in response. But there are three major themes that can be seen to dominate.

The first theme arises from his claim that philosophy is entirely descriptive and should be neither analytical nor critical. Wittgenstein says:

> Philosophers see the method of science before their eyes, and are irresistibly tempted to ask and answer questions in the way science does. This tendency is the real source of metaphysics, and leads the philosopher into complete darkness. I want to say here that it can never be our job to reduce anything to anything. Philosophy really *is* 'purely descriptive'.[24]

Or in an alternative statement:

> The solution of philosophical problems can be compared with a gift in a fairy tale: in the magic castle it appears enchanted and if you look at it outside in daylight it is nothing but an old bit of iron.[25]

Yet, this claim is deceptive in that it does not take into account the context of his "investigations". They may be descriptive within some post-hermeneutic framework yet they are critical in other contexts. He was dealing with questions presented by analytic philosophy in a post-transcendental idealist mode and was implicitly following a critical-reflective method; although because he avoids giving any critical context, this not at all obvious. This view of Wittgenstein is shared by Charles Taylor who regards some of the arguments of the later Wittgenstein as forms of transcendental argument, although he does not spell out in any detail what he means by this assertion.[26]

The second, following from the first, was his denial of, indeed revulsion towards, any theory in philosophy. Theory always further mystified problems for Wittgenstein, whereas the role of philosophy was to de-mystify, to make clear the source of the confusion. He is on record many times, both through his writings and the reports of his students, as saying that philosophical problems were really confusions or puzzles expressed as questions: 'Our problem is not a scientific one, but a muddle felt as a problem'.[27] When the source of the confusion is clarified, usually by getting the language straight, then the philosophical question dissolves. This, he says, is why there seems to be little or no progress in philosophy; the questions dissolve and there can be no record of their "answers".

Wittgenstein wrote in 1946:

> Getting hold of the difficulty *deep down* is what is hard.
>
> Because if it is grasped near the surface it simply remains the difficulty it was. It has to be pulled out by the roots; and that involves our beginning to think about these things in a new way. The change is as decisive as, for example, that from the alchemical to the chemical way of thinking. The new way of thinking is so hard to establish.

> Once the new way of thinking has been established, the old problems vanish; indeed they become hard to recapture. For they go with our way of expressing ourselves and, if we clothe ourselves in a new form of expression, the old problems are discarded along with the old garment.[28]

As an example, a simple question, such as "What is paper?" looks very much like the question "What is time"? Yet the former obviously admits of a precise answer, whilst the latter is an example of a confusion expressed as a question, or as Wittgenstein says, 'a muddle felt as a problem'. Wittgenstein says in *The Blue Book* that when we find out how to use a word such as "time" or "mind" properly the puzzle is clarified and we would see that the question "What is time?" without a specific context, does not make sense as a question.[29] It is difficult to call this a "method" of philosophy, yet it clearly is a form of post-Kantian critical-reflective method,

> There is not *a* philosophical method, though there are indeed methods, like different therapies.[30]

Wittgenstein's descriptive approach leading to the dissolution of philosophical problems is seductive but misleading. What is unstated here is an implicit understanding of the relationship between thought and language. It is the tension between the content of consciousness and language that is for Wittgenstein the source of "philosophical puzzles". It is only when this tension is resolved that philosophical problems can be "solved". The problems can only "dissolve" against the background of language as the transcendental medium.

This brings us to a third problem in dealing with Wittgenstein; the incompleteness of his project. This is an issue that has to be dealt with on two levels.[31] The first level is that in one sense there is no project; for Wittgenstein the philosopher is just a journeyman clearing as much useless debris as he can in allotted time. This is how he mostly saw himself, even if somewhat disingenuously.[32]

The second level relates to issues of context and focus of the work. Perhaps the intellectual achievement of commencing the Wittgensteinian project is sufficient in itself. But much of the criticism levelled at Wittgenstein and his followers is based on the grounds that the project "goes nowhere", we are left with a form of assertion and no clear lines of development. Whilst this criticism is well founded, it may not be as telling as it might if a "missing" context of transcendental idealism were to be provided. Nevertheless it can be said that Wittgenstein's work both as a teacher and writer was left incomplete. This is as much a legacy of Wittgenstein's personality and his inability to come to terms with what he should be doing as much as it was a consequence of the "method" of his work. Yet he envisaged, at least the theoretical possibility, that there could be an end to philosophy when all the confusion spawned by language was cleared up.

A pertinent observation may be made here as to the close link between Wittgenstein's own psychological struggle and his philosophical method. He says: 'The way to solve the problem you see in life is to live in a way that will make what is problematic disappear'.[33] He was always keen to make an end of philosophy; to complete the task of clearing away the debris that prevented him, and us, from seeing clearly. He so often drew a parallel with philosophy as a disease that he was out to cure, or a virus to eradicate. This was also a personal struggle to overcome his own personal confusions about who he really was and what he should really do. It is as if, for Wittgenstein, there was a belief that there would come a time when he was able to live free and clear of any psychological problems or obsessions.[34] When he had got philosophy out of the way he could get on and do something "real". Philosophy was for Wittgenstein a form of self-directed therapy and this clearly does not make a commentator's task any simpler.

These difficulties have meant that criticism of Wittgenstein has been very much confined to dealing with him in isolation from his contemporaries and from critical comparison with other philosophical movements. However, I believe that Wittgenstein can profitably be discussed in the context of post-transcendental idealism with direct connections to the Kantian legacy. In doing so the transcendental role of language, and indeed ordinary language, can be elucidated.

If Kant can rightly claim to have brought about a "Copernican Revolution" in philosophy by shifting the paradigm of philosophical truth from metaphysics to human cognition, it could be said that Wittgenstein has made an Einsteinian move to a philosophical paradigm akin to relativity. By conducting his own critique of his early philosophy he has moved the locus of critique from that of a detached observer, which Kant still maintained, to a participant-observer within the framework of a shared understanding which is both contained in, and realised by, language. For Wittgenstein there is no non-critical-reflective point from which to make judgements about the world. This is because language and consciousness are for him not separable. They are, for Wittgenstein, aspects of the same encounter, there are no Kantian noumena, no "supersensibles" that underlie experience. The world is a series of language mediated particulars. Language is a set of local language games with no underlying structure as proposed by either classical or recent metaphysics. His opposition to science and logical positivism was on a similar basis. It still was caught in the thrall of metaphysics, of trying to discover and impose a universal structure on both the world and experience.

Wittgenstein's views on the non-privacy of experience are central to his philosophy and constitute a direct link to Kant. They can be construed as a continuation of Kant's discussion of the issue, with Kantian metaphysics linguistically transformed and the critical method extended by a radical reflexivity. The importance of Wittgenstein here is that he gives an account of the "inner" or more accurately the "inner/outer" which provides the framework for both subjectivity and the self that had not previously been provided in interpersonal or communicative theory.[35] The picture that emerges is close to that of Mead but is a development of Mead in that Mead's theory still implies the existence of a "metaphysical" rather than an engaged self. Whilst Mead shows that the self is constructed in social interaction it is still a Cartesian and therefore disengaged self. Further, as previously discussed, Mead is writing as a social psychologist and in a pre-linguistic turn context. Therefore he could not fully grasp the complexity of the relationship between language and the inner. What Wittgenstein does is to go beyond Mead to a fully radical position and to write without assuming the presence of a super "I" that is observing the "I - me" and "I - you" relationship which still persists in Mead.

Wittgenstein's discussion of private language is contained mainly in the *Philosophical Investigations* and runs from paragraph 241 until about paragraph 293. It is then interwoven onwards throughout the discussions of the rest of the part one.[36] Whilst the "private language argument" as it has come to be called, is the central part of Wittgenstein's account of the self, it cannot be dealt with in isolation from the rest of Wittgenstein's work. He is equally concerned with the range of issues that span meaning, thought, psychology and language as interwoven into the lifeworld. Indeed one of the problems in dealing with Wittgenstein is how to approach these separate issues, as his thought is a complex, if somewhat fragmented, whole.[37] Johnston refers to the "private language argument" as, 'the locus classicus for Wittgenstein's attack on the traditional conception of the Inner',[38] but it is much more (and perhaps much less) than this; it is also a positive thesis about the relationship between consciousness and language.

There has been some difference of opinion as what Wittgenstein was setting out to achieve in the "private language argument" and the text does not make the issue entirely clear. Some have taken it that he was arguing that a private language is impossible, others that a private language is in some sense possible, but that it would have to be always strictly private and therefore redundant.[39] However, the argument has been misread by most commentators including, most recently, by Johnston in his generally excellent discussion. Johnston and others normally assert that the discussion of private language commences at paragraph 243; in fact Wittgenstein offers us the "conclusion" to the argument in paragraphs 241 and 242.

> 241. "So you are saying that human agreement decides what is true and what is false?" -It is what human beings *say* that is true and false: and they agree in the *language* they use. That is not agreement in opinions but in forms of life.
>
> 242. If language is to be a means of communication there must be agreement not only in definitions but also (queer as this may sound) in judgements.[40]

His argument is that if humans are to communicate they must agree in their judgements, particularly their subjective judgements, otherwise there could be no language either public or private. The position, seen in a wider context is even more radical than this, in that without communication, as the use of a language, the idea of the human would not find a place.

In the exposition of the "private language argument" Wittgenstein explores the possibility of private reference to sensations. At issue is how does one know that a particular expression or word refers to a particular private sensation. A person could use either words or other signs to refer in isolation to the having of particular sensations. Wittgenstein says that there is nothing to prevent this process occurring, but in a detailed analysis shows that it is either an idle or totally arbitrary process. If the process were to be successful it would be self-defeating and the invented 'private' language in principle communicable and therefore not a private language. Wittgenstein goes on to show that a private language is not possible because private ostensive definition is not possible. If, for instance, I were to use a particular sign to designate a particular sensation on one occasion, then again on the next, occasion and so on, there would be no reason why the sign should refer to any or each occurrence of sensation. Repetition does not here establish a private rule of reference.

Wittgenstein's example is one in which he imagines a case where "S" is written in a diary each time a sensation occurs. He continues in the paragraph where he produces this example, to say: 'But what is this ceremony for? for that is all it seems to be! A definition surely serves to establish the meaning of a sign'.[41] Which of course this process does not. There would be no way of distinguishing between the original "definition" of "S" and any subsequent registration of "S". Would each registration be a new private ostensive definition? Wittgenstein's point is that there is no way of distinguishing between the two. At best this would be an idle process, but in fact would turn out to be a totally incoherent practice. There would be no difference to be drawn between following the private rule of registration of "S" and capriciously referring to "S". Johnston says, quite accurately:

> What is misleading here is the idea of a subjective justification, the notion that the individual can establish the correctness of her judgement by, for example consulting a table in her imagination.

And:

> she [the private linguist] cannot distinguish between being inclined to apply it [the sign "S"] and being justified in applying it.[42]

In the "private language argument" Wittgenstein, through the close critique of the use of language referring to private experience, shows that there is something fundamentally wrong with the way we regard the self and inner states. On close analysis the normal language that is used to refer to the inner states such as pain simply does not work. What this shows is that the model of the detached observer does not work. We do not sit as a detached observer of our own inner states assigning names or applying words to them. The whole framework of the Platonic model of the self fails, and so do more elaborate models of it that find expression through both rationalism and empiricism. Descartes' model, as an instance of a model within the Platonic framework, is clearly not appropriate, as it presupposes the existence of a "superself" within. It is this model of the "superself" within that is the source of much that misleads philosophical discussion. It is for instance the source of solipsism and the magnetic pull that it has in so many discourses of subjectivity.

Empiricist models also suffer from the same delusion. Locke's view of the self as an extensionless point in space and time which is the possessor of experiences is perhaps the clearest example of the fiction of the "superself". It is worth noting that Hume's more subtle insight prompted him to demur from this model of the subjective self in favour of a reflectively constructed self. However, he was not able to free himself from the overall paradigm and thus was, as Kant so exhaustively has shown, unable free himself from a sceptical solipsism.

The cultural implications here are at least as profound as the philosophical. They would relate to approaches to art, sciences and the law but further consideration is beyond the scope of this discussion.

Wittgenstein does offer the commencement of a positive thesis about the self and the relation of the self to subjective states as part of his overall view of language and philosophy in general. The "thesis", if it is indeed proper to call it so, is complex and infuriatingly abstruse.

There are a number of reasons, and possible reasons for this. Firstly, as Wittgenstein had sought to abandon metaphysics entirely he did not have the option of putting his thoughts into a framework or theory in any conventional sense. His method had to proceed, as it were, via the concrete; the processes of removing confusions and curing the diseases of thinking. He had become, in a sense, a victim of his own methodology. Secondly, having made the breakthrough that language was part of the world, including the "inner" world, and not just a means of describing it, he faced a task of daunting complexity; more complex than language itself. This task reflected the virtually infinite diversity of dealing with language in all the subtlety of its uses. Any luxury that might come of forms of reductionism or simplification was anathema. A language game based thematisation was all that could be followed and appropriately followed, but this seemed to pale beside the grand theories of metaphysics.

Other possible reasons for the unclarity of his positive view relate to his situation both personally and intellectually. Monk reports that in his later years Wittgenstein was constantly plagued by doubts about his sanity and the worth of his philosophical enterprise. This state frequently kept him from working for long periods. Between the period from his resignation from Cambridge in 1947 until his death in 1951 he was virtually homeless and plagued by deteriorating health and bouts of melancholy.[43] However we see in the published posthumous manuscripts that this was a period in which he was struggling to offer a positive novel view of the philosophy of psychology.[44] Yet, as outlined above, this was all carried on in an implied context of a critique of transcendental idealism. This element can be most clearly seen in *On Certainty* where the agenda is clearly a refutation of G. E. Moore and his philosophical method. For instance he accuses Moore of making serious misuse of the expression "I know", observing that, 'It is as if "I know" did not tolerate a metaphysical emphasis'.[45] He also spends quite a bit of time in related passages of *On Certainty* refuting the notion of philosophical foundations, clearly claiming that truth claims cannot be based on a notion of foundations without absurdity.

Despite these difficulties the positive thesis can be outlined and will be further developed in the following chapter. The positive thesis centres on seeing language as part of the world and not a means of describing it. But it is more than this, it involves understanding the complexity of language and the interwoven language games. Some are descriptive, others participative, others normative and so on. In real life it is common to play many such games at once; as it were to participate in many layers of experience. To use a Kantian analogy, here experience is not structured by the intuitions of space and time, rather by the use of language which is the complex intuition which shapes reality. We each relate to it as players in the web of language games. It is the playing of language games that shapes the experience of each person and not the "rules" of the game. There is in language games an irreducible practical element; an element of action and engagement with the real human world. Except for deliberately formal games like mathematics or computer languages the rules are second order factors, derivative of the playing of the games. He says, in illustration of the variety of language games and rules:

> And is there not also the case where we play and-make up the rules as we go along? And there is even one where we alter them-as we go along.
>
> 84. I said that the application of a word is not everywhere bounded by rules.[46]

In addition to the element of practice there is another important factor lying behind this observation. It is that there is not just a single meaning of a word or an expression. The same word or sentence has different meanings on each occasion of its use depending on a range of factors including, context, the purpose of the speaker, stress, tone of voice, accompanying gestures. What is more one cannot single out a particular instance of an expression as the cardinal or defining use. The meaning is the use in real employments of the word or expression.

It is difficult to judge whether or not Wittgenstein's positive thesis is merely rudimentary or not. The difficulty here is one of expectations. If one expects a full scale new post-metaphysical direction in philosophy then Wittgenstein has made only a tentative beginning. He may be acknowledged for his genius in making a breakthrough, but thereafter ensnared in a linguistic trap of his own making. If, on the other hand, one were to accept that following his post-metaphysical breakthrough the whole way of philosophising had changed, then showing us "how to go on" is all one can expect. In this case Wittgenstein's close textured analysis of the use of language in philosophical problems is the positive thesis. Showing "how to go on" is all one can do and the positive thesis is complete in doing so. To follow the Kantian analogy, as language shapes experience, when we untangle confusions about words which generate philosophical problems we also change the way we experience, and act in, the world.

The evidence is clear that Wittgenstein saw himself as taking the latter approach. For instance, he says in *The Blue Book*:

> Philosophers constantly see the method of science before their eyes, and are irresistibly tempted to ask and answer questions in the way science does. This tendency is the real source of metaphysics, and leads the philosopher into complete darkness.[47]

And from writing of about the same time:

> By the way, the old idea - roughly that of the (great) western philosophers - was that there were two kinds of problem in the scientific sense: essential, big, universal problems and inessential, as it were accidental, ones. According to our conception on the other hand we cannot speak in science of a *great*, essential problem.[48]

There are many similar comments about philosophy and philosophising sprinkled through the writings which might be selected as supporting evidence of this view. But the clearest evidence is in his method of philosophising itself, which shows that he saw his purposes as clearing away confusions in philosophy but most importantly as showing others how to do so.

Wittgenstein's views here are relevant to the theory of the self through the radical shift in the ways in which the "inner" and "outer" are viewed. His concern in the later years was with the philosophy of psychology, to which he applied this method of critique. Here he claims that we have to understand that the language of psychological states is not a description of the "inner" and does not, except in unusual circumstances, refer to inner states. This is why he points out that expressions of inner states can replace pain behaviour, such as grimacing or crying out, and are learned as an extension of pain behaviour. Wittgenstein emphasises the agreement in ways of "how to go on"; agreement in judgements is the basis of establishing rules not a consequence of rules in using language. This is why it is necessary to achieve some agreement in practices in order to achieve some agreement in understanding and thus in meaning. We are dealing here with a paradigm shift in which the public use of language, with all its historic complexity, is being appropriated by the individual to not only express but also to give form to their inner states.

There are very close parallels to Kant here which are worth exploring in detail in order to clarify the significance of Wittgenstein's contribution and to demonstrate the need to ground his views. The starting point for a comparison centres on the notion of judgement. Wittgenstein, like Kant sees judgement as a separate cognitive power. It is clear, for Wittgenstein, that humans have to agree in judgement in order be able to play the language games of truth, knowledge and similar central human activities.[49] The cognitive power of judgement is reflective and there must be agreement in judgements for language to be a means of communication. Any other communication, although possible, would be less than human communication. Such communication would be like two computers "talking" to each other, or animals simply signalling to each other.[50] Thus the famous, yet enigmatic, remark of Wittgenstein, 'if a lion could talk, we could not understand him'.[51] Our bases for judgement could not possibly be comparable.

How can such agreement in judgement be possible? The answer to this will reveal humans as communicative selves. But in order to move towards an answer, it is necessary to focus more closely on Kant and Wittgenstein as the notion of judgement found in the *Critique of Judgement* lays the ground for Wittgenstein's position. Kant says:

> We can also think of this problem [How are judgements of taste possible?] as follows: How is judgement possible in which the subject, merely on the basis of his *own* feeling of pleasure in an object, independently of the object's concept, judges this pleasure as one attaching to the presentation of that same object *in all other subjects,* and does so a priori, i.e. without being allowed to wait for other people's assent?[52]

Kant's answer, as has been discussed earlier, involves considerations of the supersensible and what he calls the *sensus communis* which, he claims, is to be found in each person. Kant goes on in the next section (§39) to say that in aesthetic judgement the 'pleasure must rest on the same conditions in everyone, because they are subjective conditions for the possibility of cognition as such'.[53] Kant recognises the subjectivity of judgement and its necessity as reflective judgement for "cognition as such". He also recognises that in this case, because the imagination is free, that is the reflective dimension, judgement cannot be "law guided" by reason. Kant though, unlike Wittgenstein, locates the universality of subjective judgement in "the same conditions in everyone", by which he is taken to mean, in each person. It is in this way that he accounts for the entitlement to assume that feelings of subjective pleasure in beauty are universally communicable. The same subjective conditions in each person Kant attributes to the *sensus communis* which each human has as an internal sense.

Wittgenstein says, as means of establishing similar qualities but without anything remotely as substantive as a *sensus communis*:

> Structure and feeling in music. Feelings accompany our apprehension of a piece of music in the way they accompany the events of our life.[54]

The Kantian ring is unmistakable here, but as the remarks go on to demonstrate, the feeling and the language of feeling that give the apprehension cannot be uncoupled without the loss of both.

There is a further element in Kant's discussion of the shared basis for reflexive judgement that is rather perplexing and equally unclear, yet nevertheless tantalising. It is the element of the "supersensible within". The notion of the "supersensible within" may be a key to understanding Kant's thought as it is the means by which he closes the gap between the noumenal and phenomenal worlds. In the *Critique of Judgement,* and particularly in the second part, the *Critique of Teleological Judgement,* Kant argues that the antinomies can be resolved be seeing that the "subjective purposeness", the noumenon within, and "objective purposeness", the order in nature, can be revealed as presentations of the same supersensible. Kant, in each of the critiques, always has resort to the supersensible to resolve antinomies. What appears to be a conflict in reasoning or experience can always be resolved at a "deeper" level. Kant also uses the supersensible, or supersensibles as he seems in the third *Critique* to roll three into one, to explain that what underlies good taste also underlies, in us at least, freedom and the morally good.[55] Kant does not actually directly relate the *sensus communis* to the "supersensible in us" but the relation is clearly implied in section 40 of the *Critique of Judgement.* Thus the *sensus communis* and the capacity to make our feeling of pleasure in (good) taste universally communicable are underpinned by the supersensible in us which is the same as that underlying the beauty of the object.

The supersensible here, that is, in ourselves, emerges from the darkness of the noumenal world, because reflective thought starts to realise it. It, of course, has no empirical content but in the process of reflection the form of the reflection is as important as its content. It is as if we are given a peep at the noumenal world, sufficient to show that at core, as beings, we are part of it. Kant thought it was this element that made us transcendental beings and accounted for the apparent contradictions between freedom and reason and endowed us with the divine capacity to imagine different worlds. The communicability of subjective states, and thus communicability in general, is instanced in aesthetic judgement because each person has access both to the supersensible within and to the supersensible underlying the beautiful in the object. It is also the reflective capacity to glimpse the supersensible within that underlies the legitimacy of all synthetic a priori knowledge. As our knowledge of the world is already within us ready to be manifested via the intuition.

Kant's whole philosophical enterprise was premised on rescuing metaphysics from what he saw to be the corrosive scepticism of Hume. So clearly he did not give up metaphysics as Wittgenstein did, but in many respects he came close to being forced to accept a transformed metaphysical position, once reflective judgement and communicability had been moved to central roles in the theory. This is because the application of the powers of cognition can in fact do much that was thought to require metaphysical entities; for instance to establish the autonomy of the will and the independence of judgement.

Wittgenstein also, curiously, believes us to be transcendental beings; but this is established not by the evidence of some "inner" but by the ability to use language. The transcendental element is in, or is, the language. Our use of language transcendentalises us. The discussion of the "soulless tribe" illustrates the point that we attribute the existence of a soul or inner being to a person on the basis of their use of language; not on the basis of the direct perception of "soul" or some inner substance.[56]

Wittgenstein's position is, again, notoriously difficult, and remains a matter of interpretation due to his obscure style. Perhaps an unfortunate legacy of Wittgenstein will be that it will not be possible to say, with any authority, just what his position was on a number of significant issues. What is offered here is, of necessity, a synthesis based on a reading of Wittgenstein and reflection on his thought.

Wittgenstein's implied claim that there is no metaphysical structure, at least of the sort envisaged by the great metaphysicians, that underlies reality must be accepted. He has shown that we can get along quite well in the world without making any such metaphysical assumptions, as long as we are careful about, and understand, our use of language. Johnston says Wittgenstein has offered us, 'a belated recognition that the philosopher's claim to special authority and metaphysical insight is the product of a confused self-understanding'.[57] The role of metaphysics as Wittgenstein saw it was to "plug the gaps" in our understanding or to "cover up" confusion. As such metaphysics has served a useful role in human history and carried forward the development of culture, but often at some cost to genuine understanding. Certainly metaphysics' claim to absolute truth becomes unsustainable. The sort of conceptual analysis engaged in by metaphysicians ends up in the human practice of how we use language and thus becomes a dispute about how certain words such as "true", "time", "God", "just", "good" and so on, function in certain language games. These language games are often key language games with respect to culture or social institutions, such as religion, science, law and politics, but their core is found in human practice and language games are embedded in that practice.

One element of language games not noted by Wittgenstein is their strategic importance. Habermas has drawn our attention to the strategic communication which builds on the apolitical Wittgensteinian model. It does matter who is coerced into playing certain roles in various language games and indeed who determines the rules of the games and which games are played at various times and places. Yet, this extension of the "language game" theory, if it can be called that, is quite consistent with Wittgenstein's position. In fact it is likely that he would have welcomed a development of his discussion of language games to cover their strategic use.

Wittgenstein himself seems to have been of an apolitical mould. He regarded modern times as bankrupt of culture and values, and famously refers to "the darkness of this time" in the preface to *Philosophical Investigations.* The horrors he had witnessed in the First World War had influenced him deeply and he certainly saw Nazism as a great evil. He is on record as saying to Drury: 'Just think what it must mean when a government of a country is taken over by gangsters', and predicted 'such horrors as people being burnt alive as witches'. But he had no great faith in democracy as a force to prevent such evil, he saw it as 'resembling a form of inefficient gesticulation'.[58] He held that the problems of modern times lay far deeper than even the devastating events of his time. The root cause could be found in metaphysics, particularly in its expression as science and the form of reason that went with it, with all its problems and evils. This form of reason, which Habermas has clearly defined as instrumental reason, Wittgenstein saw as leading to gravely inhuman consequences. He says, 'Man can regard all the evil within himself as delusion', by which he means being deluded.[59]

The importance of these considerations is that they lend weight to a conclusion that there must be some underlying transcendental element in Wittgenstein's philosophy. This becomes especially evident when one introduces either hermeneutic or strategic elements into Wittgenstein's discourse. The radical nature of Wittgenstein's philosophy is most clearly recognised by realising that he does not do away with metaphysics but rather externalises it, thereby rendering it impotent. The denial that there is an "inner" core of sensation such that private ostensive definition is possible strips metaphysics and transcendental philosophy of its noumenosity. Yet there is in his philosophy a linguistically transformed transcendental element. This element is revealed in the forms of life in which the players of language games participate.

Karl-Otto Apel recognises this element in his critique of Wittgenstein's "method" against a background of the hermeneutic tradition of Schleiermacher, Droysen and Dilthey. Apel says: '...the implicit question of whether it is possible to reveal the nonsensicality of metaphysical questions without adopting, in a disguised form a metaphysical - or for that matter, philosophical - standpoint oneself, appears to be the decisive question that Wittgenstein passed on to contemporary philosophy'.[60] Apel's answer to this question is, with qualification, decidedly that a 'disguised form of a metaphysical standpoint' survives in Wittgenstein's philosophy. Within the context of hermeneutic understanding the language game model locks us into understandings which occur within pre-existing language games; a move which Apel claims takes us into the "transcendental language game" or "language game of language games". However in order to understand this fact we need to step into a new language game (of understanding the previous language game). This leaves us with the options of either moving into the historically objectifying language game and thus admitting a hermeneutic model or accepting the absurd position that each language game must be supported by another language game if it is to be understood. Apel's conclusion is that there must be some precondition for understanding; some precondition for "intelligible meaning" in language games and this precondition is to be found in the 'historical mediation between language games' and 'mediation between the form (the *a priori* rule) and the content (the objectified meaning) of human life forms'.[61]

Apel's conclusions here point to the problem with Wittgenstein's "theory" as he presents it. That is, there has to be some precondition to be fulfilled in order for language games to be played which include the human dimension of understanding. To say that language games are rooted in "forms of life" as Wittgenstein does, is finally, not sufficient to ground or support the notion of language game. Here the term "language-game" is meant to bring into prominence the fact that the speaking of language is part of an activity, or form of life.

It indicates that Wittgenstein thought that the notion of "language game" needed support, but the introduction of the term "form of life", whilst it points to a grounding in practice, does little to help.

There are two reasons why it does so little. Firstly, Wittgenstein, throughout his work does nothing to elucidate the term, regarding any elucidation as an unwarranted degree of complication. So the term itself remains somewhat ineluctable. Secondly, the resort to "forms of life" could leave Wittgenstein open to accusations of behaviourism, that he so definitely rejects.[62]

What, however, Wittgenstein's vocation of forms of life does point to is that the necessity for agreement in action, in the context of a linguistically mediated community, is necessary for the playing of language games with understanding.

Thus, Wittgenstein has not escaped the necessity for some transcendental grounding in his approach. Even primitive language games such as that of the "builders" in the *Philosophical Investigations* presuppose the existence of a language using community. The a priori here is not in the underlying conditions of cognition as the Kantian model presupposes, but "up front" as it were, in the language itself. There is here presupposed an interactive framework which is neither subjective nor objective. Wittgenstein is successful in showing that an a priori does not depend upon the existence of inner states in the communicators but in a way he falls foul of his own private language argument in reverse. The publicity of language must stand in need of justification otherwise there would be no way of one builder knowing whether he was brought a "slab" or a "hammer" a building site of Babel could exist under Wittgenstein's "theory".

Notes

1 Monk, Ray (1990), *Ludwig Wittgenstein; the Duty of Genius*, The Free Press, New York, p. 401.
2 Ibid., p. 496.
3 See Janaway, Christopher (1989), *Self and World in Schopenhauer's Philosophy*, Oxford University Press, Oxford, Chapter 13. Janaway points out that Wittgenstein had thoroughly absorbed Schopenhauer's systems and this is reflected in the Tractatus and more strongly reflected in the early Notebooks. He shows that there are many points of close coincidence but also points of difference. Also see Pears, David (1971), *Wittgenstein,* Fontana, Glasgow, p. 45.
4 Monk, Ray (1990), *Ludwig Wittgenstein; the Duty of Genius*, The Free Press, New York, p. 36.
5 Ibid., p. 322.
6 Ibid., p. 30.
7 Ibid., p. 37
8 Pears, David (1988), *The False Prison, Volume II*, Oxford University Press, Oxford, p. 289.
9 Putnam, Hilary (1995), *Pragmatism; An Open Question*, Basil Blackwell, Oxford.
10 Ibid., p. 41.
11 Rorty, Richard (1982), *The Consequences of Pragmatism*, Harvester, Brighton, p. 20.
12 The Anschluss had made it impossible for Wittgenstein to return to Austria and his haven in Norway was becoming less secure. He was reluctant to resume the academic life as he had always been deeply ambivalent about what he saw to be the artificiality and intellectual pretentiousness of it all. Indeed, Monk makes the point that Wittgenstein was an intellectual, a creative philosopher and possibly a genius, but he was definitely not an academic in the traditional sense. His method of philosophising, tolerated at Cambridge would definitely not have been acceptable at the then more scholarly Oxford.
13 For instance, he was constantly in search of an identity, yet at the same time took pains to deny to himself and to others his true origins, either those of wealth and privilege or of being partly Jewish. Monk comments "...Wittgenstein himself felt that he was hiding something - felt that he was allowing people to think of him as an aristocrat when he was in fact a Jew". Whilst of course nothing whatever to be ashamed about, Wittgenstein felt that he had somehow misrepresented himself.
14 See Apel, Karl-Otto (1980), "Wittgenstein and Hermeneutic Understanding", in *Towards a transformation of philosophy*, trans. Adey, Glyn and Frisby, David, Routledge and Kegan Paul, London. Here Apel links Wittgenstein to the tradition of German philosophy since Schleiermacher.
15 Taylor, Charles (1995), *Philosophical Arguments*, Harvard University Press, Cambridge, Mass, p. 21. The view that Wittgenstein is operating in the context of a transcendental framework of argument has recently been put by Charles Taylor. "I think that some of the arguments adumbrated by the later Wittgenstein, and

which have been taken up by others from him, can most illuminatingly be spelled out as arguments of this[transcendental] mold."

16 For instance see Kripke, Saul A. (1982), *Wittgenstein on Rules and Private Language*, Basil Blackwell, Oxford. He presents an example of an excellent analysis and discussion of Wittgenstein but in the tradition of an analytic problematic.

17 Wittgenstein, Ludwig (1966), *Lectures and Conversations on Aesthetics, Psychology and Religious Belief*, ed. Cyril Barrett, Basil Blackwell, Oxford, p. 17.

18 Monk, Ray (1990), *Ludwig Wittgenstein; the Duty of Genius*, The Free Press, New York, p. 404.

19 It is always difficult to illustrate points from Wittgenstein's works as the context of remarks is often a long run of discursive exposition and the selections standing alone can seem to signify much less or much more than they actually do.

20 Wittgenstein, Ludwig (1961), *Tractatus Logico-Philosophicus*, trans. D. F. Pears and B. F. McGuinness, Routledge and Kegan Paul, London, pp. 147 - 149.

21 Wittgenstein, Ludwig (1969), *On Certainty*, eds. Anscombe, G. E. M. and von Wright, G. H. trans. Denis Paul and G. E. M. Anscombe, Basil Blackwell, Oxford, p. 63e.

22 Gullvåg, Ingemund (1981), "Wittgenstein and Peirce", in *Wittgenstein - Aesthetics and Transcendental Philosophy*, eds. Kjell S. Johannessen and Tore Nordenstam, Verlag Hölder- Pichler-Tempsky, Vienna.

23 Ibid., p. 81.

24 Wittgenstein, Ludwig (1958), *The Blue and Brown Books*, Blackwell, Oxford, p. 18.

25 Wittgenstein, Ludwig (1980), *Culture and Value*, ed. von Wright, G. H., trans. Peter Winch, Basil Blackwell, Oxford, p. 11e.

26 Taylor, Charles (1995), *Philosophical Arguments*, Harvard University Press, Harvard, MA, p. 21.

27 Wittgenstein, Ludwig, *The Blue and Brown Books*, p. 6.

28 Wittgenstein, Ludwig, *Culture and Value*.

29 Wittgenstein, Ludwig, *The Blue and Brown Books*, p. 6, also see p. 26 ff.

30 Wittgenstein, Ludwig (1963), *Philosophical Investigations*, trans. G. E. M. Anscombe, Basil Blackwell, Oxford, p. 51e.

31 This view is taken by Thomas McCarthy of both Wittgenstein and Peter Winch. See, McCarthy, Thomas (1981), *The Critical Theory of Jürgen Habermas*, MIT Press, Cambridge, Mass., p. 168-72.

32 See *Culture and Value*, p. 47, here Wittgenstein says "And my conceit of being an extraordinary person has been with me much longer than my awareness of my particular talent."

33 Wittgenstein, Ludwig, *Culture and Value*, p. 27e.

34 See Monk, op. cit., especially Chapter 18.

35 I here use Paul Johnston's terminology in dealing with the Wittgensteinian discussion. These terms reflect Wittgenstein's language and avoid some of the difficulties encountered in reference to "self", "subject" and "Ego". I will return

to some remarks about these terms later. See Johnston, Paul (1993), *Wittgenstein: Rethinking the Inner*, Routledge, London.

36 Wittgenstein, Ludwig, *Philosophical Investigations.*

37 Ray Monk, Norman Malcolm and others have drawn attention to the way in which Wittgenstein collected his writings, by cutting out single sentences or sometimes paragraphs from notebooks and tying them together.

38 Johnston, Paul, *Wittgenstein: Rethinking the Inner*, p. 18.

39 See Kenny, Anthony (1973), Wittgenstein, Penguin, Harmondsworth, Chapter 10.

40 Wittgenstein, Ludwig, *Philosophical Investigations*, p. 88e.

41 Ibid., para 258.

42 Johnston, Paul, *Wittgenstein Rethinking the Inner*, pp. 21-22.

43 See Monk, *Ludwig Wittgenstein; The Duty of Genius*, Pt IV. See particularly p. 522.

44 A further possible element was the influence of Cambridge philosophy on Wittgenstein. It is conventional amongst Wittgenstein scholars to assume that Cambridge was pretty kind to him and that he was indulged there, even if he was not suited to the academic life. The view has been put that Wittgenstein's complaints about Cambridge arose principally from the eccentricities of his personality. However there is one sense in which Cambridge had a clear effect on Wittgenstein and that was in the setting of the agenda for his philosophising.

45 Wittgenstein, Ludwig, *On Certainty*, para. 482.

46 Wittgenstein, Ludwig, *Philosophical Investigations*, p. 39e.

47 Wittgenstein, Ludwig, *The Blue and Brown Books*, p. 18.

48 Wittgenstein, Ludwig, *Culture and Value*, p. 10e.

49 This can be illustrated by many passages for example, "If someone says he knows something, it must be something that, by general consent, he is in a position to know". *On Certainty*, para. 555.

50 The evidence would seem to be clear now that all communication in the higher animals has a degree of complexity that approaches human communication, although genuine language seems only to be conclusively human.

51 Wittgenstein, Ludwig (1982), *Last Writings on the Philosophy of Psychology, Volume 1*, eds, von Wright, G. H. and Nyman Heikki trans. C. G. Luckhardt and Maximilian A. E. Aue, Basil Blackwell, Oxford, para. 190.

52 Kant, Immanuel (1987), *The Critique of Judgement*, trans. Werner S. Pluhar, Hackett Indianapolis, p. 153.

53 Ibid., p. 159.

54 Wittgenstein, Ludwig, *Culture and Value*, p. 10e.

55 See Ibid., p. 14. The relevant passage is quoted at length in the previous chapter.

56 Wittgenstein, Ludwig (1988), *Wittgenstein's Lectures on the Philosophy of Psychology 1946-47,* Harvester Wheatsheaf, Hemel Hempstead, p. 288.

57 Johnson, Paul, *Wittgenstein: Rethinking the Inner*, p. 237.

58 Bouveresse, J. (1991), "Wittgenstein and the Modern World", in *Wittgenstein Centenary Essays*, ed. Griffiths, A. Phillip, Cambridge University Press,

Cambridge, pp. 19 - 21.

59 Wittgenstein, Ludwig, *Culture and Value*, p. 67.

60 Apel, Karl-Otto (1980), *Towards a Transformation of Philosophy*, trans. Glyn Adey and David Frisby, Routledge and Kegan Paul, London, p. 19.

61 Ibid., p. 37.

62 See Johnston, Paul, *Wittgenstein: Rethinking the Inner*, pp. 205-210. Here Johnston shows that Wittgenstein recast the Inner/Outer distinction rather than denying the Inner. See also Armstrong, David (1968), *A Materialist Theory of Mind*, Routledge, London; Armstrong accuses Wittgenstein of behaviourism.

10 Conclusion: An Interpersonal Theory

In this chapter a positive proposal is put for an interpersonal theory of the self, based on the development of the transcendental theme established in preceding chapters.

What will be proposed is a form of transformed transcendental synthesis of selves, based on imagination, incorporating previous discussion and some further insights from Wittgenstein and Kant's last works. The self is to be established via a transformed transcendental reflection on the diverse selves that we present in concrete situations and the constitutive conditions required for those situations. The positive theory offered argues that certain conditions have to be met in order for an interpersonal theory of the self to be established. These conditions are the cognitive capacities required for language use and the conditions of freedom and imagination, which must be added to interpersonal theory in order to complete a theory of the self. Such a theory will be adequate to support communicative theory and accommodate an expressive component that would meet Taylor's objections to communicative theory.

It is necessary here to again examine closely some aspects of the late philosophy of Kant in the light of Wittgenstein, Apel and communicative theory. Also relevant to the discussion is Kant's attempt to complete a theory of human cognitive powers. The most significant works for the completion of his theoretical suite are the *Critique of Judgement* and parts of the *Opus postumum,* sometimes referred to as the incomplete fourth *Critique.* In this last work, Kant not only tries to unify his critical philosophy, but extends his discussion of the cognitive powers to include the idea of self-creation in a communicable world. It is also here that he makes an attempt to manifest the " supersensibles within" through the imagination in the process of self creation. However, this late work is regarded as problematic in terms of its quality and completeness and it is necessary to provide some comment on the status of this work prior to engaging in more detailed discussion.

Following the completion of the *Critique of Judgement,* Förster notes, Kant saw that there was a further gap in critical philosophy and set about a work that would close that gap.[1] This was the manuscript of the *Opus postumum,* left incomplete on his desk at the time of his death.

From correspondence reported by Förster it seems that Kant sought to unite physics and metaphysics in a unified whole which would be the synthesis of his whole critical philosophy. A fascinating history of the manuscript is related by Förster in his introduction to the work. He explains how significant sections of the manuscript were effectively " lost" for many years after Kant's death as the manuscript passed through various hands. He also recounts how the sequence of the leaves became disordered as Kant's relations attempted to profit from sale the of the manuscript and how the ill-founded opinion was formed in academic circles that the work was the product of a senile mind. In fact, the majority of the manuscript was written before 1801, when, it is recorded, that Kant's mental and physical health began to deteriorate. Finally disputes between publishers and editors delayed the publication of the work until 1936-38. The current text represents the first English translation published in 1993. As Förster comments, what one makes of the manuscript depends on how one relates it to the body of the philosophy, and in particular the major critical works. There are certainly developments of major themes from earlier works that warrant serious examination.

In 1798, so Förster informs us, Kant wrote to Christian Garve of the 'pain like that of Tantalus' on seeing before him 'the unpaid bill of my incomplete philosophy'.[2] Kant was referring to the necessity he then perceived to prepare a major critical work to complete his philosophical project. Kant's intentions in the last proposed major work are not fully clear, but two elements are evident. Firstly, he wanted to write a critical account of natural science equivalent to the three major critiques. Secondly he wanted to unify his work in a way that now seemed clear to him. As his correspondence informs us, he saw the late work as, 'a chief work, ...which was an absolute whole completing his system'.[3]

The *Opus postumum* might, on first sight, appear as a rather fragmentary work with a long section on physics followed by a discussion of transcendental philosophy, then of the self-positing subject and finally a self-positing God. Yet there is a unifying theme to the work which can only be evaluated in the light of the three *Critiques*. Roughly, the theme can be outlined as follows. In the *Critique of Pure Reason* , the presence, within us of the intuitions of space and time allow for the possibility, a priori, of physics in which our form of cognition makes the experience of the empirical world possible. Here then is a necessary link between the cognitive power of humans and knowledge of the physical universe. In the *Critique of Practical Reason,* read in conjunction with the *Groundwork*, it is established that humans are free beings and thus determine their will as actors in the universe. This capacity for freedom renders us capable of using the knowledge of the physical universe to create and reshape it according to the laws of nature. The *Critique of Judgement* establishes that humans are beings that are capable of reflective understanding and therefore, capable of recognising themselves, and others, as beings, in a world of common understanding. In the fourth "critique" Kant recognises that the worlds of physical, rational, moral and aesthetic experience are unified in transcendental philosophy via the synthetic a priori, and have their essence in common supersensibles that may manifest themselves differently.

An indication of this development in Kant's thought can be seen in the following passage:

> Space and time are products (but primitive products) of our imagination, hence self-created intuitions, inasmuch as the subject affects itself and is thereby appearance, not thing in itself.[4]

The influence of his later thought, particularly the development of the cognitive power of imagination in the *Critique of Judgement,* can be seen here as a reconstruction of the "Transcendental Aesthetic" of the *Critique of Pure Reason.*

In completing his system Kant says that the unifying principle in which all supersensibles adhere, finally, is God.[5] He gives a glimpse of his vision of the complete system in the following passage:

> Transcendental philosophy is the act of consciousness whereby the subject becomes the originator of itself and, thereby, also of the whole object of technical-practical and moral-practical reason in one system - ordering all things in God, as in one system.[6]

From the point of view of his philosophical system the figure of God becomes important in the later philosophy as the unifying principle of all things; especially of the unification of the cognitive powers, both within themselves, and with the underlying elements of the objects of cognition.

There are also some important additional elements to Kant's scheme which emerge in the late work. One is the elevation of transcendental philosophy, again in Kant's carefully defined sense, over metaphysics. Kant says: 'Transcendental philosophy bears this name, because it precedes metaphysics and supplies the latter with principles'.[7] Another is that persons, as beings and as subjects, are both self-positing and self-determining. This is because they have the power not only of gaining synthetic a priori knowledge, but also of unifying it, both subjectively and objectively. Kant is not fully clear in his exposition of the self-positing being in the *Opus postumum* but some elements can be discerned. The key to self-positing being is that humans are capable of transcendental thought and that is through transcendental thought that they are capable of "self-creation". He says, by way of illustration:

> Transcendental philosophy is a principle which constitutes itself, in a system of ideas, into the totality of beings; the latter is not [derived] from experience but is thoroughly self-determining *a priori* for experience and its possibility - [as] an absolute whole in experience.[8]

Here, it may be noted, Kant presages some elements of Hegel's transcendental phenomenology, but here he is clear that it is the capacity for transcendental thought that provides the objects of experience and self determination. Metaphysical thought and its objects are only available to us via transcendental reasoning. In this sense transcendental thought is both ontological and epistemological. The ontological is prior, but the being of the objects of knowledge is created by the being of the subject of transcendental thought which has the objects of knowledge available to it a priori.

Wittgenstein's position is similar to Kant but for him the ontological collapses into the epistemological as meaning and use coincide in the subject as a user of language. The passages in the *Opus Postumum* frequently have a "Wittgensteinian" character about them, both because they are rather fragmentary and repetitive in presentation, and more importantly, because they address some of the same issues regarding the relation of the "inner" to the "outer" and the place of human experience in the world, or in Kant's case, "the universe". Kant here did not abandon metaphysics, as Wittgenstein did so definitively, but the inexorable development of his critical philosophy leads him to a position where metaphysics is superseded by transcendental philosophy. The "method" of critical reflective transcendental thinking becomes a more significant factor in the relation of consciousness to the world than the understanding of metaphysical elements. In this late philosophy the system of relating to the world becomes primary, with metaphysics providing principles of understanding. Once Kant had reached the position of accepting that humans were autonomous beings with communicability as a basic principle of judgment, the next step to, as Kant says, "make oneself" becomes inevitable. In this development of thought, metaphysics becomes a set of synthetically constructed principles for the cognitive powers and not a determining framework.

The character of this development is illustrated by the following key passage:

> Transcendental philosophy is the capacity of the self-determining subject to construe itself as *given* in intuition, through the systematic complex of the ideas which, *a priori,* make the thoroughgoing determination of the subject as object (its existence) into a problem. *To make oneself,* as it were.[9]

Unfortunately, Kant, in this incomplete work, does not provide the sort of argumentation that would support and elaborate the insights that appear. Yet, some conclusions can be drawn which show that Kant took significant steps towards establishing a framework for communicative theory and provide a transcendental basis for an intersubjectively based self. These steps will be explored through an examination of the way in which Kant supplants the centrality of metaphysics in his scheme.

What would be the consequences for Kant's system if metaphysics were to be "overcome" or withdrawn from the system?

In the philosophy up until the *Critique of Practical Reason,* that is, the pre-critical works, the *Critique of Pure Reason* and the *Groundwork* the consequences would have been devastating; the whole structure could not be maintained without a noumenal world and the metaphysical support for the categories. After Kant recognised the priority of freedom over reason and the autonomy of the will in the second critique, the necessity for a metaphysical structure starts to fade, although, of course, it never disappears altogether. In the *Critique of Judgement*, whilst a metaphysical framework is still clearly present, in the discussion of the "supersensibles" for instance, the system of transcendental critique is becoming more important as evidenced by the discussion of the *sensus communis* and the principle of communicability of subjective states. In the Introduction to the *Critique of Judgement* Kant distinguishes between a transcendental principle and a metaphysical principle. The context of the distinction is the outline of "The principle of the formal purposeness of nature" which he wishes to distinguish from practical purposeness such as that present in the determination of the will.

He says here, by way of definition:

> A transcendental principle is one by which we think the universal a priori condition under which alone things can become objects of our cognition in general; on the other hand, a principle is called metaphysical if it is one [by] which [we] think the a priori condition under which alone objects whose concepts must be given empirically can be further determined a priori.[10]

It is clear here that the transcendental principle refers to the cognitive powers and their capacity to generate universals, whilst the metaphysical principal requires empirical content.

When the third critique is read in conjunction with the political writings it is clear that a metaphysical framework is now not crucial to the critical works. For instance, in *Perpetual Peace* Kant draws upon the notion of the purposiveness of nature to, 'permit harmony to emerge among men through their discord, even against their wills'.[11] This purposeness he says is driven by a "transcendent idea", even though there is some implication of metaphysical content in its reality.

It is clear that Kant never rejected metaphysics. In fact he thought he had saved metaphysics from the scepticism of Hume. But as his work developed along the path towards the critical-reflective method, metaphysics becomes less and less essential to the success of his daunting project and is as it were relegated to the function of ensuring empirical knowledge, rather than providing a underlying ground for all cognition. The significance of this shift in Kant's thinking is that it paves the way for a critical reflective approach to the self and the subject. An approach which does not depend upon the existence of some "self-substance" or on a substantial ego, as supposed by Descartes.

It is at this point that there is a continuity through to the work of Peirce with his insights into "autonomy" of signs, to Wittgenstein with his insights into the nature the subject, experience and language and to the communicative theories of Apel and Habermas.

Apel's position on the self and self-consciousness is probably the most Kantian developed in recent philosophy and represents a pivotal point in attempting to incorporate elements of Peirce and Wittgenstein in his communicative theory. He opposes the idea of an unengaged ego outside the world and asserts a progressive transformation of the Kantian approach to the determination of a subjectivity. Apel believes that the actual content of the Kantian system is incorrect, because the notion of "things-in-themselves", which are available only via the transcendental deduction, marks a retreat back to a form of Cartesianism, to an ego disengaged from the world of reality. However, Apel also believes that, 'the critical and metaphysical deep meaning of the Kantian system', must be respected.[12] Apel's view is consistent with the full implications of Kant's statement that every thought is accompanied by "I think" and not just the "cogito" and, also, is further consistent with Kant's late philosophy. Apel's transformation of this observation by Kant establishes, via the notion of the "ideal communication community", intersubjectivity as a precondition for meaning and thus a precondition for self-consciousness. Apel uses the device of a critical re-appraisal of a hermeneutic position to, in part, establish his claim by appealing to a "hermeneutic synthesis of understanding" to establish the unity of intersubjective consciousness. Kant in the parallel case would have appealed to the synthesis of apperception to establish the unity of individual consciousness. It is surprising however that whilst he uses Kant's notion of a "fact of reason" to lend support for the "a priori of the communication community". Apel does not invoke the *sensus communis* nor the principle of universal communicability from the *Critique of Judgement* to support this central notion.[13] His reasons for not doing so are far from clear.

For whilst the *sensus communis* may have Cartesian vestiges, the principle of universal communicability has within it the concept of the "a priori of the communication community".

Apel's most productive response to Kant lies in the discussion of the transformation of the subject of consciousness. According to Apel's account, the unity and coherence of consciousness is now to be found in a post-linguistic "hermeneutic synthesis of communication". It is only as members of the communication community, via the playing of language games, that we are able to differentiate self-consciousness and other consciousness. Non-linguistic animals, for instance, would not be able to do this. Apel, it would seem, is saying that we must first, by a priori reasoning, postulate the communication community as a "we" and then through the pragmatic-reflexive use of language establish an "I" as a point within the community. This pragmatic-reflexive move upon further reflection establishes the transcendental communication community as the condition for the postulation of other "I's" within the community. Such other "I's" must necessarily exist, on the same terms as the "I" of the subject. This view is captured in Apel's statement that 'the purposive-rational understanding of subjective, nature-manipulating actions and their results must be linguistically articulatable even to be comprehensible to the individual subject of knowledge'.[14] And thus he claims, as discussed earlier, that the intersubjective subject of understanding must be presupposed. This view of Apel goes beyond Mead, for instance, in that he attempts to offer an a priori ground for the reflexive self in the "communication community". But this is only a partial explanation because Apel finally remains too Kantian in his approach. His "ideal communication community" is still locked into a transcendental idealism closely akin to the "transcendental synthesis of apperception" of the *Critique of Pure Reason*. Apel's transformation of Kantian philosophy, particularly with respect to the self, is not nearly as complete as he supposes it to be. He may have shown the necessity for 'the primacy of *communicative intersubjectivity*',[15] but he has not given a non-idealistic account of it.

"Communication" here is being used in a general dialogical sense that goes beyond, yet can incorporate, communicative reason and communicative action. Dialogic communication is a step prior to the reflexive self-identification of the communicators and thus to the presupposition of an intersubjectivity as prior to subjectivity.

In a recent discussion which takes a universalist communicative position, but contrasts with the transcendentalism of Apel, Seyla Benhabib argues for a socially embedded self. In *Situating the Self*, she argues for a universalist position for a socially and morally embedded view of the self which she calls "egalitarian reciprocity". She sets out six principles which formalise the notion. The last two set out a current version of mutual respect that derives from notions of a kingdom of ends transferred into communicative theory context. To quote in part from these:

> 5. ...we ought to *respect* each other as beings whose standpoint is worthy of equal consideration and that furthermore.
> 6. We ought to treat each other as concrete human beings whose capacity to express this standpoint we ought to enhance by creating, whenever possible, social practices embodying the discursive ideal (the principle of egalitarian reciprocity).[16]

In defence of communicative ethics against criticisms levelled by Albrecht Wellmer, Agnes Heller and Otfried Höffe, she points out that her view, as distinct from that of Habermas, emphasises the 'rationality of the procedure for attaining agreement', rather than agreement itself. It is essential to modern universalist ethics, she claims, that the emphasis be on 'sustaining those normative practices and moral relationships within which reasoned agreement *as a way of life* can flourish and continue'.[17]

There are strong echoes of Kant's political philosophy here, particularly with respect to freedom and the notion of "the public use of reason". It will be useful to explore further Kant's notion as a background to Benhabib's notion of "social practices embodying the discursive ideal" as yet another element of the communicative self.

In the essay *What is Enlightenment* Kant takes the notion of "general communicability" first developed in the *Critique of Judgement* to the public sphere. Here he distinguishes between the "*private*" and "*public*" uses of reason. The distinction, which is far from fully transparent, relates to freedom as the basic requirement of enlightenment. The public use of reason is always free and unrestricted, directed to the world at large, whereas the private use of reason is always restricted, particularly by some external requirement. The example Kant gives is to contrast the activity of the scholar, who uses public reason to address the world at large with that of the civil servant who's use of reason is private because restricted to his or her role.[18] The distinction is confusing, despite Kant's explanation, because it would seem that the civil servant is playing a public role. It may be an anachronistic use of language because "private" here means restricted rather than inward in any sense. There is a sense, outlined by Kant, in which the civil servant can employ the public use of reason as a private person. It is, however, what Kant has to say about the public use of reason, rather than the distinction which is of real interest. The interest lies in the fact that Kant is proposing that freedom is the basis of enlightenment and the free use of reason is the public use of reason. The public use of reason presupposes the existence of a community at large, which in turn presupposes the existence of an audience of persons who are similarly free to use their reason publicly in debate.

Kant here links freedom and reason to a criteria of both communicability and publicity. Whilst being careful not to offend his political masters, whose authority he genuinely respected, he sows the seeds for a more radical political agenda based on something approaching, 'reasoned agreement as away of life'.[19]

Benhabib's emphasis on the conditions for agreement rather than consensus itself is correct, and is supported by Kant's later philosophy. Her support for practices embedded in a way of life, based on the notion of "a Kingdom of ends" is a significant advance. Yet once again, as with Apel, there is lacking here a theory of intersubjectivity sufficient to support the "reasoned agreement as a way of life".

Against this theoretical landscape how can a universalist theory of the self be constructed?

It is a commonplace amongst philosophers, from Aristotle to Putnam, to note that as human animals we are born with a set of basic capacities and genetic inheritances. These include the capacity for sensory experience, including basic perception and emotion. We also, as claimed by Locke and later Peirce have, as a species, the capacity to represent experience in signs, most frequently in words. For non-Cartesian theories of the self, including communicative theory, selves are generated from the material of experience in interaction, usually with other selves, in a social world.

To account for how such theories are possible it is necessary to take the lead from the Kantian model and Apel's treatment of it, a linguistically mediated transcendental theory can be constructed. In this case the conditions; that is the transcendental element, must come from an actual human lifeworld.[20] It is contended that the presupposition of any form of self, even a Cartesian or Lockean self, must also presuppose a lifeworld of free autonomous beings who are capable of mutually constructing their own world. It is further contended that the self must be social in a form such as that proposed in a paradigmatic fashion by Mead. By contrast, a self which is based on a mere contractual model such as the self of the classical theory of Hobbes, or a self based on an introspective model such as Descartes', is incoherent. As previously shown it would fall foul of the "private language argument" as any process of self identification/re-identification would fail.

Mead can be credited with the paradigm shift to an intersubjective view of the self. However his theory was finally restricted by his "behaviourism". He was left with the position that the self was socially constructed out of the "I - me" relationship in which behaviour was seen as an important reference for other identification. Mead was influenced also by Darwin and the social behaviourism of his time. He thus looked for a locus of the self in the biological existence of the individual. The intersubjective self, for Mead, became a social epiphenomenon on the behavioural relationship.

There are however many elements in Mead that prepared the ground for future developments. For instance there are some very distinct echoes of Wittgenstein and "forms of life" in Mead. He discusses the importance of the game in the acquisition of concepts and the sense of self by the child. There is also a strong presence of his pragmatist roots as he stresses the role of the community from a pragmatic point of view, as the medium in which selves, as socially constructed, are generated and flourish. But all these elements did not fully reflect the 'linguistic turn' pioneered later by Wittgenstein. Nor did they fully reflect Peirce's radical treatment of signs as Mead continued to see signs as things that were instrumentally used to communicate concepts; not as intrinsic to the concepts and the conceptualiser.

Wittgenstein's contribution to the intersubjective theory of the self is most significant. It was he who made the critical step to radically transform transcendental philosophy by a new understanding of language. He was to see language as part of the world and not simply as a description of it. We see through his philosophy that there is no "noumenal world" of things underlying language. The illusion of a noumenal world is created by the externality of meaning to the subject of consciousness; a model which Wittgenstein has shown to be fatally flawed.

Following Wittgenstein we can see that language is the "transcendental" medium by which we persons construct the world and literally are in it. Selves are, as Habermas claimed, socially individuated autonomous beings, but they are only so because they can each be reflexively identified as self-creating against the transcendental presupposition of autonomous self determining beings, who create that being by creating their world through the essentially intersubjective medium of language.

Kant in *The Critique of Judgement,* distinguishes between the *sensus communis* or community sense and its opposite; what one might call a "sensus privatus".[21] The "sensus privatus" has a very restricted range in that it refers to the very narrow reference of a subject to immediate experience. When that experience is generalised in any way, such as "this is pleasing" or "this is good", even to "me" the *sensus communis* is invoked, in that this judgement is in theory communicable to all others. It is also, Kant claims, the *sensus communis* that leads us to adopt three maxims. First that reason is never passive and it is therefore autonomous and not prejudiced, second that we should adopt a "broadened way of thinking" and thus judge from a "universal standpoint", and thirdly that we should be consistent in our way of thinking.[22] The second maxim is of great importance for all of Kant's philosophy but particularly his political philosophy such as, in *Perpetual Peace,* it comes to constitute the "transcendental formula of public right". Kant says: 'All actions that affect the rights of other men are wrong if their maxim is not consistent with publicity'.[23]

Whilst the principle of communicability applies in the first instance to aesthetic judgements, Kant also clearly says that it is a principle that applies, via the imagination to cognition in general.[24] But communicability leads to sociability as being at the basis of humanity, not just in an emotive sense but as a requirement for reflection, by taking the general standpoint, and thus for all cognition including the power of reason. Kant here has moved a vast distance from the first *Critique* in which the self was considered a shell or organising principle for the synthesis of the manifold, to the self as a communicating social being. Here, in Kant, we find the beginnings of a communicative theory, incorporating a unity of reason, morality (and action) and judgement, particularly aesthetic judgement.

It is worth noting that it would seem to be a significant oversight on the part of both Apel and Habermas that in their development of communicative theory they do not pay sufficient attention to the late works of Kant and in particular to the *Critique of Judgement.* and the political essays. Even in Habermas' recent writings, where, for instance, he seeks to establish "a new paradigm, that of mutual understanding" in the essay "Themes in Post-Metaphysical Thinking", he fails to provide any discussion of Kant's development of the principle of communicability as a basic transcendental principle.[25]

Kant himself was, as has been noted, already well on the way to a transformation of his own philosophy. He was, characteristically, reluctant to admit that he was in fact revising any of his earlier views. He always insists that each development is a further move towards the development of the unity of the system in which earlier views are incorporated in a larger architectonic. Whilst Kant can claim that he was continuing the process of the development of transcendental philosophy there were significant revisions of his work. Reason is progressively dethroned as the sovereign cognitive power, by its being subjected first to the critique of freedom, then to imagination as reflection, and finally to communicability as a transcendental condition. Also, the place of metaphysics as an underlying structure progressively gives way, first to the autonomy of the will, then in the final sections of the *Opus postumum* to transcendental method. Kant did not anticipate the "linguistic turn" in philosophy as he continued to see language as representing concepts, nor did he give up his belief in fundamental essences, such as that of the self as the basis of each individual. He was however, a much more complex thinker in respect of the constitution of the self than most commentators allow.[26]

Habermas has turned to Mead and Apel to the "transformation of the transcendental subject" to provide a intersubjective self that can stand as the subject of communicative theory. Other thinkers such as Joas and Honneth have looked in similar directions to support a theory of the modern identity, with Benhabib moving to a substantive socially grounded version of communicative theory.[27] Whilst other have looked in completely different directions; for instance Charles Taylor takes a genealogical approach and supports an expressivist view of the self as the potential bearer of a substantive good.

None of these attempts have been fully successful to date. Thus philosophy remains in a parlous position with respect to asserting human self-respect and creative self-assertion in a world which is increasingly becoming "globalised", where sovereignty is becoming increasingly corporatised, where knowledge as "information" is becoming increasingly reified as a commodity, where the rich versus poor divide widens and takes new forms and where personal identities struggle to find recognition. The replies of non-subject centred theories in ethics and policy have remained attenuated and problematic due to a lack theoretical grounding.

Communicative theory as applied to ethics, policy, law and science offers the best prospect for a coherent theory that steers between on the problems of traditional objectivist or relativist theories. At the heart of communicative theory is an intersubjective theory of the self, but as has been indicated, such a theory has not, to date, been adequately articulated. The problem with intersubjective theories, is that they do not take a sufficiently radical line with respect to the combined issues of privacy of experience and subjectivity. It is only by taking a development from the later Wittgenstein, and to a lesser degree Peirce and Kant, that the issue of the non-privacy of experience can be put into perspective and lead to a "publicity" of understanding and justification for the self. Mead, who has been so heavily relied upon by Habermas and recently by Honneth,[28] has sketched an outline of an intersubjective structure that relates the ego to the "generalised other" in the process of social integration. He also recognised that language was of importance for this process. But, significantly, he did not provide a theory that is capable of accounting for the existence of autonomous selves in an intersubjective framework. Kant's problem as how the qualities of humanity in general can be related to individual persons remains for Mead and Habermas.

The transition to a theory of the self, sufficient to support intersubjectivity and thus communicative theory, can be made by "transcendentalising" the private language argument. As previously proposed, Wittgenstein should be read as offering a critique of transcendental idealism. In the framework implicit in Wittgenstein's later philosophy is a view, to put it crudely, that language is experience. That when I use the word "I" to communicate that my consciousness is experiencing, I am appropriating to my experience what is already in language. Wittgenstein's lengthy and abstruse discussions of experience, including pain, colour and subjective states are attempts to express what is extremely difficult to express. Not just that we are language, but how we are so. Language is complex, multi-modal; it is both "inner" and "outer". The private language argument shows that strictly private reference to the inner is not possible, but it in turn eventually loses its way as an argument about the nature of language and language use. This is because the use of a proxy form of private definition to illustrate the eventual futility of such a process, turns out to be as non-sensical as the claim that experience could exist without any language. Wittgenstein does give us a sketch of "how to go on", he says:

> 381. How do I know this colour is red? - It would be an answer to say: "I have learned English".[29]

The act of imagination required to grasp this position can be sketched as follows. If we are not able to communicate a content to others we could not communicate it to ourselves either.

Does this mean that we would not see the colour red or feel this particular ache?

This was the sort of issue that Wittgenstein struggled with, but failed to resolve clearly. The reason he failed to resolve it is that he could not resort to a non-descriptive philosophical position. There was in his theory no "stepping out" of language; no getting behind it to see if what we mean by "red" is really red. Peirce had reached a not totally dissimilar position when he claimed that we cannot think outside signs.

At this point one must step finally and radically away from the Platonic and Cartesian views of the self or human essence. Descartes answer to the question "What then am I?" is deeply misleading. He would have been closer to the mark if he had answered, rather than I am a being that thinks, feels etcetera, along the lines that feeling, thinking, reasoning and using language creates a being, but even this would still have been misleading. The *cogito* is deeply confused because it again offends fundamentally against the principle of the impossibility of a private language. The reference of the first "I" is precisely the sort of private ostensive definition that Wittgenstein has shown to be incoherent. The reason why the "argument" has travelled so far in modern philosophy is because this is the sort of deluded ostensive definition of which each person believes themselves capable. In Wittgenstein's terms this is a paradigm case of the "beetle in the box" for each person. The thinking of a conscious subject of consciousness is so deeply ingrained into our ways of being, institutions and culture that a radical reconception is hard to maintain. It is only possible because we are able to use language in an intersubjective mode. It is at this point that we must give up the Augustinian "inwardness" or Taylor's resort to a divine presence within. Such claims to an inner presence would again require a similar radical critique.

Wittgenstein was right that our way of using language can mislead us. And, it might be added, languages themselves, as living historical organisms, can be full of traps. He was also correct to point out the all pervasiveness, great complexity and diversity of language. In dealing with philosophical issues; this factor cannot be underestimated; it is not merely an observation about the procedure but also about the critical-reflective method of philosophising that the linguistic turn requires. It is particularly important not to think of language only as set of signs and rules. This would be to ignore the fact that language has very many dimensions in its actual use. As it is also important not to be caught just in formal or abstracted uses. The philosopher's task becomes like that of navigator of both familiar and unfamiliar landscapes; a tour guide of human life.

As indicted in earlier chapters Wittgenstein should be read against the background of transcendental philosophy. The transcendental element in Wittgenstein emerges in his insistence on "meaning as use" and his other discussions of the situated quality of language use; such as pointing out that people do not use expressions like "I am in pain" as a standard expression of pain. Wittgenstein is most often not viewed in a transcendental context because the transcendental element is either silent or disguised. What misleads us here is that the context of language use does not look like a feature of transcendental philosophy, yet it must be more than just a context; something has to be acknowledged to set up the conditions for the meaningful use of language. We are in something of a similar position with respect to Wittgenstein as Kant was to Hume. Kant was able to show that Hume's philosophy could not be as radically empiricist as Hume claimed, in that there must be conditions for the having of impressions at all. These conditions must come from the structure of human cognition, and eventually from the essence of humans as transcendent (that is capable of a priori knowledge) beings.

Wittgenstein takes a radical post-metaphysical position, in some respects not that dissimilar to that of a post-linguistic-turn Hume. He wants to establish that cognition could not be intelligibly separated from language use without presupposing something like a metaphysical "ether" in which meaning occurs; which, of course he strongly and systematically opposed. He maintained that there are no "meanings" of words apart from their employments. When we deal with definitions of words we treat them in the way of their standard employments, abstracted from their actual employments. Thus, changes in the meanings of words would be changes in the employments of those words, which may in turn lead to redefinition. But in natural languages definitions do not prescribe meanings. Wittgenstein was so determined in his position that he very carefully developed a method of philosophising that would make it extremely difficult for any later commentator to revise his work into any metaphysical framework. In this respect he succeed to the extent that his work can stand alone, or be read in many widely different traditions. But in order for it to, as it were, reveal its worth it must be exposed to the process of critique.

The process of critique can follow Wittgenstein's own beginnings of an internal critique against a background established in the classical Kantian manner. Wittgenstein's focus on psychology and inner states can here form a starting point, not that far from Kant's position in the *Critique of Judgement,* where he asks how it is that feelings towards the beautiful can be both subjective, inner states, and at the same time universal. The answer, as we have seen, lies in the fact that they are communicable. This communicability Kant claimed required a *sensus communis* that took the same form in each individual. We saw, via the pragmatists and then Apel, how the presupposition of a "communication community" could form a transformed transcendental framework for communicability and the employment of language games. Whilst these moves must be acknowledged as steps toward establishing an intersubjective ground for the self, the key to the connection between subjective experience and the publicity of language has not been established via this path of inquiry. This is because they all seek to establish a base for understanding and thus meaning and truth outside human linguistic experience.

Wittgenstein in his aversion to any theory in philosophy implicitly denied the existence of any preconditions. The only "conditions" Wittgenstein would allow were the facts of the human lifeworld or forms of life, which he saw as a joint construction of nature, and contingencies of history and culture. These conditions certainly were not for Wittgenstein pre-conditions in any transcendental sense. However, reflection shows that some important conditions are present in the practice of linguistic usage. Wittgenstein implicitly places any conditions within language and not in cognition. It is for Wittgenstein, and correctly so, the use of language that makes us conscious, cognising beings not our being conscious and cognising that allows us to use language. But such an insight, profoundly transformative as it is, stands in need of a critical framework of understanding.

Kant, in an inspired insight, provides a clue as to where to move in providing the framework for a critical transformation of the Wittgensteinian insight, by claiming that through transcendental philosophy we can construe the subject as object in self-constitution.[30] Elsewhere Kant says: 'I am an inner and an outer for myself'.[31] Though only fragmentary, the latter section of the *Opus postumum,* more than any other part of Kant's work, indicates the way in which Kant sought to tie together the elements of his whole philosophy. The elements for the completion of an interpersonal theory are to be found here: the self-determining subject given in intuition; the systematic complex of ideas which a priori determine the subject as object, and the recognition that this is problematic for being.

Placed in the context of this discussion it provides the critical ground missing in Wittgenstein and not fully grasped by either Apel or Habermas in communicative theory. The use of language presupposes a humanity of other language users who must be in the "language game" before they can make such a supposition. This is truly a priori in that each player of the language game must presuppose the humanity of other language users in order to play. The meanings already exist "external" to the language game player in the language. This is how we can have knowledge prior to experience and is the true source of the a priori.

Yet, at this point, the image of a language game becomes misleading. It gets us started in thinking the right way about language and its users, but it is not a game, there is no opting in or out; there is no "extra-game" place to be. Apel's reference to the "language game of language games" as the transcendental framework is on the right track, but misleading in this way. He can only avoid an infinite regress of language games by vaguely grounding the transcendental language game both in the, "ideal communication community" and in 'a genetic starting point'.[32] Yet this is too much of a Kantian model, again idealising the transcendental in order to create an apparent ground. It is for these reasons that Apel's promising project is finally enmeshed in a transcendental idealism from which he does not escape.

The notion of a "community" used as a ground by Habermas and Apel is also misleading in their appropriation of the notion from Peirce and Mead. The notion of a community is useful to the point where it indicates the existence of a real a priori ground for language use, but, as a concept, it rather begs the question by importing too much into the notion of grounding; assuming more about language users than is justified. It is misleading to presuppose that there is a community of language users, this is a deduction from the use of language in practice. The communication community, whether real or ideal, is a posteriori, not a priori. The notion of an "ideal communication community", attractive as it is, therefore does not serve Apel as well as it might in this regard and tends to mislead him into thinking that there is in fact a community that is, at least logically, prior to language usage. Reference to a "communication community" permeates his writing but he simply imports this notion from

Peirce, who used it rather loosely and infrequently, and does not engage it in a concerted discussion of the notion.

Habermas commenting on Mead's "commonwealth of rational beings" and its implication for communicative action says:

> In communicative action, the suppositions of self-determination and self-realization retain a rigorously intersubjective sense: whoever judges and acts morally must be capable of anticipating the agreement of an unlimited communication community, and whoever realizes himself in a responsibly accepted life history must be capable of anticipating recognition from this unlimited community.[33]

One can strongly agree with this view of Habermas as a means of furthering justice, moral action and fully realised persons. Communicative theory does provide a new understanding of rationality, action and morality but not because it is an a priori ground of intersubjectivity but because it is a consequence of intersubjectivity and intersubjectivity is to understood through a critique of Wittgenstein's treatment of language.

The notion of "community" also imports too much into the case for a grounding of consciousness. There are so many things that constitute communities that the concept becomes easily confused. It is true that communication works better in a community, but one is actually entitled to presuppose no more than that there are other users of the language. Perhaps there is in this sense a "linguistic community", but such a community need only be very basic, as Wittgenstein shows in the *Investigations*. Yet, it must be explained how we can be the sort of creatures who are in language as indicated by Wittgenstein. It is here that freedom and imagination become important notions as they are at the core of communicability, the key to intersubjectivity.

What one must presuppose is that consciousness has a purpose or intentionality that becomes self-conscious through the communicability of that purposeness. The key to understanding this is via imagination based on Kant's development of the concept in the *Critique of Judgement.* The concept of a purposeness in consciousness can be extrapolated from the *Critique of Judgement,* where Kant says that objects given in experience can present a purposeness for experience: the purposiveness in consciousness.[34]

What is presupposed in any use of language is that what can be said, can be understood and it is here that there is a freedom in the purposeness of consciousness. Humans do not respond like trained animals, they respond with a freedom to understand and respond. That freedom is, as previously quoted from Kant: 'the capacity of the self-determining subject to constitute itself as given in intuition'. The "intuition" required for language use, or in Wittgenstein's framework, language games, is that of freedom. The freedom to be, in the Kantian sense, an indeterminate being. Freedom and imagination are here combined, as one is only free to intuit self-determination when one can imagine the other of understanding. In this act of reflected self creation, imagination is the more fundamental capacity, because without it freedom would have nothing to determine.

To illustrate the importance of the move proposed here we can return to the parallel between Hume and Kant on experience. The transcendental element lying behind Wittgenstein's linguistic insight is based on the combined elements of freedom and imagination as the basic constitutive elements of human consciousness, which allow for language use. Freedom and imagination, as two sides of a coin, are what we add to consciousness to make it human consciousness. Language is the medium of this contribution and language only exists in (non-private) communities. Freedom and imagination allow for the construction of human communities but do not themselves require the pre-existence of communities as assumed in the communicative theories of Apel and Habermas. These communities become communities of interest in the mutual self-determination of subjects. Communities are the canvas upon which freedom and imagination find expression. It is not so much that the "outer" takes precedence over the "inner" but that the other becomes, in imagination a subject for me. Freedom and imagination as the intuitions of self and being are essentially linked in that imagination could not create or "image" a consciousness other than the given, if it were not free and freedom could not be without the presence of images. The capacity to understand at all implies the capacity to understand differently, to see differently, to believe differently, to feel differently with the presupposition of the intuitions of freedom and imagination. The presence of a subjectivity at all implies a possible different subjectivity which in turn implies a different subject. Each act of understanding implies the situating of an "other" subject; the focus of the purposeness of the consciousness has moved. The situating of the "other" subject here represents the linguistic moment in which I represent an imagination content as other. No human consciousness is privileged over any other in this process.

To return to the Kantian example, the *sensus communis,* is the common language. The reason why subjective states are universalisable is because each person uses the common language, not because they each have the same sense within. The means by which we create, in understanding, the other manifolds of which we are subject is the same as the means by which we understand other persons as subjects. In this way language is public and shapes the content of the purposeness of consciousness. Of course, I am not the consciousness of another, yet their linguistic moment is open to me in the use of language.

Notes

1 Förster, E. (1993), in Kant, Immanuel (1993), *Opus postumum*, Introduction, Cambridge University Press, Cambridge, p. xvi.
2 Ibid.
3 Ibid., p. xvii.
4 Kant, Immanuel (1993), *Opus postumum*, Cambridge University Press, Cambridge, p. 176.
5 Ibid., p. 243.
6 Ibid., p. 245.
7 Ibid., p. 247.
8 Ibid., p. 250.
9 Ibid., p. 154.
10 Ibid., pp. 20 - 21.
11 Kant, Immanuel (1992), "Perpetual Peace", in *Perpetual Peace and Other Essays*, trans. Ted Humphrey, Hackett, Indianapolis, p. 120.
12 Apel, Karl-Otto (1980),*Towards a transformation of philosophy*, trans. Glyn Adey and David Frisby, Routledge and Kegan Paul, London, p. 233.
13 See Ibid., p. 271 - 274.
14 Ibid., p.235.
15 Apel, Karl-Otto (1992), "Normatively Grounding Critical Theory", in *Philosophical Interventions in the Unfinished Project of the Enlightenment,* Honneth, Axel et. al., eds., trans. William Rehg, MIT Press Cambridge, Mass, p. 159.
16 Benhabib, Seyla (1992), *Situating the Self*, Polity Press, Cambridge, p. 31.
17 Ibid., p. 38.
18 Kant, Immanuel (1983), "What is Enlightenment", in *Perpetual Peace and Other Essays*, trans. Ted Humphrey, Hackett, Indianapolis, p. 42.
19 Kant states in "What is Enlightenment" that "this age of enlightenment, the century of Frederick", p. 45. It seems that he genuinely respected the authority of the monarchy.
20 I am using the term "lifeworld" here in a very general sense which could include Wittgenstein's notion of forms of life. It is my intention to refer to an unmediated realm of human experience as a basis for further theoretical development. To this extent my use does not conflict with Habermas' lifeworld/system distinction, however I would not wish, at this point, to endorse the further ramifications expounded by Habermas.
21 Kant, Immanuel (1987), *The Critique of Judgement*, trans. Werner S. Pluhar, Hackett, Indianapolis, p. 89. Here Kant distinguishes between such a sense and a private feeling.
22 Ibid., pp. 162 – 3.
23 Kant, Immanuel (1983), "Perpetual Peace, Appendix II" in *Perpetual Peace and Other Essays*, trans. Ted Humphrey, Hackett, Indianapolis, p. 135.

24 See *The Critique of Judgement*, sections 40 and 41, also sections 83 and 84 for comments on culture and the perfection of "man".
25 Habermas, Jurgen (1992), "Themes in Post Metaphysical Thinking", in *Post Metaphysical Thinking*, trans. William Mark Hohengarten, MIT Press, Cambridge, Mass, p. 35.
26 Two notable exceptions here are Hannah Arendt and Cornelius Castoriadis.
27 See Honneth, Axel (1995), *The Struggle for Recognition*, trans. Joel Anderson, Polity Press, Cambridge. Mead is used here in an Hegelian context.
28 Honneth, Axel (1995), *The Struggle for Recognition*, trans. Joel Anderson, Polity Press, Cambridge.
29 Wittgenstein, Ludwig (1958), *Philosophical Investigations*, trans. G. E. M. Anscombe, Basil Blackwell, Oxford, p. 117e.
30 Kant, Immanuel (1993), *Opus postumum*, Cambridge University Press, Cambridge, p. 180.
31 Ibid., p. 191.
32 Karl-Otto Apel, "The Communication Community and the Social Sciences", in *Towards a transformation of philosophy*, p. 167.
33 Habermas, Jurgen (1992), "Individuation Through Socialization: On Mead's Theory of Subjectivity", in *Post Metaphysical Thinking*, trans. William Mark Hohengarten, MIT Press, Cambridge, Mass, p. 192.
34 Kant, Immanuel (1987), *Critique of Judgement*, trans. Werner S. Pluhar, Hackett, Indianapolis, p. 32.

Index

9781138713246